AMERICA, AS SEEN ON TV

America, As Seen on TV

How Television Shapes Immigrant
Expectations around the Globe

Clara E. Rodríguez

NEW YORK UNIVERSITY PRESS
New York

NEW YORK UNIVERSITY PRESS
New York
www.nyupress.org

© 2018 by New York University
All rights reserved

References to Internet websites (URLs) were accurate at the time of writing. Neither the author nor New York University Press is responsible for URLs that may have expired or changed since the manuscript was prepared.

ISBN: 978-1-4798-5682-4 (hardback)
ISBN: 978-1-4798-1852-5 (paperback)

For Library of Congress Cataloging-in-Publication data, please contact the Library of Congress.

New York University Press books are printed on acid-free paper, and their binding materials are chosen for strength and durability. We strive to use environmentally responsible suppliers and materials to the greatest extent possible in publishing our books.

Manufactured in the United States of America

10 9 8 7 6 5 4 3 2 1

Also available as an ebook

*To my precious family
and to future global generations
of media watchers.*

CONTENTS

Introduction

I begin by sharing a story that illuminates for me the focus of this book. As I was conducting my research, an article in the Columbia University student magazine *The Eye* caught *my* eye.[1] It noted that one-third of all Columbia students were now international students. The same article quoted one international student from Guangdong province, China, as saying that before enrolling at Columbia, he hoped to immerse himself in American culture in New York City, where he expected to make White friends who have "blue eyes, yellow hair, and a hairy face." Since arriving, however, he had come to accept a different social reality: he had not ventured far from his network of Chinese friends. What was striking to me was not that his network was mainly Chinese, for as strangers in another land we tend to seek out those who speak our language and share our customs. What was striking to me was his expectation that American culture in Manhattan would be filled with White friends with "blue eyes, yellow hair." Many variables may have contributed to his preconceptions of the United States in general and of New York City in particular. The article didn't address this, but, I wondered, how had his expectations been informed by his viewing of US television? To what degree *was he aware* of the influence of American television on his perceptions of what New Yorkers would be like? Did his preconceptions—and those of others who have also come to study or work in the United States or New York City—limit or open up his understanding once he arrived? Finally, to what degree were his preconceptions and views similar to or different from those of millennials raised in the United States? Do US millennials from other states also anticipate New York City (or the United States, for that matter) to be similarly populated? And to what degree are they aware of the influence of US TV on their own perceptions?

The Foreign Born and American Television

My research had shown me that many Chinese students watch American TV as a way to learn the English language and American customs (Gao, 2013).[2] My research had also taught me that in some countries with restrictive government policies (like China) or where television has been limited—by law or otherwise—US TV programs are viewed on the Internet, cell phones, and computers more often than through traditional TV channels. In many countries, and in many regions (e.g., Eastern Europe), translation cells (often social groups) have sprouted up to add subtitles to US television programs and make them available—for free—to anyone with an Internet connection. Websites, such as Hulu in the United States, have also made television programs readily available for viewing and downloading. Films have been similarly subtitled and distributed, but television is still in many cases more economical; and, unlike movies, TV programs allow viewers to develop a more continuous familiarity (and perhaps an ongoing identification) with characters and plots—often in weekly segments.

But, as I read the article in *The Eye*, I was struck by what seemed to be an unconscious residue of this student's watching American media, perhaps television in particular. This was his somewhat innocent expectation that, after coming to New York City, he would be surrounded by and become immersed in an American culture where he would make White friends with "blue eyes, yellow hair, and a hairy face." Having lived in New York City for almost all of my life, I have known it to be a majority-minority city for decades. Indeed, few people who visit fail to notice this. Why, then, would this Chinese student have such a different idea about the type of people he would meet? I wondered: is it that our American media project the city so differently from the way it is—and has been—in reality?

Patterns Found in US TV Serial Programming

For quite some time, a number of works (including my own) have examined racial, ethnic, gender, and class representations in US media and in network television. A consistent finding has been the underrepresentation of these groups relative to their proportion of the US population—and relative to their actual (proportionate) presence in the settings that are featured on US TV programs.[3] It has also been found that the way in which gender and particular racial and ethnic groups are portrayed tends to convey and reinforce views of these groups as marginal, of lower social status, and irrelevant (as groups) to the main story lines. Researchers have also found that when racial and ethnic characters are included, they tend to be cast not in lead roles but in supporting or silent-extra roles.[4] In addition, the way that certain racial and ethnic characters are drawn (e.g., as Latina/o villains, vixens, or victims; or, as Zia [2000] notes in the case of Asians, as gangsters, gooks, geishas, and geeks) often suggests that they are not or should not be seen as an integral or important part of the "legitimate" social structure that is central to the story on the screen. They are, in essence, "othered"—depicted as being "other than us."

These misrepresentations have powerful impacts, as Merskin (2007:135) reminds us when discussing accumulation theory:

> [I]f the mass media, including advertising, present information in ways that are consistent, persistent, and corroborated, this instruction is likely to have long-term, powerful effects. Stereotyping, as a media effect, gains power and credibility the longer and more regularly the same information is presented, in the same way, to the same audiences. These (re) presentations remain largely unchallenged so that carefully cultivated cultural constructions of race, ethnicity, sexuality, and gender become normalized in the American popular imagination.

In addition, although we are increasingly taught that race and gender are both social constructions, most of us still tend to look for markers of race and gender to evaluate people.[5] We are still a race-conscious and gender-conscious society (Ryan, 2010:54). And, as many others have noted, the media, or the "Fourth Estate," not only reflect and sustain such predispositions but also produce them, making them appear universal and a natural reflection of reality (Hall, 1982).

How do people in other countries receive these patterns that have been identified in US TV? Does the overrepresentation of White (male) characters in lead roles come to stand for or represent the universal, normative, average person? In the global market, does US Whiteness represent or signify the successful, modern human? How does the way that US media portray women and people of color influence people in other countries?

Also, how does US TV's coverage of controversial topics—e.g., crime, education, religion, and class—influence perceptions of "othered groups" in the United States and in other countries? Chavez (2013) provides an interesting illustration of how the coverage of immigration hyperbolizes and sensationalizes certain dimensions of immigration, while ignoring other aspects. He notes that when the Minuteman Project volunteers arrived in Tombstone, Arizona (population 4,800), in 2005 to monitor the border and the flow of illegal immigrants from Mexico to the United States, "The number of media members here Friday to cover the volunteer border patrols nearly outnumbered the Minutemen. Reporters from around the world descended on Tombstone."[6] Indeed, one of the organizers of the Minuteman Project, Chris Simcox, who was also editor of the *Tombstone Tumbleweed*, a local paper, seemed to blame the media for manufacturing the event when he wrote: "The media has created this frenzy and this monster. They are looking for Bigfoot, the Loch Ness monster, the vigilant."

In this case, the focus was on the Minutemen as opposed to the struggle of immigrants to survive economically or politically in their home countries. The story was not about the contributions of immigrants to the US economy, for example; it also wasn't about the role that US businesses play in contributing to undocumented immigration, and the advantages that they net when hiring the undocumented.[7] But the question here is this: How influential is such media coverage? Does coverage like this influence views on immigration and immigrants in other countries? Stated more broadly, how does US television—including entertainment programming and coverage of news events—affect the views of people from other countries about immigrants and gender, racial, and ethnic minority groups not only in the United States but also in their own countries? And do these views change (or not) after these global viewers come to the United States?

The Sun Never Sets on TV ... the TV Is Usually On ... and It Continues to Show Mostly US TV

The impact of television is generally omitted from studies of globalization, the second generation, transnationalism, and diasporic communities. This may be due in part to the view that TV is seen by some as dumbed-down nonsense and that the Internet has taken viewers away from TV—both in the United States and abroad.[8] Yet people in the United States, as well as in other countries, still spend many hours consuming television content.

TV Viewing in the United States

Despite a clear shift toward more social media, recent Bureau of Labor Statistics data show that in 2015 Americans still watched television an average of close to three hours a day, with daily TV viewing increasing on weekends. Indeed, as Figure I.1 indicates, "Watching TV was the leisure activity that occupied the most time . . . , accounting for more than half of leisure time on average, for those age 15 and over"—with young adults (20–24) watching more hours than youths (15–19). This included watching television over the air, through cable, fiber optics, or satellite, on a television set or computer, and on a DVD player or other device (Bureau of Labor Statistics, 2016). Can we think of any other non-work activity (except sleep) that we participate in for close to three hours every day? Do students spend that much time on their homework assignments?

Moreover, despite the shifts to cable and to TV alternatives (e.g., social networking and web-based activities) in the United States, the major network shows still, as they say in advertising, brought in the greatest number of eyeballs.[9] For example, hour-long prime-time dramas still averaged between 12 and 19 million viewers in the United States in the spring 2012 seasonal Nielsen ratings—much above their highest rated peers on cable.[10] Also, many viewers of network and cable shows now access them via the Internet. So, despite the much-merited excitement about YouTube viewing, downloading, online gaming, social media, and Twitter—to name just a few alternatives—the death of TV, in particular TV content, has been greatly exaggerated, to paraphrase Mark Twain.[11]

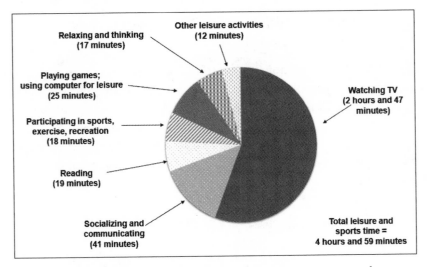

Figure I.1. Leisure time on an average day. Data include all persons age 15 and over. Data include all days of the week and are annual averages for 2015. Source: Bureau of Labor Statistics (2016).

Moreover, in order to understand the intersection of old and new media, we need to cover the history and the reality of the BT (or Before Twitter) period.[12] It used to be that you watched TV together in your living room and (maybe) shared your reactions to the programs you saw with the other viewers there; or you discussed them later with friends and colleagues on the phone, at school, at work, or in your everyday travels. Now you can tweet your reactions in real time and reach thousands of people; or you can post them on blogs, Facebook, and websites. You can also watch alternatives to network programs or access the same or different network programs on the Internet.[13] Again, TV is not dead; what has changed is how we share our reactions and how we access TV. Consequently, in this text, "watching TV" refers to consuming US TV programs, regardless of how they are, or were, accessed.[14] And my focus is on what viewers take away from the content they view in terms of their perceptions of race, ethnicity, class, and gender.

In addition, although their preferred sources differ, many people in the United States and other countries still get their news about national and international issues primarily from television programming.[15] Furthermore, although viewers are increasingly turning to Netflix and other avenues to access programs not available on "regular" TV, the digital divide[16]—both in the United States and throughout the world—prevents many viewers from having steady, reliable access to content online. There are also issues of preference for live-time viewing and an aversion to the multitude of programming options available on the Internet— what some refer to as "choice paralysis." This is to argue not that Internet (or TV) viewing will cease to grow but that different arguments can be made as to the *rate* at which they will grow, where they will grow most, and, ultimately, what role traditional US TV programming and content will continue to play in both arenas.[17]

But more relevant to the focus of this book is the fact that, to date, many of these programs are also lacking with regard to racial, ethnic, class, and gender representation (Hunt and Ramon, 2015; Kim, 2016).[18] In essence, content is king, and the content with regard to these particular variables has been slow to change (Edgerton, 2007).[19] In addition, it is important to focus on TV because, as Edgerton (2007:415) has noted, "Television is still the 800-pound gorilla because of how much the average person is exposed to it." It is also, in many ways, the common denominator, what ordinary citizens—including youths—watch or are exposed to the most in the United States, and what viewers in other countries may have the most access to as well.[20] It is also, for many, the most economical source of entertainment.

TV Viewing in Other Countries—Also Widespread

Europeans also watch a considerable amount of television. For example, according to one estimate, the average German consumes more than three hours of television a day, placing Germany third in the world, after the United States and Britain (tied for first) and Italy (second).[21] Although precise numbers are difficult to obtain, American TV is also both readily accessible and widely consumed in non-European countries outside of the United States. According to one study, globally 86 percent of TV viewers still watch TV live and on television screens, although the percentages vary considerably by country. For example, viewing TV on desktop computers and laptops is more common in China (52 percent) and Russia (43 percent), while streaming from the Internet to TV screens is more popular in Turkey (44 percent).[22] Titcomb (2015) also noted that, according to the 2015 International Communications Market Report, the United States and the United Kingdom were both leaders in terms of the number of hours spent watching television. Who actually watched the most depended on whether just live TV was measured, or if hours spent watching recorded programs, live television, catch-up television, and online streaming were combined—if combined the United Kingdom led the pack, otherwise the United States did. As Woods (2016) notes, these countries were followed by Japan, Italy, Poland, Russia, the Netherlands, and Spain, all of which watched over 239 minutes of TV a day in 2014. Countries in the Asia-Pacific region and in Australia also watched TV, with China watching up to 157 minutes per day, South Koreans up to 196 minutes, and Australians just over 204 minutes. In essence, as Woods concludes, "people all over the world are watching more and more TV, whether it is live television, recorded or indeed streaming online."

Concerns about the Dominance of US TV

Countries have taken action to deal with long-standing concerns over the dominance of American TV, and some have established quotas for how much US TV can be aired on television. For example, quotas of 50 percent European content were originally enacted by the Council of the European Community, which in 1989 established a single European Union market in television and the Television without Frontiers (TWF) Directive, now referred to as the AVMS (Audiovisual Media Services) Directive.[23] As Jones (1997) notes, the TWF Directive required member states to "ensure 'where practicable' and 'by appropriate means' that broadcasters reserve for 'European works' a majority of their transmission time, exclusive of news, sports events, games, advertising, and teletext services." The intent of the directive was dual: (1) "to protect 50% or more of transmission time" from non-EU competition and (2) to counter the "threat to cultural and linguistic diversity in Europe" (Jones, 1997). This policy evolved as a result of the overwhelming dominance of US TV in the European community and growing concern about that trend, which surfaced during the late 1980s and early 1990s, and which has continued despite changes in technology and the increased ability of consumers to access the kind of TV content they want, when they want it. Canada also requires that 60 percent of all programming and 50 percent of prime-time programming be of Canadian origin (Picard, 2011:226).

Despite the quotas imposed on American TV products and the fact that member countries are periodically reviewed to see if they have met their local content quotas, the number of hours of American programming on major European networks increased from 2000 to 2008.[24] Indeed, as recently as 2011, the Council of Europe still acknowledged the continuing prominence of US TV in Europe, saying: "American programmes and formats have retained their prime position in European TV Programme Schedules and in the list of the most-watched programs."[25] Kuipers (2010:183n1, 180) also notes that although "figures on television imports are hard to come by and not easily comparable," there is general agreement that "Hollywood is still the largest exporter of TV in the western world" (Kuipers, 2010:180).[26]

In addition, numerous US studies have shown that most countries love US popular culture—regardless of what they may think about US foreign policy (see Cohen, 2009; Wike, 2013). As one reporter put it, Batman is Batman, regardless of who is in the White House (Arango, 2008). In sum, for many years American TV has been a commonplace, steady part of life in many countries. Moreover, it is often viewed as representative of a, if not *the*, major political and economic world power of the day. But, regardless of viewers' perceptions of the US position in the world, US TV often reflects a life quite different from what exists in the viewers' countries in terms of gender, class, race, and ethnic relations. Consequently, American TV has influenced and, in many cases, continues to influence how America is seen by people who have never been to the United States. It may also influence, in terms of social/psychological remittances, people who are not in the United States but who are in touch with others from their countries who are in the United States (Levitt, 2001).

People in other countries also worry that US TV may crowd out their own cultures and traditions. Indeed, in the Pew Global Attitudes study, majorities or pluralities in 17 of 20 countries said "it is a bad thing that U.S. ideas and customs are spreading to their countries" (p. 4). The researchers further noted that although American "soft power" (especially as expressed through the media that are exported) may be appealing, there are concerns about the impact of Western media in some countries. Of particular concern in some countries is the fact that US media—both film and television—are particularly appealing to young people in other countries (Pew Global Attitudes Project, 2012:24).[27] In a more recent series of face-to-face interviews conducted with a nationally representative sample of 3,649 adults in China, researchers also found that most "believe that their traditional way of life is getting lost and that it needs to be protected against foreign influence."[28]

So, in effect, in spite of the increasing popularity of other media, TV content still occupies a huge amount of our waking life, and it is per-ceived by many in other countries as having substantial effects, such as challenging the way in which their citizens, in particular their youth, think about their own cultural and social traditions, personal goals, and preferred lifestyles. It may be that as Wike (2013) concludes, "The reality is that resistance to American culture often goes hand in hand with a strong attraction to it."

Clearly, there are also economic concerns (e.g., trade imbalances), and there have been attempts to address this dominance of American TV in several countries. Changes have occurred with, for example, the development of domestic, glocal, and diasporic programming, and joint partnerships between US media companies and media companies in other countries.[29] But the fact remains that globalization is a worldwide phenomenon within which US media have played, and continue to play, a dominant role (Liebes and Katz, 1990; Imre, 2009). This is not to deny the ability of peoples to filter media in their own way (Bielby and Har-rington, 2015) and thus ignore or counter hegemonic narratives and de-velop hybridized programming or their own independent programming (see Straubhaar, 2007; Esser, 2010; Steven, 2003; Artz and Kamalipour, 2007). But, regardless of the precise nature or degree of global media im-pact, the fact remains that US media have an influence that is relatively understudied.

In addition, the US populace seems to have little awareness of what the impact has been, or what questions might be raised in relation to this situation. For example, has the United States' success in exporting its popular culture been more effective than "boots on the ground" in terms of spreading views of democracy and equal rights for all groups, such as women, gays, transgender people, and those of African or indigenous descent? Or has it retarded such movements? Has it inflamed or reinforced opposing views?[30]

To what extent are world leaders influenced by American TV content? Some thought-provoking examples of this can be found in the *Financial Times'* March 9, 2014, article on "Why China's Leaders Love to Watch 'House of Cards.'" This article notes that "Xi Jinping, the Chinese president, reportedly considers the American classic *The Godfather* his favourite western cinematic indulgence," and "Wang Qishan, the former vice-premier of finance and ultimate arbiter for discipline on the Communist party's standing committee, is said to favour *House of Cards*," telling those in "the cloistered leadership compound, to keep abreast of the Netflix hit" and instructing his staff to check the release date for season 2. Although this American TV show is adapted from a BBC series from the 1990s, the article goes on to say that it is likely viewed as "quintessentially American" (Campbell, 2014).[31] We do not know to what degree leaders or their followers are influenced by American TV content—and in what way—but clearly it should not be dismissed as mere entertainment by those who seek a better understanding of international relations.

I do not mean to imply that the primary intent of American TV is to influence people around the world in any particular way. For while this book examines various results of watching TV, it should be remembered that American TV is a business (Picard, 2011) and, therefore, is driven by business interests. Corporations produce media and sell them to viewers and advertisers in order to make money.[32] In other words, regardless of the mode of distribution, such as cable, Netflix, Apple, Amazon, Hulu, or traditional network channels on the terrestrial TV set, and regardless of the content delivered, the driving forces are, simply and always, the seeking of revenues, net earnings, and other value by the various players.[33]

Beyond the political, economic, and cultural considerations, are there other, perhaps more social or psychological, consequences to the steady diet of American TV that many countries consume? Is this a diet mainly enjoyed by the privileged in some countries? Does watching American TV influence the views that citizens of other countries have of the United States; and how does it influence the expectations they may have of the United States before coming to country? What surprises them the most when they come to the United States? Do they see US TV as help-ing them to be more economically mobile, to better integrate into the United States or into global occupations? Does watching American TV in their home countries influence their own aspirations, desires, con-sumption practices, and preferred lifestyles? If so, does it, in this sense, operate as a form of soft power that contributes to the view or notion of American exceptionalism?[34]

Given the patterning we have discussed in US TV with regard to race, ethnicity, class, and gender, how does watching American TV influence their views in these areas? What happens when these global viewers come to the United States? Are their media-inflected views of the United States altered? Do they now see US TV as encouraging or discouraging "otherness"? Do they now see US TV as accurately reflecting racial and ethnic relations in the United States? What do their US counterparts, that is, youths of similar educational or socioeconomic backgrounds who also watch US TV, think about these same issues? This book seeks to address these questions.

Why Study This? Why Now?

International Students, Faculty, Researchers, and Other Professionals

Beyond their clear academic value, why are these questions important today? They are important because clearly we live in an increasingly globalized world.[35] A growing number of international students, faculty, researchers, and other professionals are collaborating with US colleagues (both in the United States and abroad) to drive research, financial mar-kets, and corporate expansions. This has been particularly evident in the upper tiers of our educational institutions.[36] In-depth academic research on these groups has been limited. So it is important to study this rapidly growing group of international scholars, students, and foreign nationals who have come to study and work in the United States, especially at US educational institutions, for a number of reasons.[37]

For one, although the 2013 Open Doors Report indicates that inter-national students made up less than 4 percent of total student enroll-ment in the United States at the graduate and undergraduate levels, their numbers have been growing significantly and consistently over the past seven years.[38] As the report indicated, "There are now 40 percent more international students studying at U.S. colleges and universities than a decade ago, and the rate of increase has risen steadily for the past three years" (Downey, 2013).

Second, there are large and increasing numbers of such students in tier 1 universities and in large metropolitan areas: "All of the top 20 host universities and the top 10 host states had more international students in 2012/13 than the previous year."[39] Large public universities are also important hosts to foreign students. Of the top 25 schools, 18 were public universities, including 8 in the Midwest (Porter and Belkin, 2013). In addition, many top-tier universities, including Columbia, New York University, and Cornell, are establishing campuses in other countries, which often encourage more faculty and students to come to the United States.

These international students, faculty, and professionals also tend to specialize in those areas that will continue to be important in future global development, that is, business, engineering, math, and computer science (Porter and Belkin, 2013; Institute of International Education, 2013). As such, we can expect or hope that they will continue to work with US and other global colleagues in these developing areas. Furthermore, and as the 2013 Open Doors Report indicates, they also contribute to America's scientific and technical research and bring international perspectives into US classrooms. In this sense, they help prepare American undergraduates for global careers, and their education and experiences in the United States often lead to longer-term business relationships and economic benefits for the United States and other countries. Consequently, it is important to study US TV and our global colleagues' perceptions of US TV as this may encourage communication and the kind of mutual understanding that could foster even more successful international collaborations.

Translating through American TV

In the course of conducting my research (more on that later), people would occasionally ask me what my research was about. When I told them, practically everyone had a story to share with me. One of those stories illustrates the extent to which international students consume US TV. An administrator at an urban university in the US Northeast was charged with shepherding the newest group of graduate business students from China after they had arrived in the United States. She did not speak Chinese. As she struggled to describe the venue where they were planning to meet later that day, one student said, "Oh, you mean like *Cheers*?" referring to the popular US TV sitcom set in a friendly Boston pub, where, as the theme song said, "everybody knows your name." She nodded "yes" and then heard from the group of 60 or so a unanimous "oh," as in, okay, now we get it. This illustrated for her how the show, which had developed its own iconic image in the United States, had now also become a global cultural metaphor. For me, it reinforced the ubiquity of US TV programming in other countries.

Implications for the Future

International students are generally supported by and come from countries that are projected to be (or already are) dominant players in the world's global economy. Indeed, the top three senders are China, India, and South Korea, and they now account for half (49 percent) of international students in the United States, with China sending almost as many students as the other top-sending nations combined.[40] What does this bode for future international cooperation and development? International students from around the world not only bring back their impressions of the United States but also often see their home countries in new ways. Since other countries often invest in such students, they may wonder how their investment is paying off—in understanding the United States and, indirectly, in feelings about their countries of origin.

Last, and as my own sample (described below) indicates, international students often come from fairly privileged backgrounds and, as such, can be expected to play important roles in the global economy, whether in the United States or elsewhere. We need to have a better sense not just of their US experiences in their educational settings but also of their absorption of US culture via US media before coming to and after living in the United States for a few years. In terms of my particular interest, what views of the United States do they bring, and how have these views been influenced by the American TV they have seen, especially with regard to issues of race, ethnicity, class, and gender? If they return to their home countries, what will they take back?

My Questions and My Methods

As I became increasingly aware of the large numbers of foreign nationals working in the United States and of international students attending US universities—and of the extent to which American TV was consumed in the United States and in other countries—I began to wonder: did the youths and young adults who came to study or work in the United States see much American TV before they came? If so, why did they watch US TV? Did it influence their expectations before they came? Did they see US TV as undermining their culture? Or did they see American TV as helping them in some way? How did their views change—or not—after they came to the United States? Did the racial, ethnic, gender, and class depictions characteristic of our media influence their views of the United States, and of the minorities in their country? What did US millennials, that is, youths of similar educational backgrounds, think about these same issues? How true to life did both groups view American TV to be?

What I did to answer these questions is addressed in more detail in the appendix, but suffice it to say that I conducted, over a three-year period (2013–5), personal and in-depth interviews with 71 foreign-born young adults who had come to the United States fairly recently and were living in the US Northeast at the time of the interview. I also administered electronically a shorter version of my questionnaire to 171 US undergraduates at a university also in the Northeast in order to see what differences or similarities might exist between my foreign-born group and the US undergraduate group with regard to how watching US TV had influenced them, and, in particular, how it influenced their views of race, ethnicity, class, and gender. I discuss the results of my analyses in subsequent chapters, but first, in the next chapter, I review and focus on those parts of the research literature in this area that pertain to my core question of how preconceptions or perceptions about race, class, and gender are influenced by watching US TV, and to what degree viewers are aware of this influence.

PART I

Overview

1

The Global Television Landscape Literature

Various works (including my own research) on racial, ethnic, and gender images led me to think about how people in other countries are influenced by American TV. But my interest in this topic has deep personal and historical roots, and my routes to this book have been many. Some have been surprising, and as I reflect on them now, some have been circuitous. I suspect that as a child I must have had some degree of awareness—as did US Supreme Court Associate Justice Sonia Sotomayor—that the people whom I saw on our small TV screen didn't look very much like me or most of the people who were part of "my beloved world" growing up in the South Bronx (Sotomayor, 2013). At some point, I began to think more deeply about what we saw on TV and question how it influenced the ways in which we see and assess ourselves and others. That intellectual commitment may have started with my reading of Marshall McLuhan, who was among the first to successfully draw major public attention in the United States to the medium (i.e., the media) not only for the messages it conveys but also for its larger impact on society—how "we shape our tools and thereafter our tools shape us."[1] But I don't think that I fully got the message that "the medium was the message or the massage" then. I was curious but still a bit unsure as to what the implications really were.[2]

My Journey *to* and *through* the Literature

Other readings, events, and comments undoubtedly influenced me along the way. The civil rights movement focused on both personal and institutional racism in its many forms. In 1968, after the race riots following Dr. Martin Luther King Jr.'s assassination, President Lyndon Baines Johnson established the National Advisory Commission on Civil Disorders, often referred to as the Kerner Commission (US Kerner Commission, 1968). Its final report shined intense light on the institutional racism that pervaded the land. One of the Kerner Commission's focuses was on the world of mass media, especially Hollywood movies and TV shows, which were critiqued for ignoring African Americans and other groups, both behind and in front of the cameras. Some changes were made, as the movie and TV industries committed themselves to add more diversity, and to better reflect the social realities of the land. As Lichter and Amundson (1994) would later point out, we saw a shift from the "All-White World" of the 1950s to the "Return of Race" in the late 1960s and early 1970s; and then, in the 1980s, came a move to the "Let a Hundred Flowers Bloom" period, which featured a variety of women, classes, and racial and ethnic characters. Although there were (and still are) problems in representation, people of color and women began appearing in movies and on TV in increasing numbers and in better roles. So change was possible, I thought.[3]

But what impact did those changes in programming have? When *All in the Family* (1971–79) aired, the show's creator said he sought to highlight the stupidity of prejudice by making its lead character, Archie Bunker—an outspoken, hardheaded, working-class White bigot— often look like a buffoon in his interactions with his family members and Black neighbors. But while the show's liberal viewers saw in this a skewering of racist attitudes, others identified with Archie Bunker and had their prejudices reinforced when they watched the show (Vidmar and Rokeach, 1974).

This led me to wonder: how did the shows that did *not* seek to be expressly "antiracist"—the run-of-the-mill shows that populated the networks and that scholars continue to fault for under- or misrepresenting race, ethnicity, class, and gender—influence viewers and society? It was when I began teaching media-related courses at my college in the early 1990s that I became seriously aware of the extent to which such non-mission-driven shows and media *in general* influence how people see the world.[4] My students moved me to ask questions like these: How come the then-popular shows *Friends* and *Seinfeld*, both set in New York City, were populated with characters who had no (with one or two transient exceptions) "friends" who are people of color? How come some of my brightest minority students who were fans of these shows never noticed this? By this time, I had woken up to the sad fact that television did not do right by the "glorious mosaic" that characterized New York City even then. I also became aware then of how much New York City was (and still is) a major setting for many dramas and situation comedies—and that it was and still is projected, to a large degree, from a less inclusive perspective. And so I continued to ask, where were "we" (the people I knew) on TV? And where were "we" as a society?

Along the way, as globalization increased, I wondered how the very issues that concerned me with regard to US TV—its representations of women, class, and racial and ethnic groups—might influence people in other countries. This awareness was likely influenced by the growing number of international students, faculty, and events in my life. But it was fueled as well by the evolving literature and discussions in the area, which pointed to how US media were influencing people in other countries because of increasing globalization.[5] One book that contributed heavily to popular and literary discussions of these issues was Pico Iyer's *Video Night in Kathmandu: And Other Reports from the Not-So-Far East* (1988). Iyer, a novelist and essayist who was born in England to parents from India and grew up partly in California, spent seven months criss-crossing the Asian continent, spending a few weeks in each country.[6] His goal was to see "how America's pop-cultural imperialism spread through the world's most ancient civilizations." He wanted to see "what kind of resistance had been put up against the Coca-Colonizing forces and what kind of counter-strategies were planned." He "hoped to discover which Americas got through to the other side of the world and which got lost in translation" (5).

What he found in his travels were images of America and attitudes about American influence that were "perplexingly double-edged," and often ripe with irony. They included the slogans "Yankee Go Home" and "America, Number One"; communist guerrillas in the Philippines fighting capitalism while wearing UCLA T-shirts; Sandinista leaders in Nicaragua waging war against "U.S. imperialism" while watching prime-time American TV on private satellite dishes; and many White people in South Africa who were still clinging to apartheid but could not get enough of Bill Cosby, Eddie Murphy, and Mr. T.—three popular African American stars of the time. Indeed, underscoring these contrasts, Iyer begins his book by describing a US veteran of the Vietnam War who returns to his old battlegrounds in Vietnam in 1984 and finds the locals jiving along to Bruce Springsteen's major hit "Born in the U.S.A." The vet says: "Our clothes, our language, our movies and our music—our way of life—are far more powerful than our bombs" (5). In essence, what he found in the 1980s was that "the takeover" had radically accelerated and intensified; there were now satellites beaming images of "America and other peoples" to the United States and to each other, faster than a speeding bullet. As Iyer notes, "suddenly then, America could be found uncensored in even the world's most closed societies" (6).

On my journey *to* the literature there were other sources that described the globalization of media and, in particular, the impact of US media. One that stands out because of its relationship to events in the United States at the time is an article by Ron Suskind (2001) in the *New York Times Magazine*. Suskind had been sent by the *Times* to study changes in the religion, lifestyles, and daily ethics of the Ibatan people, who live on Babuyan, an island in the Philippines. These people had been totally isolated from modern society until 1977, when a 29-year-old missionary arrived there with his Chinese American wife and two daughters to translate the Christian Bible into their language.[7] When Suskind arrived, the population had grown to 1,400 from 600 (since 1977) and, as Suskind relates, "400 of 1,000 were now devout Christians, a community of fervent Puritan ethicists that would make Max Weber take notice." As it turned out, he was on his way to Babuyan on September 11, 2001, the very day that the World Trade Center and the Pentagon were attacked.

What he found on the island was fascinating. As he put it, it was a "kind of a microcosm of what the world was suddenly fighting over—not simply West versus East or Judeo-Christian vs. Islam, but the very idea of modernity and what constitutes human progress." But what I found so interesting was the role that television played in the Ibatan people's understanding of the world outside of Babuyan. Since they were not on the grid, the video programs they watched were limited and somewhat dated. This was evident in Suskind's description of his arrival: "The islanders had long anticipated our arrival; they had even heard about me, a Jewish reporter from the United States, and they joyously greeted us at the airfield and accompanied us into the village." Later that evening, Ruben, a church elder, told Suskind that a "recent hit" at his house was *Ben-Hur*, "the 1959 classic with Charlton Heston as a he-man Jewish slave and chariot champion during the time of Christ." Ruben told Suskind that evening as he switched away from CNN to a station from Manila: "We thought the Jews were the world's toughest people. . . . Everyone thought you'd be bigger." This story—as innocent and/or odd as it may seem to be to some—illustrates the power of media to create and shape perceptions, especially when viewers have little, if any, contact with the people being portrayed on the screen, and especially when the media to which they are exposed are limited. Indeed, as much of our historical and contemporary literature suggests—and as our own personal experiences often confirm—the less one knows about a particular group, place, or system, the more one is likely to be influenced by what one sees in the media.[8]

The Influence of US Media in Other Countries

Having traversed these early routes, I turn now to a review of the literature that has influenced my thinking and this work more recently and more directly.[9] I begin first with a review of works that have examined how US TV and Western media more generally have impacted other countries. As is the case in many academic discourses, there are more than two sides to this issue, which continues to be debated.

Cultural Imperialism?

In the 1980s and 1990s, much of the literature was concerned with (1) the extent to which people in other countries consumed US TV, (2) whether this constituted a form of "cultural or media imperialism," and (3) how it affected people in other countries.[10] To some degree these concerns were personified in the worldwide fascination with a then hugely popular US TV drama called *Dallas*.[11] A major hit in the United States, it also absorbed numerous audiences across the globe. Indeed, in the mid-1980s, Ang (1985) counted 90 countries where *Dallas* succeeded in emptying the streets while the program was airing. The show's popularity also made for overloaded telephone and water systems during its commercials. *Dallas* failed only in Brazil and Japan. However, it fascinated a large and diverse audience, including Danish, German, English, Israeli, and Algerian viewers. According to De Bens and de Smaele (2001), this fascination with *Dallas* was still important at the end of the 1990s, several years after the show's initial run ended in the United States.

Following up on this general concern with "Dallasification," Liebes and Katz (1990) researched the question of whether *Dallas* was understood in the same way in different countries and among different sectors within these countries. In essence, they asked, did the drama evoke different kinds of understanding and response among different groups? To study this question, they chose groups of three married couples that were of like age, education, and ethnicity in Israel. These included Israeli Arabs, newly arrived Russian Jews, veteran Moroccan settlers, and members of kibbutzim (typically second-generation Israelis). The Israeli groups were matched with 10 US groups of second-generation Americans in Los Angeles and with 11 groups in Japan. In total there were 65 groups of six persons each. On Sunday night, when *Dallas* was broadcast, each group met in the home of one of the couples together with a trained interviewer, who led a discussion after the broadcast. Researchers also observed the viewers and noted their reactions to the show during the viewing.

What they found was that the groups differed in the way they received or perceived the show, and, as the authors described it, in their inclinations to retell the specific episodes. Arabs and Moroccan Jews tended to describe *Dallas* as a sociological story of family. The couples in the United States and in the kibbutzim saw it as a psychological story of personality, and the Russians saw it as an ideological paradigm with primordial themes, such as the story of Genesis and the rivalry between brothers. The Japanese, however, rejected the story's bid for acceptance as reality; they saw the show as incongruent with what they knew of Japan or the United States, in the traditional or modern sense. They also did not see it as art. They just were not fans. Liebes and Katz's work challenged the then-prevalent view of American cultural imperialism as "a hegemonic message [that] was transferred to the defenseless minds of viewers all over the world; and that this reflected the self-serving interests of the economy and ideology of the exporting country" (4).[12]

Sponges or Filters?

Many other scholars also questioned the cultural imperialism thesis (Downey and Mihelj, 2012; De Bens and de Smaele, 2001). Many began to argue that people in other countries (as well as in the United States) were "not simply passive receivers of information" and that they could alter and interpret the media they watched (Carroll, 2001; Rentfrow, Goldberg, and Zilca, 2011). Elasmar (2003:206) perhaps put it best when he quoted Browne (1967:206), who said that if a picture is worth a thousand words, "those words will not mean the same thing to everyone." I would add that if this is the case, then how many meanings will a moving picture stimulate—especially within different cultures and subcultures?

This is not to deny the fact that US TV is often framed unconsciously by viewers, as well as intentionally by producers, as a representative expression of a major power, if not *the* major power in the world, or that this context may also influence—and make for similar responses to— the "American brand." Indeed, as many of my respondents emphasized, and as Carroll (2001:1) and many others have noted, the United States is generally perceived as an exceedingly powerful country, possessing wealthy transnational corporations, great influence within and among international regulatory organizations, major military might, and the ability to structure and control economic and other interactions all over the world. This macro political and economic context is not without its own influence on viewers consuming US TV. The rapidity of contemporary transnational information flows—many of which emanate from the United States—likely accentuates this view.

Regional Markets

Still other scholars contest and complicate the literature on cultural imperialism, arguing in effect "not so fast": there are and always have been other dynamics at play that influence reception. Straubhaar (2007), for example, analyzed TV schedules he gathered for the past 10 years in over 22 different countries; he examined one week of programming in each year.[13] He did not find that US TV reigned supreme with regard to programming, but rather that there were cultural-linguistic regional markets where viewers watched mainly domestic programming. He found that in Latin America, Asia, and the Middle East, more people watched *transnational* programming—soaps, comedies, news, and variety shows—than truly global channels such as CNN, HBO, MTV, or Discovery.[14] He concluded that there was a multilayered world of television, in which what was common was not US cultural imperialism but hybridization or glocalization, in other words, adaptations or hybrids of global programs and formats to conform to local patterns. Straubhaar also countered the idea, suggested by some media scholars at the time, that people were not really watching much TV, that the medium was no longer as powerful as it once was:

> [F]or most people in most countries, television remains the central element in their consumption of the cultural industries. A television set (or a better television set) is still the main consumer priority for most people in the developing world (and still a high priority elsewhere, as large recent spending on digital high-definition television sets in the richer countries also shows). (Straubhaar, 2007:1)[15]

However, he also held that global TV involved many actors and many levels. Moreover, he argued that most people sought "cultural proximity" (i.e., how culturally similar the programs were to their own cultures) in viewing.[16] He added that although European and African countries continued to import programs primarily from the United States, this was not true in Latin America and the Middle East. Indeed, he found a "trend toward geocultural and transnational cultural-linguistic regions or spaces . . . perhaps as crucial as globalization per se" (7).

He described influences and interactions within each level of society and noted boundaries, cultural constraints or dispositions, rules, enabling forces and conditions, resources, cultural agents, and patterns that underscored continuity. He also discussed emergent changes and threshold events, such as changing technology, hybridization, and multilayered cultures and identities that influenced interactions. He called his theory "complexity theory" and was opposed to more linear theories like cultural imperialism or dependency (8). In essence, although he agreed that capitalism might be a "homogenizing culture force," one that "produced and reproduced a culture of consumerism," he maintained that this operated differently in different nations and classes (18). He categorized the world's main cultural-linguistic regions in the following way: Spanish (Latin America), Chinese (East and Southeast Asia), German (Europe), Hindi and Tamil (Southern Asia and Southeastern Asia, respectively). These regions represented different television markets.[17]

As Bielby and Harrington (2015) pointed out, the earlier works of Liebes and Katz (1990) and Straubhaar (2007) were similar in that both underscored that (1) TV was still important and (2) not all viewers would be affected in the same way by the same program. In essence, as many others have pointed out (Hall, 1981, 1990; Steven, 2003), viewers filter media content through their own culture and experiences. Moreover, Bielby and Harrington (2015) maintained that the move to different types of technological devices (mobile phones, tablets, etc.) has not substantially altered television content consumption. Focusing on youths, they say that Nielsen data indicate that despite young viewers' ready adoption of new media formats and technologies, teens consume the vast majority of their video content via traditional television. Bielby and Harrington also note, however, that "[w]ith few exceptions, globalization of TV has not received much attention" (7).

Formatted Programs

In addition to Straubhaar's (2007) focus on regional markets, other scholars began to contest the notion that viewers were empty slates upon which US or Western media would make an indelible and irreversible mark. They introduced a host of new terms to describe these perspectives and focus areas, including formatted programming and international TV, glocalization, hybridity, diasporic media, and translational media culture. For example, Esser (2010), analyzing US schedules from 2007 and 2008, found that 33 percent of prime-time programs had formatted programing, that is, shows (*Big Brother, X Factor, Survivor, Pop Idol*, etc.) that follow a particular format, such as game shows and reality shows. Not all of the formats originated in the United States, and many of them have been remade in multiple markets with local contestants. Esser noted the business incentives driving the sale of formats, for if a format becomes a global hit, revenues far surpass the money derived from canned programs. She says it is "safe to hypothesize that due to the rise of formatted programming and the continued use of American fiction, the amount of content shared by audience across the world is growing" (289). However, she also saw a "convergence of 'concrete cultural content' albeit adapted locally, reflecting knowledge, faces and dialects" (289). So in this sense, although she agreed with Straubhaar (2007) that we will continue to have national and regional TV, she took issue with him, arguing that we will also have international TV (290), that is, TV that also has common (global) links in programming.

Glocalization

Other authors focused on the emergence of *glocal* or strongly localized and hybridized adaptations of global patterns.[18] Indeed, Štětka (2012a, 2012b) refers to the shift from the earlier one-way street of US TV to the now more common media freeway or expressway by referencing Tunstall's 1977 book, *The Media Are American*, and his 2008 follow-up, *The Media Were American*. Although Štětka found that in films the United States was still king in 2011, TV presented a different picture, with more domestic products emerging in other countries. Indeed, the author described three stages of media globalization: (1) emerging globalization, (2) increasing globalization, and (3) declining globalization. This last period is marked by an increasing number of local adaptations of global TV formats, such as *Dancing with the Stars* and *The Voice*. Downey and Mihelj (2012) also found in their analyses of TV programming in Central and Eastern Europe that the top 10 programs tended to be glocal, that is, imported or domestic shows with transnational formats.

Some authors have examined the *specific* impact of glocal media in different parts of the world. Lewis and Martin (2010), for example, examined the role of "lifestyle advice television" programming—cooking and health shows, reality-style makeover shows, and consumer advice programs—in Australia, Taiwan, and Singapore. They found that what united these shows was their concern with instructing their audiences in everyday life skills while showcasing the latest consumer products and services. In their article they argued that, by instructing ordinary viewers in the "art of living," these shows play a significant role in shaping social identities, consumer practices, and personal lifestyles in the region. They also stated that these shows contribute to the formation of new consumer-oriented middle classes comprising people whose lives and aspirations are continually influenced by the varied local, national, regional, and global formations of lifestyle culture and consumption.

Kraidy (2008) provides an interesting example of the extent to which glocalized formats can come to be of huge importance to their audiences, as well as to political actors. He uses as a case study based on *Superstar 3*, a popular pan-Arab reality show (similar to *American Idol* in the United States and based on the British show *Pop Idol*) that was hugely popular in both Lebanon and Syria. He examines how at one point the winner of the show influenced the politics and political identity of audiences and high-level politicians. He begins with an analysis of how and why there were two small spontaneous riots in Beirut, Lebanon, over the elimination of the Lebanese contestant and the elevation of the Syrian candidate who won. Providing a historical context for the tensions between the two countries, he notes that France created Lebanon by carving territory out of Syria during World War II to make a place for Maronite Christians. Syria was generally seen as more powerful than Lebanon, and it consequently controlled Lebanon, which feared Syria's secret police. Kraidy (2008:10) points out that the fact that groups as disparate as Hamas, business owners, and governments felt compelled to intervene in the dispute over the winner of an Arab reality-TV contest testifies to the power that these groups ascribed to popular culture and to the political and economic advantages they believed they could reap from participating in such a debate. As he notes, the show was a magnet for social and political actors who knew that having a voice in the debate would yield them greater media coverage and better opportunities to mobilize their supporters.

Diasporic Media and Hybridity

The rise of diasporic media further challenged the notion that Western media were conquering and homogenizing the world.[19] Dudrah (2002) focused on Zee TV–Europe and the construction of a pan-European South Asian identity. Zee TV has as one of its goals the development of a world identity for South Asians similar to that being developed by indigenous people worldwide or by people of African descent. Zee TV–Europe shows South Asians living in other parts of Europe celebrating similar holidays but with different (acquired?) accents. Dudrah argues that for South Asians these programs expand or change concepts of who they are. Thompson (2002) also focused on people who had originated in the Indian subcontinent (South Asia) but who were living in Western countries (especially the United States and the United Kingdom), and examined their media consumption through their use of new technologies, such as the Internet, and older technologies, like the video player, cable or satellite television, radio, and telephone. He found that, contrary to what assimilation theory might have predicted, that is, the replacement of the ethnic immigrant culture with that of the culture of the host nation, in contexts where multicultural policies were supported, viewers' habits and preferences may accentuate ethnoreligious differences rather than blur them and may lead to new hybrid identities and cultures. In addition, he found that middle-class immigrants were more inclined to resist cultural assimilation than their lower-class counterparts. Georgiou (2012) also examined diasporic media and focused on transnational Arabic soap operas. She studied their appeal to young women born in the diaspora in terms of raising both critical perspectives as well as cultural connections.

International Connections

Some authors argue that the perspective and media of diasporic communities challenge the traditional ways of conceptualizing, regulating, and running national television.[20] In essence, while some argue that diaspora media reflect an intermixing of cultures to sustain traditional cultural closeness, others argue that such mixing of cultures may make for a change in home cultures and be empowering for those looking to escape cultural isolation and enter into a larger transnational conversation. Li (2015) provides an example of this view in describing Makmende, who is seen as a Kenyan superhero but who emerged from a mixture of cultural appropriations and remixes of music and film references, including Clint Eastwood's catchphrase, "Make my day."

Some also view Spanish-language programming and the creation of programming in English or Spanglish for Latinos/Hispanics as media of the diaspora because they are created to appeal to people of Latin American or Spanish descent in the United States.[21] However, who creates diasporic media is complex. They might be the result of a grassroots movement of people creating TV shows who have come together and would like to view more programming that reflects, reinforces, or appeals to them culturally or nationally (see Prey, 2011). Or they might be the result of large conglomerates that develop programming, for example in Venezuela, Mexico, or Brazil, for the consumption of Spanish-speaking audiences in the United States or other countries. Then again, the media might be the development of US corporations that are seeking to capture this market in the United States by developing Hispanic-oriented media, including NBC's Telemundo, Fusion, NuvoTV, and others.[22]

MTV

MTV was also seen by some to have been an agent of cultural hegemonic forces, introducing youths of other countries to US youth culture and in the process challenging or corrupting their traditional values, styles, preferences, and behaviors. But *New York Times* journalist Deborah Sontag has maintained that it actually played an important role in the creation of diasporic media. This was perhaps best articulated in an article she wrote on MTV World in which she described the *diasporic* dimensions of the *glocal* phenomena in the United States (Sontag, 2005). According to Sontag, in the late 1980s, when MTV started to establish channels abroad, critics viewed it as cultural imperialism and an attempt to homogenize youth culture worldwide. However, MTV learned that it made better business sense to be glocal, that is, to think globally but act locally. The premise was that young people, wherever they are, would watch international acts but only for so long before they wanted to see something of their own. So each of MTV's international channels developed local talent and its own personality. Consequently, MTV Indonesia came to have a Muslim call to prayer, MTV Italy had cooking shows, and MTV Brazil was colorful and bare.

According to Sontag (2005), in its subsequent phase, MTV did "market research" through house parties and mini groups involving Asian Americans in New York and Los Angeles, and concluded that the second generations in the United States also desired their own age-appropriate connections to their parents' homeland, but they also passionately wanted to see TV programming that mirrored their own struggle to define themselves as hyphenated Americans. The assumption at MTV was that young bicultural Americans have tastes that are not only different from those of monocultural youths in the United States but also different from those of youths in their ethnic homelands. Therefore, they need a customized MTV. As Sontag notes, MTV had long exported American pop culture to the world, but now it was reversing the direction and trying to import global pop culture into the United States.

Making reference to an ongoing debate about the "cultural space inhabited by children of immigrants and immigrants," and to the extent to which "hybridity" makes it a place of its own, she noted that many US youths have a "transnational identity." She argued that this identity was encouraged and supported by those involved in jet travel and technological and global commerce. They and their children maintained vital, current links to their homelands, which they never really left behind.

Critique of the Diasporic Perspective

Ang (2003), however, takes issue with the diasporic perspective. She argues that "it is only in the past few decades—with the increased possibilities of keeping in touch with the old homeland and with co-ethnics in other parts of the world through faster and cheaper jet transport, mass media and electronic telecommunications that migrant groups have become collectively more inclined to see themselves not as minorities within nation-states, but as members of global diasporas that span national boundaries" (142). She contends that this feeds into a *transnational nationalism* that is based on the presumption of internal ethnic sameness and external ethnic distinctiveness (145). Consequently, diasporas often involve drawing a boundary around the diaspora, and this is double-edged. This can make it a site of both support—for those deemed to be within the group—and oppression—for (1) those who do not conform sufficiently to the in-group definitions and (2) those who are not members of the group and who may be targeted for their "otherness" (142). This construct, he maintains, reinforces the differences of the group from others and so perpetuates their "otherness" status. It also reinforces sameness within the group and constricts the options of those within the group. In essence, within this view, "[d]ifference is absolutized" (146). She advocates "moving beyond diaspora, into hybridity" (153).

Corporate Dominance: Does It Continue or Extend Cultural Hegemony in the 21st Century?

Although many authors have rejected the idea that US or Western media were hegemonic, other authors have continued to express concern with the dominance of US global and corporate media and its impact on other countries (Noam, 2009; Wu, 2010; González and Torres, 2011). Barber (2001), for example, in his book *Jihad vs. McWorld: Terrorism's Challenge to Democracy*, described McWorld as representing universalizing markets and as making national borders porous from without.[23] He wrote in the 1995 edition of his book that "the cultural wars are being won hands down by American television" (102). Indeed, he saw the Americanization of global television as "proceeding even faster than the globalization of American films" (101). Although he was writing more broadly about media and not just television, he contended that television had a particular influence. For example, he noted that while films were McWorld's preferred software, television was its preferred medium. In essence, while films were one-shot deals, television was a permanent ticket to ceaseless film-watching anytime, anywhere (101). In America, he wrote, "it is often television that makes policy" (112) and the corporate sector (or business) that is the major beneficiary of global media. Acknowledging that technological changes had ushered in greater global diversity and changes in content, such as global rap, his bottom line was that, despite what viewers perceived, business or corporations were still in control. He also argued that McWorld was rooted in consumption and profit, and that in this world, everyone was a consumer but no one was a citizen (6–7ff.).

After the fall of the twin towers in 2001, Barber's publisher issued a second edition of his book. Here Barber wrote:

> The struggle of Jihad against McWorld is not a clash of civilizations but a dialectical expression of tensions built into a single global civilization as it emerges against a backdrop of traditional ethnic and religious divisions, many of which are actually created by McWorld and its infotainment industries and technological innovations. Imagine bin Laden without modern media. . . . Imagine terrorism without its reliance on credit cards, global financial systems, modern technology and the Internet. (xvi)

Barber is not opposed to capitalism in the world of media—actually, he sees capitalism as an economic engine that drives change. His objection is with "unrestrained capitalism counterbalanced by no other system of values that endangers democracy." His concern was to "prevent monopoly control over information, and to interdict that quiet, comfortable coercion through which television, advertising and entertainment can constrict real liberty of choice" (296). The titans of media today, he argued, are far more powerful than earlier barons like Rockefeller or Vanderbilt because their power is over pictures, information, and ideas.

A Medium in Transition

Still other authors have focused on television as a medium in transition amid new global media formations. For example, Picard (2011:233ff.) maintains that although US-produced media content and services dominate the global trade in television programming, dominant ownership of media and content firms is increasingly non-American. Artz and Kamalipour (2007) also argued that the new global media formation was marked by the collaboration of capitalist classes across national borders. This, they argue, will lead to transnational media formation in which global media become quite similar and national media production is diminished.

Numerous other works have also examined and raised concerns about the consolidation of media companies (Noam, 2009), the power of US media to frame terrorism and legitimate US intervention (Freedman and Kishan Thussu, 2011), and the control of information by the media (González and Torres, 2011). Kuipers (2012), however, argues that the extent to which global media replace media of the nation-state depends on how close (or far) the nation-state is to the geographic and cultural center. Focusing on the reception in various countries to the film *The Lord of the Rings: The Return of the King*, she finds that "relatively few people have a primarily global identity" and that national repertoires of evaluation can supersede global or transnational "repertoires of evaluation."

Lotz (2013) provided something of a summation with regard to the state of the media literature in this area when she reviewed recent major volumes on global TV. She found a "medium in transition," one that had moved from mass- to niche-audience norms, with viewers less concerned with "liveness," that is, seeing programs when they first air. But she also found that changes in TV systems—the development of new ways of viewing TV and new ways of producing and distributing it—were nation-specific and viewer-specific. Her answer to the question of "what (or where) is television today" is this: it very much depends on where you are (192). For example, in some countries, the "absence of better TV" influences the degree to which people in that area like US TV. This was clearly a theme that resonated among some of my respondents and explained why they watched and liked US TV—in other words, they said it was the best option, given what was available in their country. However, in some countries, Lotz noted that well-made domestic shows (e.g., telenovelas) beat out US TV, but it was not clear if this was true of all age groups. Scheduling also influenced consumption of US TV. For example, if US TV shows aired during prime time, they were more likely to be watched.

Lotz (2013) also observed that TV studies published in the post-broadcast era have pushed beyond the Anglo-American nexus and been very aware of TV as a digital medium that viewers can access in a wide variety of ways—via mobile phones, game consoles, iPads, YouTube, Hulu, Joost, the BBC's iPlayer, Microsoft's Windows Media Player, and Apple TV, among other options. She concluded that we don't know much about how the attributes and features of digital TV affect viewers and societies. But just because "audiences can use a DVR to watch a show created by a broadcast network does not erase the fact that the program was created within the industrial logics of broadcasting" (196). Finally, as this review has indicated, the literature on how US or Western media influence people in the United States and in other countries is wide ranging and, as Lotz (2013) concludes, we don't yet have "widely shared terms." However, Lotz interestingly adds, "nor should we, necessarily" (195).

Summary

During the mid- to late 1960s, McLuhan and Fiore's book *The Medium Is the Massage*, the National Advisory Commission's report, and other works brought to the fore the role and the impact of media on our lives and perceptions. At about the same time, media were becoming a truly global phenomenon. In this early period, the United States dominated the production of TV and movies, and a growing number of scholars took a critical look at the impact of US media on the lives of people throughout the world. Concerns were raised by literary critics and by leadership in other countries about cultural imperialism and how this went hand in glove with US economic and military imperialism.

As the 20th century entered its final decade and the Cold War thawed a bit after the Reagan presidency, scholars began to critique this view of cultural imperialism. In a somewhat dialectical manner, they began to draw attention to the agency that global viewers had and brought to their viewing of US TV. Others focused on the filters that accompanied such viewing, regardless of whether viewers lived in the United States or elsewhere; and many concluded that not all viewers would be affected in the same way by the same program. The business of TV also became more global in this post–Cold War period, as other countries turned to developing their own media productions. Countries began *adapting* US TV, not just adopting it. Global citizens exercised their agency, critiqued US TV, and began developing their own TV shows. The changes to the titles of media scholar Tunstall's books on the media reflect this major shift. In 1977, his book was titled *The Media Are American*; in 2008, it was *The Media Were American*.

In the 21st century, the business of TV has become even more global. Scholars have written about corporate dominance and control, and the growing consolidation of the TV, movie, and other media industries via multinational corporations. As we move further into the 21st century, the migration of countless people around the world has led to diverse and increasingly heterogeneous populations in countries that had come to view their populations as homogenous. This has created diasporic communities in many countries and new forms of hybridity throughout these countries, which in turn have led to the creation of new media and new media forms—and all of these changes have been assisted by changes in technology. These new developments in the media landscape have also become areas of scholarly study and led to new discussions about a "medium in transition" (Lotz, 2013). In describing my journey *to* and *through* the literature, I have not attempted a comprehensive review of the literature. Rather I have focused on the literature that examines the influence of US media on viewers in the United States and in other countries. In the next chapter, I focus on the literature that has most directly influenced the construction of my questionnaire in this work.

2

Building on Previous Studies in the United States and Other Countries

As noted previously, my reading of works by Iyer (1988), McLuhan and Fiore (1967), and Suskind (2001) sensitized me to the influence of US media throughout the world. The studies I reviewed impressed upon me how important TV viewing has been and continues to be—despite the changes in technology, access, and ownership, and in how programming has been developed and distributed since the 1960s. TV's influence has been pervasive and for decades now has helped shape our perceptions (and misperceptions) of race, gender, class, and otherness more generally, and of ourselves and our place in society. But it was the more empirically based work of others in the United States and in other countries that inspired me to set up my research questions as I did.

For example, the Liebes and Katz (1990) study on *Dallas* (1978–91) drew my attention to the process of *collective meaning making*. This refers to how when people watch TV together, they connect with other viewers on a common subject, the program. Liebes and Katz argued that this process of collective meaning making was especially important for those who felt marginalized as their views were likely reinforced by others while watching the same program.[1] This is a bit like today's online discussions of popular TV programs. In the more recent literature, scholars have referred to this process of collective meaning making as "bonding" or "bridging" (Childress, 2012; Wayne, 2015, 2016), which has continued even with the introduction of new media and greater opportunities to watch TV anytime. Bonding and bridging over television content were evident in the interviews that Wayne (2016) conducted with middle-class Americans about their viewing of TV regardless of how they accessed TV. They can also be seen, if we reflect, in casual encounters we have with others about what we watch and our reactions to it. These conversations about programs (or films) often serve as a bridge on which we interact and, in some cases, bond with others.

As a result of the Liebes and Katz (1990) findings on collective meaning making, I asked my respondents whether they watched TV alone or with family or friends, and whether they discussed what they saw on TV with others at home, at school, on the Internet, or on the job. Their responses to these questions often gave me more insight into (1) the role that US TV had played in their lives and (2) the contexts within which my respondents lived, that is, whether they lived in countries where US TV was restricted, limited to certain class levels, or seen as relevant only to particular generations of viewers. Let me illustrate.

For some respondents, watching TV was a common, regular, family-centered event. For others, it was a solitary event wherein they watched US TV on the Internet by themselves, although they often discussed the programs with others on the Internet, at school, or in other contexts. (This was the experience, for example, of a number of my Chinese respondents whose options on their terrestrial television were often restricted by the government.) Still other respondents described intergenerational differences: They watched US TV alone (if they did not have same-sex siblings),[2] and their parents watched TV in other languages. For example, some of my respondents from Kyrgyzstan said that they watched MTV and other programs in English, but their parents watched TV in Russian, and their grandparents watched programs in Kryg. I found a similar generational and linguistic pattern among some of my respondents from Latin America, where Spanish-language "telenovelas" were consumed family style for part of the day, and then they watched US TV programs alone via the Internet or cable.

Referential Reading and Emotional Realism

Two other concepts in the Liebes and Katz study influenced the construction of my questionnaire. One was the idea of how viewers participate in *referential reading*.[3] By this, Liebes and Katz (1990:100) mean that the viewer often reads (or sees) the programs as connecting with real life. This also surfaced as a theme among my respondents, as they said they often expect places they visit to be exactly as they had seen them depicted on TV. However, just as in the Liebes and Katz study, my respondents differed with regard to whether they made referential or critical comments on the show's relationship to real life. In the Liebes and Katz study, the most critical comments were made by the Russians, then the Americans and kibbutzniks, followed by the Moroccan Jews and Arabs. To some degree, the more educated the groups were, the more critical they were (101). Interestingly, Liebes and Katz argued that respondents' critical statements and referential statements were generally equally involving: people were involved with the show, whether they made cool (cerebral/cognitive) or hot (emotional) statements about it.[4]

However, when they examined the Japanese couples' reactions to the show, they found that their critical statements were not necessarily involving.[5] Indeed, the Japanese couples made few referential statements and, compared with the other groups in the study, saw less of *Dallas*, and in Japan the show was pulled after only six months. Liebes and Katz reasoned that the facts that the show was broadcast late at night and that Japan had developed its own TV and did not then import much from other countries may have contributed to the Japanese couples' very different responses to the show.[6] This concept of referential reading alerted me to consider variables in my foreign-born respondents' lives that might have influenced their viewing of US TV; for example, the fact that many had attended American schools or that their parents were affiliated with US companies might have heightened their referential reading or increased their access to, and interest in, US TV.

In constructing my questionnaire, I was also influenced by Liebes and Katz's concept of *emotional realism*. Do viewers believe the show is emotionally genuine or in sync with their own emotional responses to the stories and characters on the show?[7] For viewers of the *Dallas* series in each of the countries Liebes and Katz studied—with the notable exception of Japan—the answer was yes. The Japanese viewers deviated considerably from the rest in their dislike of the show, and Liebes and Katz worked with a Japanese colleague to understand why. Together they concluded that the Japanese respondents saw the show as reflecting a way of life they had abandoned and which they thought the United States represented. For them, *Dallas* represented a previous era in their history. They were now grass-eating, not meat-eating people; more peaceful, less aggressive. They saw the characters as too stereotyped and therefore unreal. They also saw contradictions in *Dallas*'s depictions of characters. For example, if they were rich, why did they carry their own suitcase and set their own table? They felt the female characters were depicted as being too strong and, therefore, unattractive. (At the time, viewers in Japan, both male and female, were turned off by strong women; they saw weakness in women as an attractive trait.) They saw the sexual overtures between and among characters as too blatant. In general, they felt the show's characters were unrestrained in pursuing their passions for power, wealth, and sex—a way of living that violated Japanese sensibilities of how people should interact, publicly and privately, to achieve and maintain harmonious relationships. They also thought that the characters all looked alike and that their depictions were flat, too simple, not subtle or cunning, as in Japanese drama. They liked another US TV show, *Columbo*, because the title character showed weaknesses, as did real people. Finally, they didn't like the cliffhangers and the unhappy endings that were very much a part of the show. They did, however, like *Little House on the Prairie*, a family drama that chronicled the life and adventures of an American family in the 19th-century American West.

Curiously, the Japanese respondents did not see the *Dallas* characters as rich or upper class: they deemed their clothes and houses shabby, and the idea of marriage based on romantic love, they felt, was a middle-class view. In essence, the world presented was remote for them then—and possibly, I might add, not one that they wanted to emulate or embrace during the period in which they were interviewed. The 1980s, which is when this study took place, was a period when the economic sun was rising in the East, not the West. The results of Liebes and Katz's study in Japan and their concept of emotional realism made me more conscious of how political, economic, social, and cultural contexts influence how viewers, both in the United States and in other countries, receive US TV.

Finally, Liebes and Katz (1990) raised two key questions for me: What kind of critical viewing ability did my respondents bring to the programs watched? And what did they take away about the United States, and about Americans, from viewing programs such as these? These questions influenced my decision to craft my questionnaire in such a way as to ascertain how *aware* my respondents are of the influence of American TV in their lives, how it may have helped shape their views of the United States and their views of race, ethnicity, class, and gender.[8] Last, and perhaps somewhat inadvertently, this now classic and foundational study also touched upon the issue of race or physical difference. One of their Moroccan viewers commented that all of the actors on *Dal-*

las had "blue eyes" (46). This takeaway may not have been anticipated by the authors of the study, and they did not pay particular attention to it, yet it might have been a fairly common takeaway in the worlds of predominantly brown-eyed audiences then. And it may continue to be a common takeaway among many global viewers—as is suggested by the story noted earlier about the Chinese student at Columbia University who said he expected that, when he came to New York City, he would be surrounded by White friends with blue eyes and yellow hair.

Although Liebes and Katz (1990) were among the first to discuss these concepts, subsequent authors conducted research that continued to show that, despite changes in the ways in which American TV is accessed, consumed, or owned, TV is still an important part of people's lives; and that not all viewers are affected in the same way by the same program. In essence, media content is filtered through one's own culture and experiences (Straubhaar, 2007; Bielby and Harrington, 2015; Hall, 1981, 1990; Steven, 2003). These works reinforced my sense that this is still an important area to research, with implications not only for communications and media but also for sociology and the social sciences. These works also contributed to my interest in sampling people from a wide range of countries, as well as from the United States. In addition, the fact that other authors have continued to investigate why particular US programs, or US TV in general, have been so popular in particular countries was another feature of the literature that contributed to my assessments about sampling and questionnaire development. For example, Imre (2009) discussed why other US TV shows were, and are, so popular in Eastern Europe, and Vujnovic (2008) examined the popularity of Latin American telenovelas in Croatia.

Research on Former Soviet Republics and China

The Vujnovic (2008) study was of particular interest to me because the author concluded that Latin American telenovelas were "only partly a cultural product of Latin American identity" and were "more largely the carriers of the broader values of the Western culture industries." The flow of telenovelas to other countries appears to have preceded the influx of US TV in certain countries, particularly those with strained political relations with the United States, like the Soviet Union. I am reminded of a former Russian student who shared with me a tape of a very popular tele-novela that had been dubbed in Russian and that she said was all the rage in the predominantly Russian immigrant community of Brighton Beach, Brooklyn, at the time. The student indicated that this love of telenovelas began in Russia. She recalled that when she was living there, she and her mother would wait in long breadlines. However, when the popular tele-novela was about to air, the queue would dissipate, as everyone rushed home to catch the latest installment of the show. According to her, in addition to being drawn to the melodramatic class- and gender-based plots, Russian audiences were also fascinated by the backdrops, that is, the material comforts of the characters' homes and clothing, which were not available to the everyday Russians at the time.

The dissolution of the Soviet Union resulted in the "fast and furious" arrival of Western media to countries that had not previously received much US TV. This, in turn, provided scholars an opportunity to research the impact of Western and global media on these countries in a some-what controlled manner (see Havens, Imre, and Lustyik, 2012; Downey and Mihelj, 2012). Tomascikova (2010), for example, explored the impact of British situation comedies on perceptions of class in Slovakia. Zand-berg (2006) focused on the advertising accompanying television in the United States and Poland.

Some studies assumed that globalization of markets would be ac-companied by a defense or strengthening of local cultural, ethnic, and national identity. A postmodern shift in theorizing globalization also suggested that cultural heterogeneity was produced even when local cul-tures assimilated and adopted Western popular culture. For example, Ramet and Crnković (2003) argued that this resulted in an interactive dynamic in which US media influenced other cultures and other cul-tures' media influenced the United States. These studies made me curi-ous about how the views of people from former Soviet Republics would have changed (or not) after coming to the United States.

Another opportunity to examine the impact of Western (or now global or international) media occurred when the 2008 Beijing Olym-pics were televised internationally. Zeng, Go, and Kolmer (2011) exam-ined the impact of international Olympic coverage on China's image and found that the image remained relatively stable, but that, indirectly, awareness of China was raised in the international media.[9] These case studies on the impact of Western media in the former Soviet Republics and in China contributed greatly to my decision to make a special effort to include viewers from these countries in my sample. In addition, as I note in subsequent chapters, the perspectives of viewers from these countries were particularly enlightening, and they demonstrated the dramatic influence of US TV in areas that had had (or have) very little contact with Western media.

Works Examining the Impact of *Non-US* Media in Other Countries

In their 1994 volume *Unthinking Eurocentrism: Multiculturalism and the Media*, Shohat and Stam questioned, in a major way, the extent to which much of Hollywood and Western media were Eurocentric. Works in other countries also began to examine their domestic media and how gender, race, immigrants, and otherness in general were represented. The results of these studies are similar to those noted earlier with regard to the portrayal of gender, class, and ethnic and racial minorities in the United States. In essence, the studies found that there was much underrepresentation and misrepresentation of those deemed "Others" in almost all countries.[10] Similar research questions, about the accurate representation of gender, immigrants, and minorities (including racial distinctions), and the consumption of media among youth and members of different social and economic classes, were also being pursued.

To take gender as an example, Eisend (2010) performed a wide-ranging review of the literature on gender stereotyping in radio and television ads in different countries and found that although some change had occurred over time, gender stereotyping was still prevalent in advertising. Similarly, Steinhagen, Eisend, and Knoll (2010) examined gender stereotypes in ads and focused on German TV. She did *not* find fewer stereotypes on public TV but did find that the ads differed in terms of the types of gender stereotypes that predominated. Private TV channels emphasized role behavior and physical characteristics, while public channels showed genders in more stereotyped occupational statuses. These approaches and findings did not differ substantively from research on gender stereotyping in ads in the United States. Likewise Franco (2008) analyzed the *Extreme Makeover* series in countries in Western Europe and found that even though there were some cultural differences evident between the Western European countries that aired the show and the United States, the "formulaic narrative structure" of this format perpetuated traditional gender and class norms. Moreover, she argued that even though participants undergo a transformation, they are not necessarily empowered or endowed with agency.[11] So, at the same time that media scholars and writers were developing and expanding the literature in different directions in the United States, scholars in other countries were studying how their domestic programming was influencing viewers.

Different Areas of Research

Scholars in other countries pursued some questions and areas of research that differed from those explored by researchers in the United States. This was due, in large part, to the fact that different countries have different media histories. For example, in the European literature there was a focus on what "state media policies" were or should be, with greater distinctions made between public and private TV content.[12] But the US government does not generally articulate a state media policy as the media in the United States are overwhelmingly commercial. However, many countries in Europe have a strong tradition of public broadcasting. There was also work on (and critiques of) how the media projected the idea of European homogeneity and "homogenous" immigrant groups (Ogan, 2011; El Sghiar, 2011; Vidmar Horvat, 2010; Kydd, 2001; Haag, 2010; Goren, 2013).[13] This was clearly a factor of interest (and perhaps concern) after the creation of the European Union.

Homogeneity

In the US literature, scholars have also been critical of the tendency to view minority or immigrant groups as homogenous; however, this has been more evident in the racial and ethnic studies literature, and is not a well-established theme in the mainstream media literature. This tendency to view immigrants or ethnic groups as homogenous is similar to the tendency to consider all Africans, all Latinos, or all Asians as if they all came from a single place called Africa, Latin America, or Asia.

Kosnick (2004) focuses on Islamic immigrants in Germany and writes that seeing them as homogenous reinforces essentialist notions of groups. She looks to the television media that different groups produce to illustrate her point that Islamic immigrants are not homogenous entities. The author examines two Alevi Turkish migrant programs in Berlin on open (free) channels. One program emphasizes how Alevi Turks are different from Sunni Turks. For example, they don't pray five times a day; they build schools not mosques; there is no separation of women and men; women don't wear special clothing; and they don't regard drinking alcohol or eating pork as wrongdoing. This program emphasizes how similar Alevi Turks are to Germans and how they might be seen as a model minority in the country in contrast to the stereotypes of Islamic immigrants in Germany. The other program, however, seeks to emphasize the immigrant group's similarities to all Turks and to being Turkish. These two programs have different audiences and underscore the different strategies for coexistence. One is the model minority (or benign Islam) vis-à-vis Germans, and the other highlights the moral and sexual integrity they have, like Turks in their homeland. Kosnick (2004) notes, however, that there is a third strategy for Alevis: to stress their political history of suffering to mobilize Alevi solidarity. However, Norris and Inglehart (2009:304) take issue with this view in that it often falsely assumes a zero-sum game in which one has to choose between identifying with one's country and feeling part of a broader world community.[14]

These strategies are historical and familiar to researchers who study assimilation and bicultural models of adaptation. Some groups or individuals will seek to assimilate quickly, while others wish to retain their unique differences, language, and culture. What is different today is that we have media outlets that reflect and reinforce these two general strategies. These types of programming are similar to those adopted in the US Latino media community, and in other immigrant communities in the United States. Some programs (and individuals) emphasize the community's similarities to all Americans; others accentuate their uniqueness and difference from "the Americans." Historically, much Spanish-language programming has accentuated differences and English-language or "Hispanic" programs have emphasized similarities, while the newer hybrid, or Spanglish, programs (i.e., those programs that incorporate both the Spanish and English languages and cultural views, e.g., *Jane the Virgin*) project a middle road.

State Media Policy Analysis

In terms of media policy analysis, the European Commission (2009) undertook a nine-month study to analyze 150 diversity media initiatives undertaken in the (then) 27 European Union (EU) member states plus Iceland, Liechtenstein, and Norway. The study's researchers recommended 30 of the best practices that they felt would lead to greater social cohesion, preventing conflict and improving the ways in which groups facing discrimination were represented. Their objective also included "hardwiring effective practices into media management processes" (p. 6). Frachon, Vargaftig, and Briot (1994) also surveyed 15 countries in Europe on differing national responses to issues of ethnicity, cultural diversity, and migration, and the media's handling of such matters, and ter Wal (2002) presented an overview of research and examples of good practice in six countries in the EU from 1995 to 2000. This latter project was called the MEDIVA research project and focused on media and migration between the Maghreb and Southern Europe. Niessen and Huddleston (2009: chap. 2) outlined strategies to improve integration in the EU. As is suggested by these studies, it is clear that the EU has studied the issue of diversity and the media from a policy perspective, and different countries have developed distinctive policy approaches. Some of these approaches have changed over time. For example, Awad and Roth (2011) discussed the shift in the Netherlands in media policy from targeted minority media to cross-cultural media targeted at multiple (and in many cases all) social groups. In this case, instead of a focus on one minority, media policy was now aimed at all minorities and, typically, at the majority audiences simultaneously.

The subtle, but important, implications of such a shift from allowing (or developing) media of (and by) particular minorities to a focus on multiple groups as part of a whole are illustrated by Haag (2010). He focused on an Australian song ("I Am Australian") and a German commercial ("You Are Germany"),[15] both of which stressed the message that "we are one but many." Selecting examples from both Australia and Germany, he illustrated how this phrase—and its accompanying campaign—was used to construct national unity through diversity. (This is in some ways reminiscent of the US motto, *e pluribus unum*—out of many, one [Schlesinger, 1992].) Haag's examples reflect the shift described by Awad and Roth in terms of how diversity perhaps should and would be viewed in the media, that is, from a focus on particular groups to a focus on all groups within the same context.

Clearly there is debate within Europe on the benefits and disadvantages of multiculturalism (Horsti, 2009). Indeed, as numerous articles in the *Economist* have noted, the issue of *how to address* diversity (because of increased migration) has affected not just European nations but other countries as well.[16] Shome (2012, 144) offers an interesting take on this issue. She questions whether the multicultural approach taken in Anglo-American national cultures is an effective way to "map and address relations of cultural otherness." Shome says multiculturalism in the West is so nation-bound that it is inadequate to comprehend the logics of non-Western cultural inequality. Moreover, she says, other countries, such as Singapore, Malaysia, Hong Kong, and India, have their own histories of conflict and accommodations that are now "intricately woven into the fabric of neighborly belonging." She maintains that the concept of integration, which underlies the Anglo-American concept of multiculturalism, assumes that new groups will integrate (or should be helped to integrate) into the majority culture. This, she argues, may contrast sharply with approaches that have been developed in other countries.

Prey (2011:110–11) provides an interesting point of contrast in this debate. Conducting an ethnographic study of multiethnic media in South Korea, he found that while Europe was bemoaning the failure of multicultural approaches for their immigrants,[17] South Korea seemed to be welcoming immigrants. He also observed that in South Korea "life with difference does go on in relatively convivial terms" (Prey, 2011:111). Then again, although it is important to study the micro level—the everyday practices of multiculturalism—it is also important to understand these practices within the macro context. South Korea is known to be one of the most ethnically homogenous nations in the world, with one of the world's lowest birth rates and a rapidly aging society. It has been dependent on migrant workers to do the "so-called 3D jobs" (dirty, dangerous, and difficult) (Prey, 2011:113). South Korean men have also imported women from other countries for marriage. As a result, South Korea's immigrant and migrant worker population has increased in a major and necessary way. The migrations are also mainly South to South and not South to North, as is the case in migrations to the Western or Anglo-American countries.

Taking a longer-range view, Malik (2010) reviewed the development of multicultural programming in Europe. She examined how the traditional analogue national broadcasters had to contend with the changes that the 1990s introduced because of the introduction of satellite, cable, and digital commercial channels—and from which diasporic TV also emerged. She concluded that, prior to the 1990s, the United Kingdom, Germany, and the Netherlands took an assimilationist approach (aka integration) and sought to have immigrants identify with the nation. That changed, however, during the 1990s. Malik stated: "Like the UK, regions such as The Netherlands and Sweden proclaimed themselves to be multicultural societies and to favor positive discrimination for their ethnic minorities" (125). Germany and Austria incorporated multicultural programming as a form of public television. Accordingly, they developed programming that sought to present the nation as multicultural. Interestingly, she notes that France, Belgium, and Spain, on the other hand, took an individual integrationist approach and emphasized "common aspects of humanity such as love, death, birth and friendship" (125).

However, according to Malik (2010:125), in the years following the 1990 Broadcasting Act, multicultural programming in Europe was undermined by the emerging cultures of commercialism triggered by increasing competition, greater technological development, and less regulation. Diasporic television, Malik argues, changed media in these countries and challenged the nation concept. This seems similar to the role that some say Univision, Telemundo, and other networks aimed at Latinos in the United States play in that they challenge English-dominant public and commercial television. But recently in the United States, we have seen change occurring in the opposite direction. Several English-language broadcast TV shows have incorporated Spanish-language network models or language (Diaz, 2011). For example, *Jane the Virgin, Devious Maids, Cristela, Modern Family, Ugly Betty*, and *Telenovela* all have or have had characters who openly and consistently speak Spanish and refer to their cultural backgrounds or distinctiveness.

Moran (2009:84–88, 102–9) offers a striking case of how one television show defied national boundaries and spread around the world in the 21st century. He describes *Ugly Betty* as unique in terms of transnational flows of programs in that it originated in Colombia before being exported to various countries in Latin America, including Chile, Ecuador, Venezuela, Bolivia, and Argentina, and then to Central America. The Colombian original also appeared in the Philippines and Spain; the following year, it was shown in Brazil as *Betty, a Feia*, and on cable channel Telemundo in the United States in Spanish. By 2003 dubbed versions of the show were broadcast in Hungary and Bulgaria, and by 2004 in Turkey, Italy, and Japan.

The show was then remade in the United States, where it appeared from 2006 to 2010. The US version was also sold in the United Kingdom, Canada, Australia, and Hong Kong. In 2005, a German network began airing a local version called *Verliebt in Berlin*; this version was hugely successful, and a dubbed version of it was exported to other parts of Europe, including Hungary, Switzerland, France, Belgium, and Slovakia. A Dutch version also began in 2006, and Greece franchised the show in 2007. Turkey and Russia then adopted versions of it. In total, 21 countries aired a version of this program. Although this may be a unique case and not represent all transnational programs, it does indicate what is possible. These works on transnational media and the transformations that occur with such programs further influenced me to investigate how programming that was simply seen as "American" might influence viewer perceptions.

Summary

Despite some differences in focus, this literature also led me to reexamine some assumptions that I had made. Given the work I was familiar with on racial, ethnic, and gender stereotypes in US media, and given my awareness of the extent to which US TV had been prominent and popular throughout the world, I assumed that the United States was mainly responsible for exporting such stereotypes. However, my review of the literature by scholars in other countries gave me pause. What was evident in these works was that all countries had their own biases and often projected their own problematic views concerning diversity and gender. A number of questions occurred to me: Were the stereotypes that I was familiar with *global stereotypes*, and were they included in glocal productions as Straubhaar (2007:7) and Kim (2008) had suggested?

Did they emanate from, or overlap with, exported US TV content? Or were they quite independent and distinct? While I discuss these issues later in the book, I don't offer any comprehensive answers to these questions, which are beyond the scope of this volume; they would require their own book.

The international literature I reviewed was also very helpful in that it reinforced my view that it would be important to ask my respondents how they perceived "home-based" diversity in their countries. So I asked respondents who the "Others" were in their home countries, why they were seen as "Others," and how the respondents thought that such groups were portrayed in their country's television programming. Although I provided my respondents with a simple definition of Others (i.e., "those who are seen to be different from your general, mainstream population"), just about everyone seemed familiar with the term. It seemed that every country had "Others." I also asked my respondents what proportion of the people in their country were immigrants, because a number of the works I consulted had immigration as a central frame, and immigrants are seen as "Others" in a number of countries.[18]

But most importantly, the literature, both from researchers in the United States and from those in other countries, led me to ask questions of both my foreign-born and US-millennial samples about *how much US TV* they watched and why; how much they enjoyed US TV; whether they thought that their watching US TV influenced their views of gender, race, ethnicity, and class; whether they saw US TV as encouraging or discouraging "otherness"; and whether they felt that US TV gave them an accurate picture of racial and ethnic relations in the United States.[19] Furthermore, the literature on consumption and corporate dominance reviewed earlier also influenced my decision to ask both samples whether they felt that their watching US TV influenced their consumption habits with regard to their desires for, or purchase of, material goods; and their views toward sex, birth control, smoking, and alcohol consumption. Because of my own earlier work on race, class, gender, ethnicity, and the media, I was also interested in examining how both the US millennials and the foreign-born groups saw the influence of US TV on their views in these areas. In short, the literature had a great impact on the questions I included in my questionnaire, and led me to expand the diversity in my foreign-born sample.

PART II

The Foreign Born

3

Enjoying American TV before Coming to America

Let us turn now to the results of the surveys and to some of the questions raised earlier: Did the young adults who came to study or work in the United States see much American TV before they came, and how did watching US TV influence them? Did watching US TV influence their expectations before they came? What did they watch? Why did they watch US TV? Did they enjoy watching US TV? If so, what did they enjoy about it?

Given that the flyer used to recruit respondents asked whether they had watched US TV in their home country, it is not too surprising that in this sample 81 percent (51 of 63) watched American shows every day or a few times a week; an additional 3 percent watched US TV but not on a scheduled daily or weekly basis. Nine respondents watched a few times a month. Only one person watched American shows once or twice a year, and this individual lacked ready access to such shows. So, this sample watched a lot of US TV.

What Did They Watch? What Americans Also Watched

When asked what two TV shows they enjoyed most in their country just before they came to the United States (whether the shows were American or not), and what country they thought produced them, the majority (54 percent) indicated they watched comedy shows, such as *Friends*, *Sex and the City*, *Desperate Housewives*, *The Simpsons*, *The Big Bang Theory*, and *Gossip Girl*. Dramatic programs were mentioned second for this group, with programs like *24*, *Lost*, and *Heroes* being cited. Crime and medical programs, such as *Prison Break*, *Bones*, *Criminal Minds*, *Grey's Anatomy*, *Scrubs*, and *House, M.D.*, ranked third. Many of these same shows were also popular in the United States, although they had generally begun earlier in the United States. Interestingly, documentary and news programs were also talked about by 29 percent of the group.

Most of those in the sample mentioned only US TV shows, but some did reference shows made in their home country (e.g., local news or sports programs in their country's language), shows on the BBC, and programs dubbed in their home country's language but made in the United States. Eva, a graduate student from Russia, said that the show she enjoyed the most before coming was a Russian reality show called *Mexican Holiday*, because the people on the show lived in a house in Mexico. She added that although she had seen it as a Russian show, she thought the concept was similar to the US show *Jersey Shore*. So, the show that she enjoyed the most was a global production.

Favorite Shows

I also asked whether they had an all-time favorite US TV show. Most of the respondents, 90 percent, answered yes and indicated that these were the same shows that they had watched just before coming to the United States. They mentioned a few other shows that, although they had not mentioned them in response to the first question, were also popular in the United States. These included (in order of the most mentioned) *Frasier, American Idol, Family Guy, How I Met Your Mother, The Sopranos,* and *The X-Files*.

Temporal and Geographic Contexts

It was clear from some of the responses that the respondents' temporal and geopolitical contexts, that is, *when* they watched US TV and whether they watched from a country that had a close relationship to the United States (or not), were important variables influencing what they viewed. The following three examples illustrate this.

Nanette was a 24-year-old graduate student majoring in international relations from the Yukon in Canada. When I asked if she had a favorite show, she said, "Yes, growing up, the show I watched every week was *One Tree Hill*—which takes place in one of the Carolinas, but I had no idea [it was set there]." When I asked how she knew it was a US TV show, she said, "I had no idea [that it was a US TV show] until I learned about it in school—they're the same-looking people, they talk about the same things, so I didn't realize until high school, it did not even click in my brain." So, for Nanette, growing up in the 1990s and watching US TV (in a rural part of northwest Canada) was a very routinized part of her everyday life. The fact that her favorite show was set somewhere in the United States was somewhat lost on her.

For Eva, another 24-year-old graduate student, watching US TV was a very different experience in her native Russia. When asked how she knew the shows she watched were American, she said, "I don't know. I just thought that everything of this sort, of this kind of stuff, was American, if it was cool. And if it is on MTV, it's [an American] program, or if it is a TV series, a sitcom, you can realize it's American, judging the settings." She added, "I like that it's some kind of unusual settings. It's not like soap opera [in Russia] where it is mostly about gender relations, but it's something new, new characters." By way of illustrating the contrast (between the United States and Russia), she referred to *The Big Bang Theory* and said, "I don't remember any other comedy [in Russia] about scientists."

At the time of the interview, Eva, who was pursuing a graduate degree in media studies, said that her favorite program before coming to the United States was the news show *Anderson Cooper 360°*; she also said she liked to watch sitcoms, like *The Big Bang Theory*, *Gossip Girl*, and *Teen Mom*. When I probed why *Teen Mom* was a favorite, she said:

> I think I have more [of a] research perspective on *Teen Mom* now, as I am doing media studies, and I did media studies in the Moscow State University too. I did journalism and so I watched it more from a research perspective. I've seen how violence is portrayed, how gender relations are portrayed, about how all these things, like victimizing, work. And then I get engaged in this show. I feel for the girls. So it's not only just cold research but it's also, I'm a human being, I feel for the girls. And it's nicely done. It's well produced, good music, nice girls, and really troubled life situations. I like this show.

Eva's experience contrasts very sharply with that of Nanette, who barely noticed a difference between the characters on US TV and the people in her country. Eva's comments suggest that she perceived clear (and important?) differences between people in her country and people in the United States, but that in viewing these US TV shows she was also able to see commonalities in both peoples because of the stories, characters, and situations depicted on these shows.

In contrast to both Eva and Nanette was Irina. A professional with an MBA in business, she was raised in Latvia during the 1980s. When asked what her favorite show was, she said: "It's hard to go back to those times [under Soviet communism]; we used videos and gathered with people to watch." She added that accessing shows was difficult and said: "There were only three to five TV channels when I was growing up. One was a local station. TV started at 5 PM. There were few shows from 12 PM to 5 PM [and often you heard] only a long beep [during those hours]." US TV was not readily available, Irina said. Nonetheless, she did have favorite characters and shows. She liked Lisa in *Saved by the Bell* and Phil Donahue, the host of the eponymous talk show. When asked why these characters appealed to her, she said they were motivated, goal-oriented, strong, funny, and aggressive. Donahue was also "handsome," she added, and Lisa was good at "defending herself." She also liked that Donahue did not "shy away from asking provocative questions"—which may have been rare in her home country's media at the time. Interestingly, she echoed Eva's views of how, despite differences between the United States and Russia, there were so many commonalities. As she said, "Every human is the same, just the environment changes." Indeed, for her, the major lesson that she took away from US TV was that she "saw people as similar, regardless of the country they were from."

The temporal context was also important in these three cases. For the younger respondents, US TV had become much more accessible. Yet, the impact of US TV was similar. When asked if they discussed US TV shows with others on the Internet, both Nanette and Eva said yes, but Irina said email and the Internet were not yet available in Latvia when she was growing up. Nevertheless, she too discussed the shows with friends at school, just as Eva and Nanette did.

How Much Did They Enjoy US TV?

Although I did not directly ask whether they felt that US TV was undermining their culture, the majority of respondents said they very much enjoyed US TV. Respondents were asked to rate on a scale from 1 ("did not enjoy at all") to 10 ("enjoyed very much") how much they enjoyed watching American TV shows when they were in their country. It is clear that they enjoyed it immensely because the sample registered a weighted average of 8.76 (with a standard deviation of 1.13), with more than half of the respondents (54 percent) rating their enjoyment a 9 or 10!

Why Did They Like US TV?

Their responses to another question I asked give us some insight into *why* they enjoyed American TV as much as they did: "Tell me what pops up first when you hear the following question: Can you give me one word or one sentence that explains why you watched American shows?" They were then asked to elaborate on their response. In examining their responses, I discerned five major categories (listed here in descending order of number of times mentioned):

> Production Values
> Seeing a Different Lifestyle and/or Culture
> Entertaining and/or Funny
> To Gain Knowledge
> Scheduling or Access[1]

As we will see below, this sample did not apparently see US TV as undermining their culture; or, if they did, they accepted that. A number of them saw US TV as helping them gain useful knowledge and better integration into US culture and society and as a way to gain other useful knowledge, for example, English fluency.

Production Values

The fact that respondents mentioned production values came as a surprise to me for a number of reasons. One is that so many of them made reference to it.[2] (The phrase "production values" generally refers to the quality of the lighting, sound, scenery, and props used to create a film or TV show. In this text, it also refers to the general quality of the production, including plotlines, characters, and dramatic action.) Creative types and people who work on TV productions are aware of the high production values of US TV, but I have tended to take this for granted and have therefore not been particularly conscious of their significance. US TV programming has been the main TV that I have been exposed to, and I guess you don't always appreciate what you have. While some respondents used the exact term "production values," others used similar terms, such as "quality," "nicely made," "nice story, plots were well adapted," "good stories and good quality of production," and "energetic, fast-paced, vibrant structure of show."

In addition, when describing *why* they watched US TV, many respondents contrasted it with their own domestic TV programming. For example, a 30-year-old female administrator from Turkey said:

> Creative—find them to be creative. The subjects and ideas put forward were so different from those in Turkey, which showed classic and boring themes—you could anticipate their endings from the first. With US TV, you have unexpected themes. The themes and what was discussed could not be figured out at the beginning. What would happen at the end of the show was also unexpected, e.g., the antagonist might be the protagonist at the end.

A number of other respondents echoed this idea: they enjoyed not being able to predict the action or the ending.

A 25-year-old Portuguese female architect said that she watched US TV because she found the shows to be "[w]ell-written, easy. A lot of them [are] better than the Portuguese ones." I probed, "Easy?" and she responded:

> Don't have to think about them too much; helps you to clear your head, shut down what you're thinking. Portuguese media is similar to a really bad [version of the] *Oprah* [*Winfrey Show*]. Production values are very bad. Maybe adequate to the audience—grandmas love them, but young people do not like them.

A Chinese female undergraduate student majoring in business said US TV programs were "[f]ast-paced—most of the Chinese media was sentimental, clichéd; I hate to watch other people cry or take a long time to die." She added, they were "boring."

Kemi, a 30-year-old Nigerian businesswoman who had spent a lot of time in Britain, contrasted US TV with British TV and said she liked

US TV better because it was "different" and she enjoyed the accents. She said that the "sayings were more glossy and more perfect [on US TV]. UK shows were more raw and gritty." She also felt that the quality of filming was better. "For example," she said, "a US show had movie quality; a UK show was like shot with a small camera."[3]

The following response from a female graduate student from Peru also speaks to production quality and values and provides some interesting insights into how American TV is accessed by different classes in Peru:

> The script and how people talk is more elaborate, and there are interesting stories. Peruvian TV is focused on low-income people who speak in slang, while American shows focus on professional people doing something with their lives. Peruvian shows all have similar scripts of rich families not accepting poor families. Peru may not be a good example, because many people in Peru do not watch Peruvian TV, just Peruvian news. Many people watch cable TV. In shantytowns, people tape shows and show them each week, one week late. [They do this because only a few can afford cable.] Even in shantytowns, people watch American shows. Some channels are in English and Spanish (possibly Fox), and you can choose. Many channels are in English but with Spanish subtitles.

Some respondents cited more than one reason, combining elements of some of the most common responses. For example, a graduate student from Russia indicated that she enjoyed the production values of US TV but also watched it to gain knowledge:

> I like to watch American news shows because I think they are balanced in opinion, and they give very up-to-date information and also they are independent. If I am to talk about entertainment shows, I like them because I think they are produced nicely; they have good pictures, good cameras. They have a certain kind of plot; you feel really engaged in this show and want to follow the stories. I would say that they are done really professional.

Contrasting Cultures—Seeing a Different Lifestyle and/or Culture

A number of respondents said that seeing a different lifestyle and/or culture was a major reason they watched American TV. They gave responses like the following comment by a 31-year-old financial analyst from Spain: "Entertainment, laughing, problem-solving, curiosity, different cultures, different approaches to solving problems," and he added, "A team solving approach." A female graduate student from Brazil, who referred to shows depicting teens in high school or college, said: "Liked the story—fun; had curiosity with regard to living in a dorm. Don't have these in Brazil [even] if you are going to an expensive private school. Also [in Brazil] people are not 'working in cafes' while they go to school; society is against this, and you don't do this if paying money for a private school."

A male software engineer from Kyrgyzstan described US TV as "interesting, because we see different behaviors of people from what I grew up with—for example, saw school parties, drinks, buildings, cities, and fancy cars; clothes were different." I asked him how the parties depicted on US TV contrasted with what he experienced in Kyrgyzstan. He said, "In Kyrgyzstan, [we] would have had a gathering of school friends in a house, and there would be no drinking. Music would not be too loud, and adults would be supervising."

Coming from a country where the government censors the media, a Chinese female graduate student responded:[4]

It [US TV] covers almost all kinds of topics—corruption, sex . . . I was very shocked when I watched *Prison Break*. I couldn't believe that the government would allow this topic on TV. It basically tells a story that the vice president did a lot of bad things to people for her own good.

Finally, a female graduate student from India responded: "They are interesting. The Indian shows always have a common theme," she said, citing the often-depicted "mother-in-law and daughter-in-law clash," for example, on Indian shows. She said that "on US TV the shows were diverse and unpredictable."

Entertaining and/or Funny

Those who indicated that they enjoyed US TV because it was entertaining or funny were fairly straightforward and direct in their responses. They either used short answers, such as "funny" or "liked the humor," or expanded on this by adding comments that referred to the entertaining plot or settings. For example, a 40-ish female undergrad from Brazil said: "Just fun." She noted that she "liked the fiction of having a problem that was resolved in 30 to 45 minutes." A male graduate student from Austria said: "Entertaining—just used to relax when [I] get home. *Mad Men* was more intelligent—it shows personal development. It [i.e., whether he enjoyed a program] depends on the show."

Others spoke about how the humor in American TV contrasted with their own country's programming. For example, a young female graduate student from Paraguay said: "Funny and interesting." She liked the humor because she was never allowed to watch Latin American soap operas. Her "father felt that they lacked content," she said, and so instead they watched comedies. A female senior business consultant from India said: "Fun, nicely made. Indian media is all very similar; all the drama and acting are the same. US shows were made well, tight." A 30-year-old female graduate student from Serbia offered a one-word response: "Funny." As an example, she mentioned the show *Frasier* and the title character's lifestyle and social life. "He leads a bohemian lifestyle," she said, "he goes to concerts, theater, and [meets] nice people. Has coffee shop he always goes to, where everyone knows him."

Another female graduate student from China used the word "relaxed" and added that "there are common factors in the shows" such as *Friends* and *How I Met Your Mother*. "Each episode ends on a positive note; and they are funny, not heavy like in the movies; they are real-life stories; together [the characters] fight, but get back to be happy; each episode had a positive message." She added, "In China it is different; actors are very expressive with their emotions." By that she meant that the emotions the actors expressed were projected as deeply felt emotions, not light and transitory. Finally, a Russian female grad student used the word "humor" and said she liked comedies, and that in American TV "the sense of humor was really unique—a little sarcastic, but smart." She also added: "The Russian shows that are similar are not so funny; also the writing in the US is better, shorter, scripted."

Learning a Different Culture or Language, or Gaining Knowledge

Although some responses (like those above) focused on "contrasting cultures," the theme of "learning a different culture" also surfaced in other responses. For example, among those who watched US TV primarily to gain knowledge or language, some also mentioned learning about another culture. A 24-year-old visiting graduate student from Italy said she watched US TV "first of all to learn English, secondly to try to understand a different culture." A male Japanese undergraduate said he watched "to learn about culture and language," and he added that he wanted to "communicate better" and that watching US TV gave him an opportunity to learn and "to see things from a different perspective."

Some respondents gave more explicitly utilitarian reasons for watching (or liking) American TV; they indicated that they wanted to gain knowledge of some sort. These responses were generally simple and to the point. For example, one male Chinese grad student in business said: "Learn English; [plus I] liked drama and story line." Another's reason was "to know about the US." For these respondents, gaining knowledge meant acquiring or developing language skills, cultural knowledge, or some other useful information. Indeed, when asked if they had watched US TV or movies in English for the purpose of learning the language before coming to the United States, 57.1 percent said they had watched US TV and 61.9 percent had watched movies in English. They also engaged in other activities to learn English. For example, they attended English-language classes, made friends with English-speaking students or people working in nonprofit organizations, or read in English. However, watching English-language movies and viewing US TV were the second and third most cited activities, respectively, after reading newspapers, novels, or magazines in English, which many did as part of their English classes in school.[5]

Access or Limited Options

Some watched US TV because they had few other options—often because of scheduling or access issues. For some, US TV was what they could watch during the times they had available to watch TV. As one female grad student from Canada said: "Access. Much of what was broadcast was US [TV]. Had to work to find programs from other countries." Another respondent, also from Canada, echoed this view, saying: "Dominance in scheduling—sometimes the only thing on—especially during the primetime slots, 8 PM to 12." These two latter views underscore the different television landscapes that exist in different countries.

As many scholars have noted, the presence of US TV is stronger in some markets than in others. For example, it is commonplace in the Anglophone world—the United Kingdom, Australia, Canada, Ireland, and English-speaking Hong Kong (Moran, 2009). It is harder to access, however, in places such as Latin America, which have their own highly developed TV networks (Straubhaar, 2007).

Habitus

My respondents' comments also suggest that class position within countries also influences what type of TV people consume, that is, their national TV or imported US TV or a combination of both.[6] For example, many of my Latin American respondents clearly distinguished their viewing of US TV from that of poorer people in their home countries; and they were aware that this had to do in part with their access to cable and to the Internet. Some were aware that this also resulted from their personal exposure to US media, literature, and educational curricula, much of which they had received in the elite or "American" schools that they generally attended.[7] But this was not limited to Latin Americans, as many respondents from Asia also noted these class distinctions and the relationship of the media they consumed to their education and class habitus. In essence, it appeared that US TV, like other "American" brands, had a certain cachet that appealed to the upper classes.

Reflections and Summary

To a certain degree, my discovery that US TV was often the preferred viewing of the elite in other countries underscored for me a particular irony in my research. My earlier work had often focused on the more disadvantaged in our society; and I had become interested in US TV because it was (or had been) such a democratizing medium, accessible to all groups and classes in the United States and consumed via free airwaves. In conducting this research, however, I became aware of how elite a commodity it is (or was in some cases) in many countries. I also became more aware of how globalization and changes in technology might be intensifying these class divisions and possibly creating an elite class of global cosmopolitans more connected digitally, linguistically, and culturally in terms of social mores and practices to each other than to those in their own countries.

In sum, the youths and young adults in this sample saw quite a bit of, and very much enjoyed, American TV before they came to the United States. None in the sample said that they saw US TV as undermining their culture—although a few acknowledged that this was a concern of older generations in their country. They were also very clear about *why they liked US TV* and *what they liked in particular*. In general, they did tend to see American TV as helping them to better integrate into US society, and when they replied to the question(s) of why they watched (and enjoyed) American TV, they spoke highly of US TV's strong production values, how it enabled them to see a different lifestyle and/or culture, how it was entertaining and funny, and how they were able to "gain knowledge" and English-language skills from watching US TV. There were, however, some who were critical of US TV. They cited how US youths were portrayed as irresponsible, immature, and spoiled and as "not appreciating things." And they noted an emphasis in US TV programs on partying and an easygoing culture that did not live up to the hardworking reality that they found when they came to the United States. At least one respondent was critical of the greater emphasis in American TV on violence and the use of guns.

The fact that US TV, like other "American" brands, had a certain cachet that appealed to the upper classes is undoubtedly also influenced by world power relations and the concept of American exceptionalism. As a graduate student from Israel said, when he watched US TV, it influenced him to think of the United States as an affluent country and one that reflected "American exceptionalism"—which he defined as being "an exceptional force for good in society, with an emphasis on individualism and the freedom to fulfill your dreams." In the end, a financial analyst from Spain best expressed why it is important to study the impact of US TV when he volunteered that he always wanted to come to the United States because "the US has a lot of soft power because of the influence of TV."

4

The Impact of American Television

Given how much US TV my foreign-born sample consumed and how much they enjoyed US TV, how did watching US TV influence them? How aware were they that watching US TV influenced their views of the United States and their own outlooks on life in general? Did they see US TV as undermining their culture? Or did they see American TV as something that would someday help them to better integrate into US culture? To ascertain the *degree of US TV influence that they perceived*, I asked respondents, "Do you think that watching these shows influenced your impressions of the US or of American culture before you came to the US?" If they said yes, I asked them to rate—on a scale from 1 to 5, with 5 indicating the most influence—how much they thought that watching US TV shows influenced their views of the United States or of American culture. All but four in the sample (or 94 percent) said that watching US TV shows influenced their impressions of the country or of American culture. In fact, 74 percent said that watching US TV shows influenced their views "a lot" or "more than a lot." However, how much and what they took away from their viewing varied—as did how aware they were of the influence of US TV on them.

Contrasting Experiences
Jane from Northern Ireland

The story of Jane, a 22-year-old native of Northern Ireland, provides one of the more dramatic illustrations of the impact of US TV. Jane was very aware of how watching a show that most Americans would consider to be fairly innocuous, i.e., *Judge Judy*, dramatically influenced her views on gender and her personal aspirations. Jane had grown up in a small town near Belfast and had gone to school in Belfast. She was part of the only Catholic family in this town at the time. When we met, she was studying civil rights law; she immediately conveyed that she

had an acute sense of the meaning of civil rights and the need to protect them in all contexts. She explained that she had understood, from
a very young age, that the rights that one enjoyed in life depended on
one's religion and gender. According to her, such was the segregation in
Northern Ireland between the Catholics and the Protestants when she
was growing up that her mother gave both of her daughters names that
sounded non–Irish Catholic, so that they could, in their daily encounters, "pass with ease" and without discrimination (at least initially, for
their last name was, as she put it, recognizably Irish). She indicated that
both of her parents had been stopped at their university by the police
various times because of their Irish surnames. She also noted that if you
didn't own property, you couldn't vote, and that many Catholics didn't
own property. She added that the government used this fact to divide
and conquer.

Jane went on to say that US TV was a common feature of her life
then. She clearly and warmly remembered watching *Judge Judy* at a very
young age with her "granny" and deciding, right then and there, that
she wanted to be a lawyer. She had never seen a female judge. As she recalled it, in Northern Ireland, women were not allowed to be judges, and
women lawyers were encouraged to practice family law, not any other
kind of law. She became determined to practice civil rights law, and she
felt that watching Judge Judy encouraged her pursuit of this goal for it
showed a woman administering justice in a legally sanctioned authori-
tative position and in areas beyond family law. From her TV-viewing
perspective, the United States seemed more progressive and open for
women. Jane's story is a striking example of the impact of watching US
TV, for she saw her decision to pursue civil rights law as directly related to her viewing this program; however, other respondents were less
consciously aware of its impact, although they acknowledged that they
watched and enjoyed American TV "a lot."

David from Colombia

David represents the other extreme; he was less conscious of the impact
of US TV. Most respondents fell somewhere between the two ends
represented by David and Jane. David was an intelligent, 31-year-old,
middle-class male from Colombia. He had been studying in the United

States for two years, finishing up a master's degree in business, when we spoke. He had gone to an American school in his country, and his English was quite good, with barely an accent noticeable.[1] He also would not be immediately identified as Hispanic/Latino, as he did not fit "the Latin look" nor were his first and last names clearly recognizable as Spanish in origin. Somewhat in contrast to some of my other Latin American male respondents, he had a strong interest in the media in general, consumed a great deal of US TV content in the United States, and had focused in his school work on media issues. At the time of the interview, he was about to begin a job with a large media company. He indicated he had watched US TV shows "every day" in his country—which I thought at the time was a bit unusual because Colombia has very extensive, well-developed Colombian and Mexican television programming, which most Colombians watch.[2] Now in the States, as a full-time student without a TV or access to cable, he still logged an average of one to two hours per day watching some of his favorite shows on the Internet. In addition, and as with many other respondents, he sometimes binged on a particular show for as many as six hours straight.

Given his strong involvement with US television content, what was most striking about his responses to the questions was how—in contrast to Jane—he had never thought very much about how his viewing had influenced his views of the United States before coming and spending time here. At the end of the interview, he said—as if he had not considered this before—"I'm not sure if it has really influenced me or not." However, he may have been reflecting more broadly on his sense of identity, his outlook on life, or his worldview. He acknowledged that viewing US TV "absolutely" influenced his consumption habits, for when you "see a celebrity or a role model," he said, "you want to do what they do." He also gave as examples the ads, in particular the junk-food ads that accompanied the programs he watched. As he said, they "make you feel you really need it and will enjoy it."[3] In addition, he had chosen to study and work in the US media field.

David's story further illustrates how, for many respondents, watching US TV was part of the social and economic environment they inhabited, took for granted, and rarely examined, that is, their own class status or habitus. The following profile of David gives a fuller picture of the type of social milieu from which many of the respondents came, regardless of their country of origin, and how they sometimes were not immediately conscious of the impact US TV had on them. However, many admitted upon reflection that they were very influenced by US TV.

David's strong command of the English language and his short visits to the United States prior to coming here to study may well have influenced his puzzlement over my question about how much US TV content had influenced him. Not only did he always attend an American school, but he grew up watching US TV and also read English music lyrics, newspapers, novels, and magazines, listened to English-language radio and music, watched US movies, and visited with friends and family in the United States for short periods prior to coming to study in 2012. When asked if he always wanted to visit the United States, he said it was a place where he felt comfortable, and he loved the city where he was living. But part of what drove his immersion may have been his stated view that accessing US TV content (entertainment or news) was a way of staying up to date with what was going on in politics, sports, science, technology, and other fields, especially in the United States. This was a view shared by other respondents. The good shows and high-quality production added to his view that the United States was the place to be. It may have also been the case that he was reluctant, as an intelligent, very media-savvy person, to admit that he might have been influenced by what he so readily acknowledged was fiction or, in the case of ads, designed to manipulate or influence viewers.

Watching Their First American TV Show

Other questionnaire responses suggested to me that watching American TV in their home country had had an important impact on this foreign-born sample. For example, when I asked, "Do you recall when you watched your first American TV show? What was that show's name, and how old were you when you watched it?" I was surprised at how vivid their recollections were—they were, after all, young adults now. I was also struck by the fact that they recalled this early viewing with such positive emotions (with joy in some cases, with a warm smile in many other cases, and sometimes with humorous recollections). In addition, 96.77 percent of the respondents—all but one—recalled the name of the show and how old they were when they watched it. I'm not sure how many of us, born and raised in the United States, could recall our first TV show that distinctly and warmly.

An example of a story that illustrates a warm and humorous recollection is that of a young researcher from Belgium, who said that when she was 6, she would run home every day from school to watch "Homer Simpson" from *The Simpsons*. To her, this show was America, and not being able to watch it was a form of punishment, one that her parents sometimes employed.

In terms of the actual shows they recalled first seeing, this was very much influenced by when US TV arrived in their home countries. Many recalled seeing their first shows between the ages of 4 and 7, and animated cartoons and children's shows figured prominently in their memories. Many of the shows mentioned will be familiar to US viewers, including *Looney Toons, Tom and Jerry, Barney*, and *Sesame Street*.[4] Those who came from countries that had been part of the former Soviet Union recalled seeing their first US TV when they were older, as US TV did not arrive until after the fall of the Iron Curtain. The shows they recalled seeing as preteens or teens for the first time included the following: *The Wonder Years, Beverley Hills, 90210, Santa Barbara, The Facts of Life, Saved by the Bell, Bonanza*, and *Alf*.[5] The following comment by Lena, a Hungarian graduate student, captures the experience of many respondents who lived through the end of communism in their native country. She said:

> I watched when I was young, 10, 12. I suppose cartoons—like the *Tom and Jerry*. The first, it was a huge thing, *Dallas*, after communism ended. The regime changed, I think in the '90s. That was the first American show that they had on the TV. I remember they had it on Friday evenings. Everyone disappeared from the playground; everyone was watching it except for my family, because my father hated it so much. He didn't let us watch it. He hated it because he was a psychiatrist, and they [the characters on the show] drank a lot. Sometimes I still watched it when he wasn't at home. Literally, I think the whole country was watching it on Friday nights.

A few respondents remembered "educational" or scientific programs as their first US TV shows. Eva, a Russian student pursuing a graduate degree in the social sciences, said:

It was in Russian, but it was translated from English. It was around 1998, and it was called *Inquiring Minds*. . . . I was 9. [The show featured a] group of two, three people, and they would explain how things work or do some kind of fun experiment of things we see in real life. They would explain how the human body works, how machinery operates.

Joseph, originally from Northern Ireland, said he remembered a show called something like "lost in space," and he remembered "at age 4 drawing flying saucers and the moon landing on the back of houses." He went on to become a physics major and work in the health field.

Conveying Differences in Lifestyles and Cultural Mores

Also curious to me was how quickly a first viewing of a US show conveyed to foreign-born viewers differences in lifestyles and cultural mores between the United States and their own country. I had seen this in earlier historical work that I had done—for I had previously examined the impact of early Hollywood films in the Spanish-speaking Caribbean during the 1920s. Many of these early films reflected the Jazz Age and portrayed women driving cars, smoking, drinking, working, and being generally more independent than had been the norm in many conservative, middle-class Caribbean settings. It was members of the middle and upper classes in these countries who could more afford to indulge in watching the "moving pictures." These films dramatically presented alternatives to the viewers about the ways in which lives were (and perhaps could be) "normally" lived. In fact, the press at the time expressed concerns about the impact these moving pictures could have on society. Indeed, one columnist in the major arts magazine of the day in Puerto Rico articulated the challenges such films presented to traditional/accepted social relations and warned parents to not allow their young girls to see such films for fear they would be corrupted and endanger societal norms. He noted "the tendency of movies to corrupt youth—especially the young girls!" and pointed out "that two months after two movie houses were established in one community, the elementary and high school teachers began to notice that the students' lessons were less well mastered; and young girls' imaginations had been sharpened—for the worse." Moreover, he argued that young girls who went alone to the movies developed prejudicial relationships. Indeed, he wrote, one of these young girls responded to her mother, who had scolded her on this issue, "[I]f you only knew what I know about life, thanks to the movies. I know more than you do!" (Rodríguez, 2007:31).

An example of how quickly a first viewing of US TV conveyed differences in lifestyles and cultural mores can be seen in the following, seemingly simple story by a graduate student from a former Soviet Republic. She described her first viewing of *The Dating Game* and how it had challenged the way that she had always understood social/dating relations between men and women, that is, how they had always been conducted in her world. She thought, "How could you go on TV to get a date? They were selling themselves, but you couldn't see them. I found it strange and stupid. You don't have to use TV to find a partner." In this era of Tinder, speed dating, and hookup apps, her first reaction may seem quaint today, even to her. But sprinkled throughout the interviews were many other comments that spoke to gender relations and the way in which they were depicted in American TV. US TV programs often altered the way my respondents thought about such relations and led many of them to want to emulate the patterns they saw on these programs, patterns that were not present in their home countries. For some, coming to the United States was a way of pursuing what they thought was possible as a result of US TV, such as living as an openly gay person or cohabiting with people of the opposite sex and not being stigmatized.

Watching Alone

Despite the warmth of the recollections and the "positivity" associated with the comments about US TV, I was surprised to see that, when asked whether they usually watched American shows alone or with others, about as many (32) said "alone" as said they "watched with other family members" (30). Watching alone also increased as they got older. In addition, few discussed the shows with others in the family, saying instead that they tended to talk about the shows with friends at school or on the Internet. This was surprising to me, given that in the past in the United States—before everyone in the household got their own TV (or, these days, tablet, phone, or laptop)—the TV was the place around which the family gathered. This practice still existed in some families (for example, in one Serbian respondent's family, "it was the custom to eat and then watch TV"), but for many in this group, "TV wasn't really a social experience." Respondents noted other instances when US TV contributed to a generational gap, with the younger generation watching MTV, for example, and the older generations watching programs less identified with the United States.

Viewers' differing preferences also influenced whether they watched TV alone or with others. Some of these differences were based on gender and grew with age, with male children, for example, wanting to watch sports and females wanting to watch dramas like *One Tree Hill*. In addition, one respondent said he watched TV on the computer, which was difficult to share. There were also generational differences, with parents liking, for example, the news or "old Russian TV and movies on history and the war," and my respondents preferring *Friends* and *Seinfeld*. Or, in some cases, the parents were busy professionals who were not interested in US TV at all. Last, some of the shows were broadcast late at night, and my respondents watched them in bed. A majority of the sample, 60 percent, recalled watching their *first* American show on local or terrestrial TV, while the remainder had watched on cable, on video cassette, on DVD, on satellite TV, or online, either on a website or as a downloaded file. How they accessed the shows also changed over time, with increasing numbers in the sample streaming from the Internet or watching via Netflix.

How Did They Know the Shows Were American?

Given that many US TV programs were dubbed and some had titles changed, how did my viewers know the shows were American?[6] Half of the sample mentioned the language (or accents). This is not surprising since many watched the shows in English to learn or to improve on the language. Another 37 percent mentioned the setting—again this was not unexpected, but what they said was very interesting. For example, a male graduate student from Moldova noticed that the houses on US TV had porches; he also saw "Do Not Disturb" signs; and certain words, such as "meat," "cheese," "flour," and "sugar," surfaced in cartoons. During our interview, he said that he still remembered the visual setting of these words. Others mentioned the sizes of the houses (big) or the presence of lockers in high school, which did not exist in their schools. A German postdoc researcher said:

> German cities look so different. Many topics were covered—schools, baseball, skyline—that are not covered as much in German TV. There are way-smaller cars [in Germany]. Even the size of refrigerators was big [on US TV]. And pickups—we didn't have them in Germany.

Still others picked up on the relations between characters. Two young women from Kyrgyzstan spoke to this. One said: "American universities and English names, and relations between students and faculty was different." The other said: "Content of language and how they spoke with each other. They were open with each other; in Kyrgyzstan people are more reserved."

One-third of the sample spoke to US hegemony in the television landscape. Although this often has been described and studied in the literature, among those in my sample there was the sense that everyone in their country knew that whatever was on television was mainly from the United States; it was taken for granted. A male undergraduate student from Japan stated it clearly: "Anything in English is American." An Israeli male graduate student echoed that comment:

> I assumed everything in English was American. Not many British or Australian programs were brought to Israel. There were also references to settings, e.g., *Dallas* in Texas, *Cheers* in Boston, and references to geography and to cities.

A male graduate student from Syria said: "American TV was the default English TV; also, the British have a different accent." Another respondent, a young male graduate student from Northern Ireland, also spoke about the "default" media setting. "[I] can't remember," he said when asked how he knew the source of the first US show he watched. "[I] knew some were American by default." He added that there were US references in the shows and gave as examples "*Scooby Doo*—found something that said USA. Also, on *Sesame Street*, characters talked about America from time to time, for example, they sang the song 'America' from *West Side Story.*" Disney programs were also immediately associated with the United States.

The "Coolness" Factor

Finally, when asked how he knew the show he watched was American in origin, a visiting professor from Paris said, "It was obvious. They were the cool shows in the 1980s; they rocked—violent story lines were good. French shows were boring." He remembered waiting for the next week to come, so he could see his favorite US shows. A White British financial consultant referred to a similar dimension, which might have been his equivalent to coolness. He liked the California lifestyle they projected and noted that in the 1980s and 1990s, US TV had been referred to as "American trash," but now the comments were more positive. Gretchen, a medical researcher from Germany, said that she would discuss the shows with her friends—they were "really cool," "really funny."

Even MTV, which has been pursuing a strong *glocal* thrust in its programming (see Sontag, 2005), was seen as American TV. Respondents also associated this network with a "coolness" factor; if a program was seen as "cool," this influenced whether they thought it was American or not. As the Russian graduate student said in a previous chapter, "everything of this sort, of this kind of stuff was American, if it was cool." A Filipina undergraduate student said: "My friends and I watched MTV, and I knew that MTV was American." Part of this coolness had to do with "what was talked about," and respondents mentioned articles in the papers and in magazines, and ads that conveyed that programs were American; according to a visiting professor from Latvia, the programs "were sold that way—as an American show." A French businesswoman said:

> You read magazine articles that described [the shows as the new American show]; also, the cinematography, plot, the subjects talked about were different. Families in the suburbs of the US were not very French [i.e., not much like the French in the suburbs], and in the US they lived in high-rises.

Cable TV was seen as being somewhat similar to MTV. A Nigerian financial professional said: "When you watch cable TV, you know everything is foreign; you also use the color of the person—if they were White, you assumed they were American and had American accents." (This was the only respondent who addressed the issue of race in US TV in this question, but race and ethnicity did surface when respondents answered other questions, especially those that referred to their experience once they came to the United States.)[7]

Finally, a professor from Switzerland who had also spent time in Poland suggested that she could tell an American TV show by the accent and "point of view" of people on the show. By "point of view," she meant a subtle pro-US perspective. She sensed this on news shows, for example, when the "commentators were America-friendly" or when someone asked, "Do we [as Americans] have to go in [to help resolve a conflict]?" Commentators on non-US shows, she said, "were not so pro-American."

Only two respondents said that they were unaware that the shows were American. One was a Greek architect, who said he "didn't know then." The other was a Canadian female grad student from the Yukon, who said that almost all of the TV shows she and others in the Yukon saw were American. Indeed, many of my respondents from Canada and Australia conveyed the idea that there was a certain seamlessness between US TV and their own domestic TV. Actually, they had to think a bit more to discern what the differences were. In the case of the Greek architect, the question of where shows were produced was just not generally discussed.

US TV Fills the Voids

I was initially surprised at how many of my respondents were aware of how much they had been influenced by US TV before they came. In my own personal experience, I have found most TV viewers in the United States are generally *unaware* of how what they watch on US TV influences their views. In part, this is why I, and others, teach students to become more critical viewers. Also, as we saw above, many in my sample enjoyed US TV because it was simply entertaining; they watched it to relax. However, upon consideration, I realized that their responses reflected the fact that they were now in the United States and therefore experiencing a challenge to, or a confirmation of, what they had expected to see, given their prior US TV viewing. This would have made them a bit more aware of what their views or expectations had been.

Respondents provided many examples of how they felt that watching US TV influenced the expectations they had before they arrived and in many cases made them feel more comfortable in the United States. For example, a male undergrad from China said that watching American TV "made me more comfortable when I arrived. [I was] very familiar with the culture and how people get along with people." An undergrad from Indonesia said that he "assumed that the slice of life you see in sitcoms was what life was really like in the US." A female undergrad from China also spoke to the more mundane but nonetheless important impact that US TV had on her expectations and behavior. When asked if she felt US TV influenced her, she said, "Definitely!" She said that instead of drinking tea, which is a big part of the culture in China, she now drank "coffee once a week or when I have a heavy workload." Bagels were often mentioned in *Friends*, but she did not know what a bagel was until she came to the United States. US TV influenced her to think about the coffee culture of America and how people spent their leisure time in coffee shops. However, now she was concerned with expenses; drinking coffee in a café every day could be expensive. But this fact was not noted in US TV. She had also become "concerned about [the potential negative] health impact of [drinking too much] coffee."

A female grad student from Italy pointed out how US TV often filled a vacuum in knowledge about the United States, especially about everyday interactions or mundane events. She said she had limited exposure to other sources of contact with, or knowledge about, the United States. She referred to the somewhat psychologically transcendent impact that watching US TV had had on her expectations: "Because of the lack of a direct/tangible knowledge of the American culture, my mind elaborated an image of America based on what I watched. For example, sometimes America is associated with terrorism, which is a feature presented in *Alias* [a favorite program of hers]. As a consequence, the first time I was on the subway in New York I thought about an episode of the show in which, due to a terrorist attack, the subway exploded." A grad student from Romania voiced a similar response when she said: "Yes, definitely. Well, the first thing that impressed me when I came here is that it looked like what was in the movies, like the suburbs. I feel like I am in an American movie right now. And then, I guess it idealizes, a little bit, how people live. Of course, depending on the show." As Holtzman and Sharpe (2014:xix) have pointed out, "While the intent of entertainment media may not be explicitly to educate us, it often fills the voids in our formal and informal learning."

Habitus and Social Milieus

Again, the world—or habitus—within which each of the respondents lived in their home countries also influenced their views of the United States and their viewing of US TV. As the story (above) of Jane from Northern Ireland illustrated, respondents' habitus played an important role in determining their views of, and their relationship to, American TV. For many of my respondents, watching American TV was part of what everyone in their milieu or habitus did. Moreover, for many respondents, US TV was the only opportunity they had to "understand American culture." As a number of respondents noted, "You don't get that kind of learning from a book." One female graduate student from Peru put it this way: "[Watching US TV] was 90 percent of my experience and exposure [to the United States]. The other 10 percent [I gleaned from] friends who had traveled to the US." Finally, a young undergrad from the Philippines said, "I didn't have sources to disprove anything," so she tended to assume that what she saw on US TV was an accurate reflection of the United States.

How True to Life?

This is not to say that respondents took US TV at face value and believed that what they saw on TV was real. In fact, when asked how true to life they thought US TV was on a 7-point scale, where 1 indicated not real, not believable, and 7 equaled very real, very believable, the group registered a mean of 3.98—or right in the middle, not skewing as true believers or as cynics.[8] A number of them commented that their views had changed after being in the United States; for example, they shifted from seeing US TV as more believable to less believable, from a 6 before coming to the United States to a 2.5 on the 7-point scale. Holtzman and Sharpe (2014:xvi) speak to this issue of viewers knowing that programs are fictional but at the same time having their sense of what is real influenced by what they view: "Even the smartest and most aware television consumers can experience television in two seemingly contradictory ways. On the one hand most of us know and can articulate the fact that the programs we are watching are fictional. Yet simultaneously and often less than consciously, we believe and internalize the subtle and often subliminal messages we are receiving." They also note, "According to the American Psychological Association, the less real-world information viewers have about a group, the more likely they are to accept the media 'reality'" (335). As Wilson and Gutierrez (1995:33–38) note this is particularly relevant to how we think about groups of racial and ethnic minorities, and different classes and genders in our own country as well as in other countries.

A Roundup on Impact

Positive Expectations

For a great many respondents, American TV presented them with perspectives and assumptions that differed from what they experienced in their own cultures. In some cases, this led to their developing a greater affinity and admiration for US culture—this represented the majority of the sample. But in other cases, respondents were more critical of the alternative views represented on US TV, especially after they had spent some time in the United States. Examples of positive comments are the following: A Syrian male graduate student said US TV "made me interested in coming to visit the US and in the US in general. [It] makes you feel like you know the US just from watching the shows. You develop an affinity to the culture." A female graduate student from Nigeria said: "US TV shows have big impact back home. Everyone wanted to be a big rap star [and] change their accent. Imperial TV fuels your appetite to see the [US] country yourself." Others spoke positively about how watching US TV shows helped them to move cultural boundaries that they felt were limiting. For example, a software engineer from Kyrgyzstan said, "Eastern culture tries to manipulate. Because of the shows, we have the freedom to [think and] critique this. Islamic versus Western culture—the shows introduce an alternative to Eastern culture."

Indeed, there were many references to the greater "freedom" that individuals or characters in the shows seemed to have with regard to their lives; this was especially the case with regard to gender roles and relations between genders. As the graduate student from Syria said: "I see it as New York; young adults living together and thinking they have knowledge." This appeared to be a reference to shows set in New York City, like *Friends* and *How I Met Your Mother*, which were often noted in the sample. A Mexican financial analyst said watching US TV influenced her to see "how fabulous New York could be with its dating culture." She was living with her boyfriend when I interviewed her. "At home [in Mexico]," she said, "this would not be acceptable." A young woman from Kyrgyzstan spoke to the impact US TV had on teens in her country. She said she had "worked with teens, saw their behavior and [how] they started to express their styles and attitudes from TV shows." She also noted that "Korean shows were popular at one point and also influenced them, [but] the US was the country of freedom— freedom of style and sexual orientation, and of speech." She said that "US TV opened her mind to these perspectives." Last, a Filipina, referring also to the freedom of being geographically mobile, said:

> You get exposed to how people really are in those shows and what sorts of things they do. You get insight into the value system and how what they do is different. For example, in the US it is common for [people] 18-plus to have a sense of independence. In the Philippines it is not the same; this usually happens when you get married and then you may still be under their [your parents'] influence. In the US, you have more opportunity to move to a different city. When you watch New York City [–based] shows, all [of the characters] have come from somewhere else. If you are born in Manila, you wouldn't go elsewhere. There is a greater sense of mobility [and freedom to do this] in the US.

Other respondents spoke to the sense of easy living that many of the shows project. As a female grad student from Romania said, "We get the sense from TV shows that life is somehow easier here [in the United States], that people enjoy their freedom more, that it's easier to become someone in life, to achieve something, that there are not so many structural barriers. This is the kind of image that the movies and TV shows are transmitting. Coming here, one of my dreams was to take a road trip and drive across the state. Route 66. What comes to my mind is this movie with Thelma and Louise. Also on [the] Discovery [channel] there were these travel shows. One was a guy traveling on a motorbike on the thruways, [to] the Grand Canyon, all of that, that sense of freedom."

It was also interesting that, in responding to *other questions*, respondents mentioned the role of US TV. For example, when asked if they always wanted to come to the United States, many spontaneously mentioned the role that watching US TV played in their decision to come. For example, the same graduate student from Romania said, "I wanted to live in the US for a little bit too, just to test out some of the things that I was getting introduced to by watching TV." A graduate student from Israel volunteered, "I was interested in the places I saw on TV and wanted to see them for real." An undergraduate student from the Philippines said she wanted to come to the United States because "it looked like a beautiful place in TV, movies, and media. Everybody is happy in the US; everybody has fun in the US." A graduate student from Saudi Arabia said that "the shows encouraged him to love New York, especially *Seinfeld*." Finally, an MBA student from China said that he liked the freedom he saw on US TV because it was "very tough for me to be a gay in China."

There are many factors that determine an individual's decision to leave his or her country, including, job offers, acceptance into educational or research tracks, and so on, so US TV viewing was not the sole factor causing people to come to the United States, but it was interesting that it was positively and deliberately mentioned to the degree that it was when respondents answered other (seemingly unrelated) questions.

More Critical Views

Some respondents expressed comments that were also critical of US TV. For example, a graduate student from Ireland said: "College scenes in the US seemed really irresponsible. In Ireland, you go straight into professional school [and are] therefore more adult, mature." Another respondent felt there were shows that projected Americans, especially youths, as immature and irresponsible in college, and as spoiled and not appreciating things. Others had mixed views. For example, an undergraduate student from China said that she liked and appreciated US TV: "It makes me know more about American culture rather than just views (from books or Americans or people who had visited America). For example, holidays are a way to socialize." But, she went on to say that she also took away impressions of the United States that were disconcerting. "Murder," she said. "In American TV people are killed; we don't have that in Chinese TV. In US, [people] can have guns. . . . [P]eople in high school spend more time at parties than studying, and they want to be heroes; people are killed [on American TV], and there is more of an emphasis on adventure." Finally, a number of others were critical of the role that watching US TV played in setting up their expectations about the United States. In their home countries, they had imagined the country to be an "easy-breezy fun culture," as one respondent put it, but instead what many found was that it was "a work culture."

The Effect of the Interview and Reflections

At the end of the interview, I asked respondents: "Is there anything that we have not discussed that you would like to talk about related to your answers or related to anything else?" I also probed with the following question: "What did the interview make you think about?" Slightly more than one-third of respondents, 36 percent (or 19), had no comments. The other post-interview comments varied widely, but a number of people spoke to how the interview made them reflect—some for the first time—on the influence of US TV in their lives. They said, for example, "[I] realized I almost exclusively watched American or foreign TV." This undergrad from the Philippines added that her fascination with *Captain Planet* and the five (very diverse) children depicted on this program probably influenced her decision to take five classes in global sustainability. (*Capitan Planet* was an animated environmentalist television program that dealt with issues of global sustainability and also featured five youth who were chosen from different parts of the globe; it was originally broadcast between 1990 and 1992.) A Nigerian woman said, "I haven't thought about the impact that TV had on me—had seen it as pure fantasy." A Brazilian woman said the interview "made me think about how much I had watched as [a] child." A Filipino, raised in Indonesia, responded that it made him think about "how I actually respond to TV rather than just consuming it as entertainment."

Some respondents also reflected, at the end, that the interview made them think about how their watching US TV influenced how they thought about race and about class. For example, Jane from Northern Ireland (described above) reflected that the interview made her think about "how much your background influences your downtime [by this she meant *when* you watch TV] and the fact that I didn't notice race back home." This was intriguing, given that she was fervently committed to practicing and defending civil rights in her country and in the United States. But it is perhaps not surprising given that we often tend to be more absorbed by our own immediate and pressing concerns.

In his post-interview comments, a graduate student from Austria returned to the issue of the influence of habitus. He said, "It made me think about growing up and the time I spend with TV." He also commented on how trendy it was to watch shows in English and that this was "becoming a class divide." A male grad student from Lima, Peru, expressed similar thoughts, saying the interview "highlighted my group in Lima and how TV shows are a part of a bigger package." He added that he realized US TV introduced a whole cultural sphere that others in his country didn't have. "Now people go to coffee shops to discuss politics, etc. It is 'cooler' in Starbucks," he said.

For many respondents, the interview experience made them reflect on how they had thought about the United States before they came, and how their views of the United States, like the views of those who shared their habitus, had been influenced by their watching US TV. It also made some of them reflect on how their views of the United States, which had been generally positive, shifted after living here for a while. Nonetheless, many were still thoughtful and hopeful.

A Series about Bipolar Illness

The interviews also made *me* reflect on how watching scripted television content may have influenced my own perceptions. In the course of conducting my research, I began to watch a new but short-lived TV series, *Black Box*, about a famous neurologist who secretly had bipolar disorder. Having personally known some people who had been diagnosed with this disorder, a number of whom had died sooner than their statistical life expectancy—some taking their own life—I was drawn to watch the show. Knowing very little about this illness, I found myself mentally referring at times to scenes from the show as a way of explaining to myself and to others why the deaths I was familiar with had occurred—and then wondering if my "TV knowledge" or exposure was at all correct. The show was clearly where my mind went and what I rested my knowledge on when I thought about this illness. In the same way, I can clearly see how people unfamiliar with particular racial, ethnic, gender, and class groups would similarly derive "knowledge" or expectations based on what they saw on TV.

Holtzman and Sharpe (2014:xvi) note the often unacknowledged impact of TV watching on the way in which people view their worlds: "[D]espite the multiple types of fictional programs and the fast-growing genre of reality television we generally are still exposed to a series of homogenous, consistent messages conveyed during prime-time television regardless of the platform, time of day, network, or program selected." Moreover, they and others have noted that even though television is a special kind of constructed reality, and even though it is only one of many things that serve to explain the world, it still has the ability to bombard, "standardize, streamline, amplify, and share common cultural norms" with virtually all classes, groups, and ages with the same perspectives (Morgan and Signorelli 1990, quoted in Holtzman and Sharpe, 2014: xvi)—whether they all receive this content at the same time (as was and is still true with real-time TV watching) or at different points of time. As applied to the foreign-born respondents, watching US TV may set up expectations that are not counterbalanced by real-life experiences until they are actually living in the United States; and even then, their media-influenced expectations may guide how they experience or view the world, especially with regard to areas not often explicitly or casually discussed in the United States, like race, ethnicity, class, and gender. The respondents' views about race, class, and gender will be addressed in subsequent chapters, for these involve a deeper level of interaction between their own developed views in these areas before coming and what they found or experienced in the United States.

5

No Way!

Surprises after Arriving

The United States is hugely heterogeneous, a nation of immigrants. According to the US Census Bureau, in 2014, the US population was 77.5 percent White, 13.2 percent Black, 5.4 percent Asian, and 1.4 percent Hawaiian, Pacific Islander, or Native American Indian, with 2.5 percent reporting two or more races.[1] Hispanics/Latinos were counted in a separate question and constituted 17.4 percent of the total US population (Colby and Ortman, 2015). Increasing diversity is projected, so that by 2044 the United States is anticipated to become a majority-minority country (US Census Bureau, 2015). Moreover, the terrain, culture, lifestyles, and even accents differ greatly across the country. So, although it may be seen as important and useful to define America in a uniform way, there are many pitfalls and challenges to doing so.

Furthermore, despite our variegated America, the research shows that we are still generally exposed to a series of patterned, often homogenous and consistent messages regarding race, class, and gender on television. This situation persists despite how TV is accessed, despite changes in the types of scripted fictional programs that have been developed—some of which more accurately reflect the racial and ethnic diversity of the country—and despite the increasing number of reality TV shows (Holtzman and Sharpe, 2014).[2] Given this, what images of America do people in other countries receive, and how accurately do those images reflect their experiences and perceptions after they arrive in the United States?

One way to start investigating these questions is to ask whether or not people still watch US TV after coming to the United States. My respondents did not watch as much and said they accessed it differently, doing more streaming than they did in their native countries, sometimes bingeing on shows on Netflix and Amazon. Do they still watch the same TV shows? A total of 28.6 percent (18) did, but more—39.7 percent (25)—did not. The remainder watched some of the same shows, but had expanded their viewing. Still others had less time to watch any TV.

Was the United States exactly as they imagined it to be? In general, my respondents said that the exported image of America lured them in, but it didn't always live up to their expectations once they began to live here. Sometimes it did, but other times it was worse and, then again, sometimes it was better. To some degree, this was affected by where they landed. Many arrived first in New York City, one of the United States' historical ports of entry.

New York City has had a large presence in the media, especially the US media consumed in other countries. It is a global city, a major center in terms of cultural production and media and financial concentration. In addition, it has been described variously as an idea, a fantasy, a promise, a lie, a cultural media production in itself, a chaotic mélange of signs and symbols, a melting pot, a refuge, an escape, and a geographical place where dreams go to thrive or die, where freedom and anonymity can be achieved, and where both free expression and oppression can occur.[3] So, there are often simultaneous, contradictory definitions of, and experiences in, America. New York City, like America, is a place that has come to mean various often contradictory things to people, often depending on the nature of their expectations and experiences. Seeing America through a New York City lens—whether that lens is the result of personal or "media-ted" experiences—can also skew what we think of as America.

Moreover, as Yang, Ramasubramanian, and Oliver (2008:247) have noted, "Decades of research have demonstrated that television may affect viewers' perceptions of social reality, with the influence of television on viewers' perceptions thought to be particularly strong when viewers lack direct experience with the content being depicted." Therefore, how people view America after arriving has much to do with *what their experiences and expectations were before coming* to the United States, as well as where they arrived or settled once here. Consequently, it seemed important to ask my foreign-born respondents what surprised them the most when they first arrived in the United States and why they were surprised. I thought that this would elicit both a sense of what their expectations had been and how much media images might have contributed to their expectations. Given that my specific interest was in how US TV had influenced their views of race, class, and gender, I followed up these questions by asking whether they thought that US TV encouraged or discouraged the integration of "Others," and whether they saw US TV as more inclusive than the media in their native country.

Part I

What Surprised You the Most about the US When You First Arrived? Why Were You Surprised?

During the interviews, we covered more than 90 questions, but it was the respondents' answers to this question that surprised *me* the most.[4] I was generally not surprised at *what* they said, but I was often taken aback by *how* they described their surprise and the examples that they used. An example of this was the simple response of an undergraduate from China who said, when asked what surprised him the most: "Black women with White children." This response gave me pause, for this is a feature of the middle-class, urban lifestyle that residents of New York City and other parts of the United States take for granted, and do not often think about, because it is such a familiar occurrence to see Black or darker-skinned nannies with White children. But for others, especially those coming from countries like China, this is not a commonplace sight. His comment made me reflect on how common a sight it is in New York City, yet we do not often see this on US TV.

What Did the Sample Say as a Whole?

As might be expected, given that they hail from 37 different countries, close to half of the respondents, 49.21 percent, were surprised by US "social norms and patterns," with another 14.29 percent (or 9) mentioning "people's interactions." The "size of things" and "high buildings" registered another 22.22 percent (or 14). Smaller percentages of respondents said they were surprised by things like "the sense of order," "aging infrastructure," "inequality," "fewer White people" and/or "different race/ ethnic composition," and "not like US TV or US films."[5] These last two categories, both of which mentioned race in their answers, accounted for 22.23 percent of the responses (or 14 respondents).[6]

The Similarity of First Impressions—in New York City and Elsewhere

What was most surprising to those who first arrived in New York City? One important theme that surfaced was size. For example, one respondent said: "The size of buildings, of things—much bigger than Europe—and the consumption practices." As might be anticipated, given that the media and TV images of New York City are fairly well known, many of those who first came to the city also mentioned its traditional hallmarks, for example, "city lights—they shined much more than I expected" and (again) "the size of things." Mario, a graduate student from Brazil, presented an interesting contrast that underscored these specific (and perhaps media-enhanced) characteristics of New York City. He said he was "impressed by how big it was, how crowded, noisy it was; also [by the easy access to] great books, magazines, movies, music, Madison Avenue, Statue of Liberty. Just loved it!" When he went to Washington, D.C., he saw "a major contrast" and noted "the calm, quiet, national malls, museums" and how he liked the contrast. Like many of the foreign-born respondents, he was also surprised by the high cost of living in New York City. Luis, a civil engineer from Venezuela, expressed this succinctly when he said that in New York City, "two beers cost $20!" Other respondents talked about the unanticipated cost of taxis and housing, especially in Manhattan, where so many of the TV characters whom they liked lived, and where so many quickly hailed a cab without a second thought about money.

Somewhat related to "size" were comments that spoke to "order," infrastructure, and how things work. As a native and resident New Yorker, I am more aware of when the trains are late than how often they run on time. But as the following comments indicate, that "regularity and order" often comes as a surprise to those from many other countries. Mani, arriving with his family from India, said in New York City "there was more organization and less people compared to India." His family "experienced less traffic," and they were surprised that people "followed the rules." Aperi from Kyrgyzstan was most surprised at how organized the station was when she arrived. As she said, "all was in order, the time and the people. Everyone did their job." But perhaps a respondent from Brazil said it best when she said that in New York "the bureaucracy worked, but if one thing went wrong, people couldn't deal with it. In

Brazil, the opposite is the case. Nothing works, and you always deal with exceptions." She also applied this distinction to the United States as a whole.

There were also at least two respondents, one from Turkey and another from Qingdao, China, who were surprised, however, that when they first arrived, New York City seemed to be behind the times and trailing their home countries in "not having free Wi-Fi and cellular service in the subway system and with some still paying bills by check as opposed to electronically." As the respondent from Turkey said at the time of the interview, she was surprised at "everything related to daily life—we [in the United States] pay bills by check, [which is] not as advanced as Turkey. And, we're still signing credit card slips in the US." And, as the undergrad from China put it: "No phone service or phone signal in subway because we have signal everywhere and US/NYC subway is very old."[7]

Outside of New York City, First Impressions

What about those who did *not* come to New York first? Many were also somewhat stunned by "size" or what some described as the sense of bigness and abundance that surrounded them. For example, a young graduate student from Kingston, Jamaica, said that she first came to visit Miami and then an aunt in Atlanta. She saw it all as glossy and shiny, but what fascinated her was the all-you-can-eat concept. She clarified that she was not a stranger to the variety and amount of food available, and she did not come from a background of scarcity, but the fact that restaurants were established around this concept surprised her. She was also struck by "choice overload" and how people consumed salads as an actual meal and not just as part of one. She had always thought of salad in the same way that many from the Spanish-speaking Caribbean think of salad, that is, as a garnish that accompanies the main meal, which consists of, for example, rice, beans, meat, and salad.

A sense of splurge or bigness also came through from other respondents who did not enter the United States through New York City. Both Kasia, a professor from Poland, and Anna, a graduate student from Russia, first went to Minnesota, and were surprised at the distances between cities and the size of the country. They found that everything—

the people, cars, houses, even household appliances, like washing machines—was bigger than they had expected or were used to seeing in their native country. They also were surprised not just by how big but also by how comfortable the houses were. How little people walked also surprised them. Landing in Arizona, Juan from Spain was impressed by the heat, dryness, and, again, the size of everything—roads, cars, and buildings.

Rosie, a graduate student from the Philippines, said the highways in the United States were so much better than the roads in her country, and the retail environment was better and bigger too; this included grocery stores, junk food, and toys—"there was so much to buy," she said. In the Philippines, she added, stores are "not as large and they have a smaller selection; some stuff is still not readily available." When I asked for specifics, she said her family would bring or send to the Philippines boxes of Fruit Roll-Ups, which were not available there. She also remembered bringing home Instant Noodles, Charms Blow Pops, Tootsie Pops, and other lollipops. She added that still today her family would ask for other food items not yet available there, like cookie butter, which is similar to Nutella. Another graduate student was similarly impressed with the bigness of everything in the United States—she had noted, for example, portions of food, roads, cars, and stores. I asked her if any of that bigness appeared on US TV in her native Russia, and she said yes, but that it didn't strike her that way when she saw the shows, only when she came to the United States.

Racial and Ethnic Diversity

Foreign-born respondents were also surprised by the ethnic and racial diversity of the US population, regardless of whether their point of entry was New York City or elsewhere. The population was more diverse than they had anticipated. New York City, for example, has been a majority-minority city for decades now, but the US TV programs that my respondents saw do not typically portray the city that way, nor do they give viewers a sense of the linguistic diversity that has been characteristic of New York City for decades.[8] But again, what was curious was how they described this diversity. For example, one male grad student from the Philippines said: "There are all kinds of racial backgrounds here. You don't feel like a foreigner because everyone looks different." A gradu-ate student from Syria said he was most surprised by the "diversity and background of people, how people look—the national ethnic/social cos-mopolitanism" in another city in the northeast. He said: "In the Middle East, everyone looks and speaks the same. The idea of people being dif-ferent is [or was] new to me." The number of different languages spoken also surprised him—he added that it was not what he had been used to. Others also commented on this. One graduate student from India said: "In New York City I barely heard English." The linguistic diversity struck her the most. And yet, much depends on where you are com-ing from. A Filipino graduate student who had gone to an international school in Indonesia was "jarred by everybody speaking English," he said, because in his home and school environment people spoke a variety of languages, and English was just one of many.

Respondents who came to the United States from more homogenous places had different impressions. A graduate student from China, for example, was struck by "people with different skin colors walking in the street," and by the fact that a stranger asked *her* for directions. It was "not like in China," where "if there is a foreign face, that person is not seen as a real person; here people trust each other." Also referring to so-cial sanctions in China, another female graduate student was surprised that "the way people dressed was very open. They seemed very comfort-able as the way they want to be, regardless of other people's attitude." A 25-year-old woman from Kyrgyzstan also made reference to diversity and dress, noting that there were a lot of Jewish people (Hasidim), Af-rican Americans, and [South] Asians, and "you couldn't see them in my country. The clothing and hair of the teens were [also] different; some were half naked."

In addition to race, language, and clothes, what surprised some the most were the evident class divisions in the city. For example, one Ger-man researcher, who came to the United States as a medical student and worked at a hospital in New York City, said that he and his col-leagues noticed first the "discrepancy between rich people and lower classes and immigrants." He commented that, regrettably, "the US is the most modern country, but . . . there was a big gap between rich and poor receiving medical care. Many have no primary physician—and so get no treatment. The American Dream is never achieved (for so many).

[The gap is] in any society, but when [you] come to NYC—in the richest country—it's really exciting, but also the gaps impress you."

Race and Diversity outside of New York City

People living outside of the city commented on race and diversity less than those who first arrived in New York, but some did bring up this topic. For example, Nance, a Canadian grad student, was surprised at the level of racial segregation that existed in the United States. She said that Toronto was more integrated and that it had a multiracial population, not just Blacks and Whites. Living in the United States, she felt she didn't have a vocabulary to talk about relations between Black and White people. She said, "In Canada, you didn't discuss 'race,' but you spoke in terms of multiculturalism. Race was implicit. In Canada people preferred to talk about cultural practices." Indeed, the Canadian census does not use the term "race" but counts "visible minorities." I probed her on whether she thought that the differences were due to the influence of the French-speaking people in Canada. She said that they did have this historical cultural difference, but that Native American indigenous languages and cultures were also historical issues in Canada, with race or color underlying them.

A Nigerian businesswoman who had studied in London and Nigeria said her biggest surprise when she came to study as an undergraduate at Clarke Atlanta University, a historically Black college in Atlanta, was the degree of [racial] segregation in the city. I asked if this had not been the case in London or Nigeria. She responded that in Nigeria there was mainly one (Black) group. In the United Kingdom, she was the only Black person in her class at school, and most of her classmates were White, but there were many people from other backgrounds, such as different countries in Asia. Nicolae, a male graduate student from Moldova, living in a medium-sized city where African Americans lived in a part of town that was separate from the university campus, said, "Safety was a problem," and "you have to be careful when you choose a place to live." The de facto segregation and the caution that he perceived others had about where to look for housing when they arrived made him wary. Others in the sample also quickly realized that there were race-based geographic lines that they had to consider when choosing a place to live.

He and others in my sample said they did not anticipate this would be a problem when they came. Despite his strong awareness of racial fault lines in the city where he was living, Nicolae did not indicate that he had experienced any racial discrimination. When asked how he thought others in the United States would racially classify him, he said as "Soviet, Eastern European."

At the same time, he spoke positively about the US image around the world and how in the United States there were higher expectations that individuals could accomplish the goals they set for themselves; he mentioned that in the United States there existed liberty and great opportunities. Although he referred generally to some administrative or bureaucratic issues that he had faced, he was very impressed with the United States, because "you are free to be what you want to be. No one will judge your behavior, beliefs, or views. And, you can express these. No one will push you to say otherwise." He added this was true in many areas, not just in politics. In saying this he was contrasting his experience in the United States with that which he had had in Moldova, where one was judged severely because of one's expressed beliefs.

Finally, Iliana, a graduate student from Romania, said:

In terms of this racial issue, discrimination, by watching the shows I was [watching], I thought the problem is not as pertinent any longer. But coming here I realize that it is still very present. And you see it play out here almost every day, in the stories and projects we hear about. [In her university town], for example, in the South side, the poorest part of the city is where there are the most African American people. They are [the] people with the [least] social security and poor access to education. There are certain areas that are inhabited by African Americans. That's where we are told is the most unsafe to live. And then, [she said she noticed] just the way that some people talk about issues with a lot of passion—both Caucasian and African American people. And, in my class, we are 130 and there are only six or seven African Americans. Lately, shows have become more politically correct, so you don't see all White actors.

Clearly, for many foreign-born respondents, the racial (and economic) patterning of life in New York City, and in the United States as a whole, came as a surprise in light of the way the United States was/is depicted in the media we export or at least on the US shows the respondents were accustomed to viewing in their native countries. This is not to say that US media are solely responsible for the expectations that respondents brought. There are many other influences, including what they learn about the United States in their schools or from their own varied domestic media outlets, from media from other countries, or from others who have visited the United States or who are still in the United States and communicate with them (Levitt, 2001), to note just a few other sources.

Social Relations, Social Norms

As noted previously, it is somewhat to be expected that foreign-born people would be surprised by different social relations or norms. Indeed, many in both groups mentioned this, but how they described these differences and what they said was surprising to them are (again) most intriguing. For example, on the age-old and unresolved debate about whether New Yorkers are naturally rude or naturally friendly, Francois from Toronto said, "New Yorkers have a negative connotation but are probably some of the friendliest people I've ever met." And David from Colombia said that he was surprised at "how people respect each other and each other's personal space. For example, on the train if a person trips, people try to help." He expected they would be minding their own business. He did not expect people to be aware of others' problems or concerns.

As may be evident from some of the comments, what people were accustomed to in their home countries strongly influenced what surprised them most about the United States. For example, Gretchen, a biomedical researcher from Germany who worked in a research lab and lived in Manhattan, found great contrasts between social norms in Europe and in the United States. "Culturally there is no difference from Europe; it is mostly White people," she said. But she was shocked, for example, at how people waste energy. She called the United States an "air-conditioning" culture and said, "In Europe, if it's hot, it's hot. You don't immediately turn on or look for air conditioning." She was also overwhelmed by the friendliness of people. She said, "This irritated me at first. . . . There is small talk a lot. They make you feel like you are best friends but you are not. In Europe, nobody would talk to you." She also said that the

"US is not [really] a free country. You don't go to the park at night or drink alcohol on the street or in the park." Finally, she was surprised that "people follow rules even if they think they're silly. No exceptions." She said, "Not sure if it is a New York thing, but in Europe, you have rules, but if you need to violate a rule, you just do it, no big deal." (Here she was referring to rules like "keep off the grass," which would have meant pedestrians following a more circuitous route.)

Class and Social Norms outside of New York City

Similar to Gretchen was a Chinese graduate student who said that she was surprised everyone was "so chatty" when she first came with her parents and visited Chicago, Florida, and Niagara Falls. She was surprised that her parents were "chatted up a lot," she said. "We don't chat so much in Asian cultures. Really, you're talking to a stranger." Despite the chattiness that she found, she also indicated that she was very surprised at how little US people knew about others outside of the United States. Other observers have commented on how the rest of the world knows a great deal about the United States—in part because our media are so predominant—and how little Americans know about other countries.

However, a Canadian graduate student who had seen very little difference between Canada and the United States before coming to the United States found people in the United States *less* talkative and more individualistic than Canadians. Indeed, she found a great many differences between her experiences in her country and in the United States, particularly in California:

In California I really thought and realized that things were different because I spent the most time there, and one of the things that I found was that religion is talked about way more in everyday life, and people identify as Christian or Muslim more openly than they do in Canada, just in my day-to-day interactions, and I found that very interesting. And I also found Americans a little bit more closed off than my Canadian friends and my Canadian family. They kind of do their own thing, very individualistic, whereas I find Canada to be a little bit more communal. Like when I would take a bus in Canada, usually people would say, "Hi, how are you?" have a conversation; but in America, people are on their phones, in their heads, and they just want to get their task done, not so much caring about the relationship part of life. I think in Canada we do value community a little bit more. I definitely see the difference between a capitalist and socialist background.

However, Hamid, coming from Kyrgyzstan, a former Soviet Republic, arrived in Iowa and was struck not by capitalism and a strong individualism but by the politeness and simplicity of people. For example, he saw people sitting on the floor in the train terminal. When I asked why this surprised him, he said, "In our country, we would see the floor as dirty."

Similar to George, who noted class divisions and unequal access to medical care in New York City, an undergraduate from the Philippines commented, "I didn't realize that there were poor people in the US. Movies and TV never show poor people. I went to LA and San Diego, and I was shocked to see homeless people." Her comment and those of other foreign-born respondents who indicated that they were most surprised at the economic divisions, inequality, and poverty that they saw when they first arrived reflect the perhaps more sanitized view of America that is exported via or along with US TV programming.

A number of respondents from Latin America were also surprised at social differences, but of a different sort. Alicia from Brazil itemized what surprised her when she arrived. She said: "When I filled in a form at Berkeley for Race/Ethnicity, I put that I was White and then found out that I was 'Latin' [or Hispanic]." She also said, "There was no body contact between people. I would go to give someone a kiss in greeting, and they would hold back. They thought that I wanted to give them a kiss on their lips—'don't you wish!'" she said she thought at the time. In addition, she noted, "You also didn't hug when meeting or greeting people." Finally, she was surprised at the difference between the countries with regard to sex and sensuality. She said, "Dance in the US was sexualized but not sensual." Maribel, a graduate student from Tijuana, Mexico, experienced a different kind of shock when she moved to Miami from Mexico. She found that, although Miami was a "mainly Spanish-speaking world," Mexicans were a minority, and the Latin Americans who lived there were from various countries.

A Serbian graduate student was also struck by how different "social life" was in the United States. She said in Serbia, students would meet for coffee after school; here they disperse, go elsewhere separately. She said she was lonely until she came to New York City and found friends in a new university and in another graduate program. A graduate student from Kingston, Jamaica, was also struck by differences in social behaviors and how impersonal people were, especially in New York City. She said that in her country, saying "good morning" and "good afternoon" to people you passed, even if you did not know them, was a normal part of everyday life. "In the United States, people would greet you by saying, 'How are you?' but it was not an actual question," she said; "it was another way of being polite." And "you come to understand that they did not expect an answer."

Media Mentions and Influence

A number of respondents specifically mentioned the media. For example, Sandra, a Nigerian graduate student, said she was "not really surprised [at the diversity] because she watched Western media a lot and had cousins and a husband who visited the US a lot." She had heard about racism from the media, but she found people were "nice." Her neighbors were nice to her, but she noted that "at home we have more communal lifestyles; here everyone stays to themselves." In thinking about the contrasts between her life in the United States and her life at home, she said her current neighbors were kind, but at home in Nigeria, "it's about thinking more about the 'we' than the 'me.'"

An architect from Greece also mentioned the media and said he noted strong differences between what the media said about US government involvement throughout the world and what he, his New York City acquaintances, and people in other countries thought about the government's actions:

There are totally different perceptions [between what the media presented and the views of the New Yorkers I had come to know]. . . . People here don't see the US as controlling others' resources but as helping other countries. People were friendly, helpful. They have a different mentality than their government. They don't care where you're coming from or what family you come from. They just care if you have a good personality, are hardworking, and comply with general social norms. They are more

open-minded than people in Greece and [more open-minded] than what
I was expecting. Also they are more about being pragmatic with regard to
business decisions. But I expected them to be more informed about how
the US operates and why it operates as it does. For example, the greater
use of resources (in and by) the US—most New Yorkers are unaware of
this. Also, I was a little blind-sided by how the media treats Israel—very
one-sided. I realize why people are misinformed. But I am cynical about
the media in Greece too.

Last, given the recent media coverage of the Black Lives Matter movement and civil rights organizations that have been critical of the way in
which people of color are policed, it was interesting to hear Steven from
Israel say that he was surprised that there was more self-policing, politeness, and respect for authority than was being conveyed in the media.
He also contrasted this with what he had experienced in Israel, where
he said the police were "less refined, polite, and uncivilized." He was not
denying that there was racial inequality in the United States; indeed,
he said that he saw that "in front of me all the time" and that this was
reflected "somewhat in the media" but that "the media did not show it
to the full extent."

Despite these "surprises," a number of respondents made reference to
how similar New York City was to what they had imagined based on the
media they had watched, and how they felt they were in a movie when,
for example, they walked across the Brooklyn Bridge and were reminded
of a particular scene. As Ileana from Romania said: "First thing that impressed me—it looked like in the movies."

Those who first landed outside of New York City also mentioned the
expectations that US media had introduced into their minds. For example, Hiro from Japan said that the United States was "different than
what they saw on TV. People are not as wealthy in America as others
think; people are not as happy as TV portrays. It's the same as other
places in the world, where people are suffering and striving to be better."
Irina from Latvia came to the United States to study in a small town in
Michigan and was surprised at "how simple and unattractive it was." She
said that she and others from her country all imagined the United States
as beautiful because of how it was represented in the media that they

saw. She said that she later came to appreciate the town where she lived, "that all was working, and people lived regular lives."

Cata, a grad student from Peru, went to Rock Springs, Wisconsin, for two months for a work-study program. She was also surprised at how very small the town was. She said that in Peru, everyone imagined the United States as just having big cities; yet she remembered thinking that San Francisco was the biggest, closest city that she knew of then and that was quite far from where she was. Eva, a graduate student from Russia, said that when she first came to the United States, "I lived in Oregon in a rural area, and this is not how I pictured the US back home. I imagined big cities, skyscrapers, movie stars, and Britney Spears. And then I came to Oregon." It was nothing like what she had expected based on her viewing of US TV.

Finally, Sabila, who traveled from Azerbaijan, a former Soviet Republic, to Manhattan, Kansas, found that Kansas was nothing like she had seen of the United States in the movies or other media. She was very specific about what surprised her and summed it up by emphasizing six things that generally reflect how our (exported) media may emphasize large urban centers over smaller, rural areas of the country: First, the area where she lived was small and rural compared to what she had seen in the media. Second, almost all of the women she met were either engaged or married, and had blond hair. (She had been told, or she assumed from her TV watching, that American women didn't marry until after they had careers.)[9] Third, people's sense of morality was religiously charged. She said: "I was stopped in the street by others who invited me to their church. Jehovah's Witnesses came to the door." Fourth, it was also more family-oriented, moralist, and conservative than she had expected. Her last two comments were particularly intriguing: Fifth, she said, "It was the first time in my life that people would offer me help without my asking." She gave as an example of how some neighbors fixed her windows, and she hadn't realized there had been a problem with them. Sixth, she was also surprised that the community seemed to have an unwritten honor code that everyone followed. In her college, for example, she said she was surprised that there wasn't a proctor in the room when tests were administered. She said it was so honest that it made the very idea of cheating unthinkable by anyone.

In short, while there were differences between what surprised people the most in New York City and in the rest of the United States, there were also many similarities. The concepts of "bigness" and abundance, for example, were common regardless of where the respondents landed; they were also generally impressed by the extent to which the US population is diverse. I was surprised that issues of race, diversity, and class were unanticipated by many—both those who first came to New York City and those who landed elsewhere in the United States. I wondered how much respondents' consumption of US media contributed to this gap between their expectations and experiences.

As I reflected on this and thought about my travels in other countries, I realized that we often bring our expectations to the countries we visit, and if these expectations are based mainly on media images (including news and entertainment media) with few personal or other contacts, we will probably be surprised by what we see when we arrive. This is not to say that US media are or would be the *only* contributor to the respondents' expectations. Nonetheless, I was a bit surprised that so many of them made references to expectations that they had because of what they had seen in US media.

Part II: Is US TV Seen as Encouraging or Discouraging the Integration of "Others"?

A Mixed Picture

Given these media references and given that my respondents were now "Others" in the United States, that is, other than American, I wondered whether they now saw US TV as encouraging or discouraging of the integration of "Others." Fully 43 percent (or 27) said US TV was "encouraging," and only 27 percent (or 17) said it was discouraging. The remainder had neutral comments or said it did both. Given the extent to which US TV and US media in general have been critiqued in the literature (see Chapter 1) and, more recently, on social media for their exclusionary practices, I was initially perplexed at how the group responded to this question.[10] However, drilling down and examining the responses more closely, a mixed picture emerged, with the country of origin and the respondents' view of otherness within their own country playing an important role in whether or not they saw US TV as encouraging the integration of Others. But almost everyone (96.83 percent of the sample) commented on this.

Encouraging

Looking first at those who said that US TV was encouraging of the integration of Others, we can see in their comments the role that their home-country experiences played in their responses. For example, Nicolae from Moldova, a country he described as fraught with ethnic divisions and competition, said, "TV is good. It integrates common interests." However, he also said that "the Internet tend[s] to isolate [people] more than TV" and that "too much TV also isolates." In other words, he felt that the Internet tends to lead people to places where others agree with them; and that too much TV also isolated people from actual personal interactions with Others. Another respondent, Leon, came from Indonesia, a country that has had long-simmering ethnic divisions. Like Nicolae, he saw US TV as encouraging the integration of Others. He said, "In programs, there is generally a theme of people bonding or working together; for example, in *The Hunger Games* [a film shown recently on TV], everyone comes together at the end to start a rebellion. In *Modern Family*, we see examples of encouraging differences; [we] see familial connections, and this adds to [the] idea of encouraging otherness."

Other respondents, from countries where residents had come to see themselves as relatively homogenous until recent flows of immigrants and displaced persons changed the ethnic makeup of the population, also saw US TV as encouraging the integration of Others in comparison to their own country's depiction. Two examples of this include Carmela from Italy, who said it was "encouraging because US TV is a portrayal of the multiethnicity of the [US] society," and Edelmira from Greece, who said US TV encourages integration "because the US is a nation of 'Others' in itself."

Some respondents were either Others in their own countries or sympathetic to Others at home. They saw US TV as "encouraging" integration because they showed Others pursuing opportunities. For example, Nishi from Nagaland said, "The cultural message [on US TV] is that, as long as you are hardworking, nothing can hold you back. Obama is an example." Nishi indicated that people from her part of India were not given the same opportunities as Others in India. Nagaland is in northeastern India, and became part of India as a result of political boundaries established by the British. However, Nishi and others from her region are generally assumed to be Chinese (and not Indian) in the United States because of their physical appearance. Milinka from Serbia said US TV was "encouraging especially with the LGBTQ population." She added that, as a result of seeing more LGBTQ people on US TV, "more people are coming out in Serbia. They have rights, and people are becoming more receptive."

Others, like Jose M. from the Philippines, were generally sympathetic to otherness and felt that US TV was more open to difference than was the case in his country, where people were less open to difference. He said, "There is a conscious choice by the writers to include people of different backgrounds (races and cultures); it is a conscious choice to have them succeed in what they are doing." Mani, an environmental consultant from an upper-class Indian family, shared a similar view. He said that on US TV, you "have people from all ethnic backgrounds; [it] doesn't matter what your color is. There [in India], 98 percent are Indian actors, but here, if you [are an] actor, you can get a job [no matter what group you are part of]." So, for many, US TV was more inclusive (of Others) than their own country's media. Actually, when asked how they thought that Others were portrayed in their country's television programming, only 10.5 percent of the sample said "well," while another 73.7 percent said they were "rarely seen," "not portrayed well," or "not portrayed at all."[11] More than 50 respondents volunteered comments about this.

Blended Comments

Additionally, some said that US TV was encouraging (or discouraging) of the integration of Others, but were quite "mixed" in their comments. Examples here include Joseph from Ireland, who said, "*Friends* was very White. . . . [On] *Sex and the City*, most characters were White. But particularly encouraging were *The Cosby Show* and *Roots*." Steven from Israel was also mixed in his response, saying US TV "advocated racial equality, but that this varied over time. . . . For example, today it is the Arabs that are [portrayed as] bad." In essence, many of those who saw US TV as encouraging the integration of Others (1) came from countries that had (or had had) a great deal of ethnic, racial, or political conflict; (2) were from countries that had until recently been relatively homogenous but now had substantial numbers of immigrants; (3) were individuals who felt "othered" in their home countries; or (4) were sympathetic to Others for a variety of reasons.

Becoming More Inclusive

A number of respondents did not say that US TV encouraged integration, but they said it was *becoming* more inclusive. They made comments like "Now [there is] a push for more integration" or "You see more different people in the shows (for example, lesbians, Black people, Chinese people, and Hispanic people)." Victoria, an undergraduate student from the Philippines who writes a blog on the media, was optimistic and spoke at length about this:

> I think that the US is beginning to encourage the integration of Others because there are an increasing number of people who are willing to speak up and give a voice to those who are otherwise unable to speak for themselves. As more people become educated in these sorts of topics, the more pressure companies are being placed under to change what they have been doing and adapt to the changing society. This way, people from countries outside the United States can see that whatever the media used to portray is not necessarily the right way to approach the situation, and I feel that as a whole, society would really benefit from that.

Her comments are consistent with the research that I and others have done, showing that there has been some improvement in the portrayal of minorities in US TV, but that they are still underrepresented and misrepresented.

Discouraging

Despite the fact that a *smaller* proportion (27 percent) of respondents said that US TV was *discouraging* of the integration of Others, those who felt this way had very pointed and emphatic comments on this. They included comments such as the following:

> I think it's ignorant. I don't think it really approaches the subject; it doesn't foster your thoughts of Others or the ideas of acceptance. It doesn't really address the issues of othering.
> —Nanette from the Canadian Yukon

> [US TV] shows and good storylines are based on cliché, and the view on TV is never seen through the eyes of an Other.
> —Atsushi from Japan

> [US TV] is not encouraging about integrating Others. Many shows don't deal with it.
> —Gerhard from Germany

> It's more of a passive thing; [many people want to] keep America the way it was 50 years ago. [US TV] primarily features shows about White people that appeal to White people. *The Cosby Show* was Black people pretending to be White people. The same people but Black. No black issues at all; [it was] all about White issues.
> —Clare from Toronto

> Not many racially diverse actors [appear on] many shows. If [success is] about money and power, White people are in control, and Others are sidekicks.
> —Ju from China

> [There is] little connection to the rest of the world [on US TV]; [characters] only talk about self and not global Others. [They] also discuss diet, but then order fries. Certain amount of hypocrisy.
> —Lamiya from Azerbaijan

> Discouraging because Others are not portrayed, usually not portrayed, or portrayed very stereotypically. So I think the TV does not enforce the integration.
> —Eva from Russia

[US TV] highlights different issues but never close it. Highlighting the issue just shows who is targeted. [Does not present a resolution to the issue.]
—Ekaterina from Russia

Minorities are not portrayed well, and the races are very segregated on American TV.
—Adnan from Syria

All in all, these comments suggesting that US TV discouraged the integration of Others, combined with the more mixed comments noted above, indicated to me that the critiques made in the literature (and discussed in Chapter 1) about the under- and misrepresentation of racial and ethnic groups in US TV were not as far from the views of these respondents as I initially thought would be the case.

Missed the Racial Dimension

Most surprising, however, were those who said they hadn't thought about race or perceived racial and ethnic dynamics when viewing US TV in their home countries. These included Anna from Russia, who said: "I don't think it matters. In Russia we don't think about inclusion. When we watch TV, we don't think in those terms about these things." However, she may have been reflecting on when she was younger and watched US TV, for she added, "This has changed now." Milja from Finland was similarly unaware of race. She said she felt US TV encouraged [racial] integration "to a certain extent," but she seemed to suggest that what was more important was economic integration, for she added: "as long as others have purchasing power." She said that she had seen *The Cosby Show* in Finland, but didn't understand the racial aspects of the show; she did not have any idea how revolutionary it was. She added that she saw Spike Lee's movie *Do the Right Thing* as depicting conflicts between different neighborhoods and classes rather than ethnic and racial tensions or differences. She said there were "tons of references I'm sure I didn't get at all!" Some of these comments came from respondents from homogenous countries or who were raised at a time when there were few people of color in their countries.

Summary

In summary, what happens after people come to the United States? Was it exactly as they imagined it would be? The answer is in some ways yes, in other ways no. What surprised them the most when they first came? As might be expected, regardless of where they landed, it was the bigness, the diversity, the economic divisions, and the differences in social norms and relations. Did their viewing of US media influence their expectations? Yes, in many instances.

Did they see US media as encouraging or discouraging of "otherness"? More (43 percent vs. 27 percent) saw US TV as encouraging of the integration of Others, but in examining the actual responses, we saw a more mixed picture, with country of origin and one's positionality there playing important roles in these more positive views. Some respondents also saw US media as improving—albeit slowly—with regard to the inclusion of Others, and some had the hope that other nations' media will do the same. Those who said that US TV was discouraging of the integration of Others were quite forceful and critical in their comments. Taken together, the foreign-born group's responses show a mixed picture with regard to whether they felt US TV was encouraging or discouraging of the integration of Others. Curiously, some respondents missed the racial dimension of some US media before coming to the United States.

How did coming to the United States affect how they currently think about race? Class? Gender? And themselves? We turn to these questions in the next chapters.

6

Say What?

Did TV Accurately Depict Racial and Ethnic Relations in the United States?

To what extent did this foreign-born sample agree with the critique of US TV that it under- or misrepresents racial and ethnic groups in the United States? The answer? To a surprising degree, very few (18 percent) felt US TV gave an accurate reflection. Many more (73.8 percent) indicated that now that they were in the United States, they did not think US TV accurately reflected racial and ethnic relations. As we will see, taken together, their comments speak loudly and simply to this issue.

Those Who Said Yes, US TV Did Give Me an Accurate Picture of Racial and Ethnic Relations in the United States

Some respondents (18 percent, or 11 individuals) did find that US TV accurately reflected what racial and ethnic relations were like in the United States, but in the majority of cases, these comments were qualified. For example, some admitted that they had had such limited exposure to people of other races that when they first saw a show like *The Cosby Show*, it was the first time they had ever seen a Black person—on TV or in person. For example, a graduate student from Saudi Arabia living in New York City said yes, US TV accurately reflected racial and ethnic relations in the United States. He then referred to when he and his friends first viewed US TV. He said this was their "initial exposure to diversity and what to expect—especially with regard to Whites and Blacks." He added, "Most American shows don't have races (separated) anymore. They show many friendships between Whites and Blacks, and I see this in real life too." A respondent from Northern Ireland also said she "saw Black and White people working together; this is probably representative of the people I meet here. [For] I probably would not associate with people who were not like that."

Those Who Said Yes and No

Some respondents felt that US TV did and did *not* accurately reflect racial and ethnic relations. For example, Milja from Finland said that shows like *Law & Order* reflected only "the little world they depict, but the stories are universal—good and bad guys in gritty, gray settings." But she went on to say that today these settings had taken on "bright, styled colors"—her reference being to the way in which contemporary music and prison settings in the media have made these shows more hip or fashionable globally. She noted that *The Wire*, a crime drama set in Baltimore, had a worldwide following. For her, *The Wire* was an eye-opener; she came to view it as depicting larger, more universal "power struggles within the 'have-nots'" and how they try to find a way to survive. She said, "This is a global situation that everyone can relate to." So, in her mind, the shows were "not so stereotypical as some say." However, she also added that despite its popularity globally, in the US Midwest, with its Bible Belt culture and small towns, she did not think this show was popular.

Steven, a graduate student from Israel, also offered a mixed assessment, and he, too, mentioned *The Wire*. He said "No, the racial inequality that I see in front of me all the time is somewhat reflected in the media, but they don't show it to the full extent. *The Wire* does somewhat. A few shows deal with it. But the frame through [which we see] *Law & Order* is not social inequality." By this, he meant that there was little attention given in these shows to the fact that Black neighborhoods are affected by larger societal forces, such as redlining by banks, insurance companies, and real estate interests, but, he said, "This is not the main issue in the shows."

Others who had mixed responses included Rosie from the Philippines, who noted that you did see some racial and ethnic diversity on US TV, but that class differences between racial and ethnic groups, and class mobility, were evaded on US TV. She said, "A lot of shows portray the shift from the upper-middle class to wealthy, but there is an entire sphere that is underrepresented, that [has] a very different racial and ethnic dynamic." She also spoke to tokenism, adding: "In shows there is always a token Asian or Black [person. Yet] outside of New York, you have greater homogeneity within groups. After moving [to New York City], I see there is an immigrant or racial/ethnic diversity that is not portrayed in mass media. There is more diversity in the US than you see on TV."

Margo, coming from Canada, also noted that racial and ethnic groups were present on US TV, but she stated that the "shows were narrow and showed each group in isolation. In *Family Matters* all were Black. In *Friends* all were White. This segregation between shows was kind of reflective [of the United States], but it misses the actual tensions that exist."

Finally, and most interesting, were those who said US TV presented an accurate reflection of what racial and ethnic relations were like in the United States because the shows depicted the racial and ethnic distance between groups. Nishi from India articulated this position best when she said that when you saw a show like *Modern Family*, you picked up on this. "You know how they are perceived. You know an American is different from an African American." Here she was suggesting that the way the characters are introduced or referred to made this distinction clear to the viewers.

The Nos Have It

The loudest and most poignant voices in response to this question were those who said, unequivocally, US TV did *not* accurately reflect racial and ethnic relations in the United States. Within this group, four major reasons were given for why they felt this way: (1) racial and ethnic relations were worse than shown on TV; (2) the shows didn't depict the positive side of diversity; (3) other types of diversity—e.g., religious and intraethnic—were not shown; and (4) the shows had a narrow focus.[1]

Racial and Ethnic Relations Are Worse Than Shown on TV

A graduate student from China concisely summed up this perspective when she said that she thought that discrimination was still very serious in the United States, but it didn't look like that on the TV shows she saw and had seen before she came to the United States. Another respondent, from Kyrgyzstan, articulated this view somewhat differently, saying: "No, in [the] shows [they] don't show ethnic problems; [they] are mostly friendly." Luiza from Brazil spoke to the issue of tokenism and how this did not reflect actual racial and ethnic relations. She said, "The Black kid always made it [successfully in a particular show]," and that was "not true in reality." She also spoke to how much US TV reinforced the idea of the American Dream, that is, that everyone could achieve the dream of a single-family home with a white picket fence in a happy and comfortable suburb. She added that she "didn't know about discrimination before coming" to the United States. "[I] thought everything was like the suburbs and in the big high schools; [I] came to see the American Dream as a myth." However, she also added that she still felt there was social mobility in the United States.[2]

The extent to which some of the respondents looked (before coming) to the United States as a place of freedom and opportunity was a theme that ran through many of the interviews, although it was not an area that I had initially sought to examine. It surfaced fairly early in my interviews and was referenced in a number of ways. For example, one respondent was struck by the freedom that a group of young people in *Friends* had in being able to live separately from their families and with each other; another respondent was impressed by the freedom women had in *Sex and the City*. However, Ada, an administrator from Turkey, said that the United States had had a positive image when she was living there, but that after living in the United States, she had come to appreciate how "free" the country really was. She said that in Turkey she did not see "freedom of expression and self" and the freedom to be outspoken as important. But the United States taught her "to be more like myself." She also saw greater diversity in the United States and greater tolerance of diversity than in Turkey, where she felt there was a greater pressure to be homogenous.

This view of the United States as a place of freedom for all also surfaced in response to the question of racial and ethnic representations on US TV. A particularly poignant story came from a woman from Serbia who said that one reason why she came to the United States was because she thought that everyone was treated equally here. She had survived three wars. And because her family was mixed, she was particularly sensitive to the lack of equality.[3] She recounted a number of stories of how her immediate and extended family had been affected by the dissolution of Yugoslavia and the subsequent conflicts between Bosnians, Serbs, and Croats that had made her very conscious of how groups were treated. Before coming to the United States, she felt that American TV showed that everyone was treated equally here; after she arrived, however, she found this was not the case. Indeed, she said that racial and ethnic relations were worse than shown on TV. She was acutely aware of how "a lot of times African Americans and Latinos are portrayed as bad guys and this influences the negative attitude toward [people of] color."

Elena, who claimed both Portugal and Macao as her countries of origin, was quite emphatic in her view that racial and ethnic relations are worse than shown on TV.[4] She said:

> They don't show the positive side of diversity; they don't show the reality. And, they touch lightly on ethnic/racial issues. The shows are racist and classist. The Mexicans are always the cooks, yet you never see them on TV as such, or even referred to as such. NYC is very dependent on Mexicans, but this is not acknowledged nor are they [New Yorkers] even grateful for this. They just take it for granted. [Mexicans] are just seen as mainly crossing borders, not perceived as a part of the legal population. They work a lot, but they are not seen as part of the working class. They are nannies, but they [their employers] treat them so badly—and then hand them their children. The contrast is strong. [On US TV], NYC is seen as very White, and the problems are the Blacks and Latinos, who are not seen as people.

Joseph from Ireland was a bit more moderate in his response: In thinking about shows that had African Americans in the cast, he recalled *The Cosby Show* but said that "it didn't go into anything in depth; [issues] came up but then were not pursued. [They] backed away from the issue." He also said that "the issues on the show were not particularly Black issues; they could be issues for any family or group." He added that, after being in the United States, he thought that the shows currently being seen in Ireland were "a little behind the times." Another respondent, Anna, also speaking of her earlier viewing of US TV but in Russia, said: "No, all the shows are about White people. There are some Black people, but there are never shows about them."

Did Not Show the Positive Side

Some respondents said that racial and ethnic relations were worse than shown on TV, but others said that US TV also did not show the positive side. For example, Paula from Paraguay said, "They don't show the positive side of diversity." This is also a critique that can be made of the written history of the United States and of the literature on race and ethnicity. In other words, that insufficient attention has been given to the extent to which groups and individuals from all ethnic groups and races have come together in the past to work, to procreate, and to resolve common issues and achieve common or mutual goals. Clearly, there have been divisions, but there have also been instances (perhaps less recorded or reported) of intermarriage, collaboration and cooperation, and commingling in neighborhoods, at schools, and at work sites.

Paula did not deny the negatives. Referring to the issue of racial divisions and racial classification, she said: "There is segregation here—am I White, Latino, or Hispanic? I think that this is one of the biggest shocks I have."[5] She also spoke to how the tension over race and ethnic differences was often handled on US TV by resorting to comedic representations. She said,

> You can see the separation in the TV shows when they are made fun of [for] being the only Latin guy in the show. On TV, the separation is seen between ethnic groups through jokes and sarcasm, but you never really make that connection [of Latins being made fun of] in the real world. It's not everywhere [on US TV], but it's there.

Laura from Russia also spoke to the comedic component and how this differed from the reality of racial and ethnic relations that she experienced:

> People of colors are not usually portrayed at all. And if they are portrayed, you understand that this is a stereotype and this is for fun. For instance, Wolowitz in *Big Bang Theory*, he is Jewish, and people make fun of him because he is Jewish, and I know that this is not true, like, this is not how people here treat Jewish people, I think. I know this is done for the show.

It is done for the humor in the show. But usually the shows don't have people of color or people of ethnic minorities at all.

Too Narrow; Other Types of Diversity Are Not Shown

Still others agreed relations were worse in reality, but they complained that this was because other types of diversity are not shown (e.g., religious, intraethnic). Carmen from Paris said that there were "no big racial messages in the shows she watched. A lot of minorities just not present." An undergrad from China agreed with the narrow depictions: "No, [there are] a lot of Mexicans and Asians in the US, especially in New York, but don't have them in the shows. Frankly speaking, major characters are really White people. Very rare to have them [Mexicans or Asians] be major characters." Similarly, Yang, a student from China, said the shows "have a very narrow focus. The main characters are always White, and in the US there are a lot more people here—not just White." Finally, an undergrad from China noted more broadly:

No, I didn't see any races other than White; there was one Asian woman on *Friends*, but that [is] not enough. [You] get [the] impression that America is dominated by [the] White race, and [there is] not much space for other races. In reality, [you] see that people of other races have their own channels to have their voices heard. [So you] have [a] race imbalance in US. [The] White race has gained a larger share of resources and greater connections—[they] can send [their] children to better schools. [And, they, the White people, are] seen by many as the social mainstream.

Alicia from Brazil was quite blunt. She said: "Everybody is White except for one; or everybody is Black." She added that she "hasn't found a show that reflects what she sees [in her life]: a variety of colors."

Nanette from the Yukon also maintained that US TV shows have a narrow focus, saying that they don't really reflect racial and ethnic relations. None of them really addressed how complex American society is, and in this sense they did not prepare her to live in the real world:

They don't really show all of the dynamics of society, all the different races and ethnic backgrounds. If you're gay or straight or transgender, that's huge now, but it would maybe be on one episode. It doesn't accurately reflect what it's like in real life; it's almost idealized on TV and [that] makes it seem easy and accepted, but people have a lot of issues, and [TV] doesn't show that in the real world. It definitely didn't prepare me. I had never really interacted with Black people, Hispanic people, Muslim people, gay people, transgender people, never. So I didn't feel that it helped me realize what it would be like to live with them and accept them.

Particularly interesting were the responses of two students from India who acknowledged that now that they were in the United States, they could better understand the racial and ethnic dimensions they had perceived on the US TV that they had watched in their native country, but had not fully understood. Mani said, "When I was in India, I wouldn't know what the ethnic background was, but now here I know." Indira also said, "No, I didn't see it [i.e., racial and ethnic representations on US TV] that way. I just saw White people. In India, if you saw a Black or a Hispanic on TV, you would assume they were from somewhere else, another country. Another surprise when I came was seeing many Asians here. I saw America as just White people. I actually thought that kinky hair was made to look that way, that it was not natural."

Other Views

Only one person in the sample, David from Colombia, took a more neutral or academic view. He had, as may be recalled, specialized as a graduate student in media communications. "Human interaction is different in real life here," he said. "On TV, you overrepresent everything, dramatize it."

All of the responses reflect to some degree what individuals bring to their viewing. But two dimensions that seem to influence their views are (1) their experiences in their home countries and (2) their "lived race" (López, 2013), or how they are racially viewed and treated by others in the United States and in their home countries. The following examples of women who identified as Black underscore the role that these variables played in their views of US TV.

We will hear more about the experience of Avis in a subsequent chapter. But suffice it to say that she had watched quite a bit of US TV while in her native Jamaica, and the fact that most of the characters that she saw had been White did not really hit her until she came to the United States and began to live in a predominantly White dorm. It was then that she wondered, "Why don't I see Black people in major roles and doing good?" She had never wondered about this in Jamaica, because "in Jamaica you are surrounded by Black people. Real life was Black."[6] TV then for her was another world, and she didn't connect the world depicted on US TV to her own world until she came to New York City.

Kemi from Nigeria had lived for some time in London, and she had a similar experience. She said, "The US TV shows I watched in the UK did not delve into these issues. Not until I got here did I think about race. I knew I was Black. But I didn't think about race until I went to the South in the US. Now some shows, for example, address the issue, but the *Housewives* shows do not address this." She indicated that she was now more aware of US race relations. When I probed her on why or how this had come about, she attributed this to the coverage of racial issues that she had seen in the news and to speaking with African Americans and hearing of their experiences, especially at the university she attended in the South.

The last example comes from Lamiya, a grad student from Azerbaijan, who said she did not realize how bad "it"—meaning race and race relations—was in the United States. Like a number of other respondents from Latin America, she said her first exposure to race was the census form. She said that people from the South Caucasus were called "Black Asses" by the Russians. When presented with the US census form, she wanted to put down "Black," but was later told by someone that she was "White." When I asked her, "Why are you called 'Black Asses' by the Russians?" she said, "Because we have black hair and eyes, but they are blond." This is, again, a reminder that it is not just the United States that distinguishes by color and creates its own constructions of race. The use of the term "asses" may reflect the complicated historical and geopolitical relationship between both countries, as well as the hierarchy within Russia that Davis and Sosnovskaya (2009) describe that places Russians at the top and non-Russians lower on the scale.

Summary

In an earlier chapter, we saw that this foreign-born group very much enjoyed US TV in their home countries, and that US TV generally played very important roles both in their habitus and in the views that they had about the United States prior to their arrival. We then turned to examine to what extent their expectations were met when they came to the United States, and what surprised them the most when they first arrived. We also focused on why they watched US TV in their home countries, what they enjoyed most about US TV, and to what extent they were aware of how US TV had influenced them. In this chapter, we examined a question at the heart of this book—whether respondents thought that US TV was encouraging or discouraging of the integration of Others, and whether US TV had given them an accurate reflection of what racial and ethnic relations are like in the United States. As we saw, with regard to encouraging the inclusion of Others, the picture was mixed, and few in the sample agreed that US TV had given them an accurate image of racial and ethnic relations in the United States. The majority stated that these relations were worse than shown on TV; some noted that the shows had a narrow focus and that other types of diversity were not shown, including religious and intraethnic diversity; and others stated that US TV didn't show the positive side of diversity. In this regard, the question posed in Chapter 1—Did the depictions of race, ethnicity, gender, and class relations they had seen on US TV actually reflect the society foreign-born respondents experienced once they came to the United States?—was answered more in the negative. And the participants' responses echoed the work of the scholars reviewed in Chapter 1 on minority under- and misrepresentation.

PART III

Comparing US Millennials and the Foreign Born

TV Matters

Race, Class, and Gender Takeaways

In this chapter we address the question of whether the foreign-born group felt that watching US TV had influenced their views on race, class, or gender; and whether they were more influenced by US TV in these areas than the US undergrads or millennials.[1] In essence, did US TV matter more to them?

The answer is yes regarding race and gender, but no concerning class (see Figure 7.1). A majority of foreign-born respondents (54 percent) said their views about race, in particular, were influenced by watching US TV; in contrast, only slightly more than one-fifth (21.8 percent) of the US millennials said that was the case. In addition, a large proportion (47.6 percent) of the foreign-born sample said their views on gender had been influenced by their viewing of US TV, while fewer than one-quarter (23.6 percent) of the US millennials said the same. These results are to be expected, since the millennials had been raised in the United States on US TV, for the most part, and had everyday exposure to a wide variety of experiences that may have affected how they view race and gender. Indeed, looking at these results in the negative, while half of the US millennials said that US TV did *not* influence their views in any of these areas, in the foreign-born sample only 11.1 percent said this was the case. So the influence of US TV was acknowledged more by the foreign-born group than by the US millennials.

However, in an interesting twist, proportionately more of the US millennial respondents (41.8 percent compared with only 30.2 percent of the foreign-born group) said US TV had influenced their views on class. This was the area of influence cited most by the US millennials. The second most mentioned area was culture or ethnicity, with 26.7 percent naming this. Nearly half of the foreign-born respondents (49.2 percent)

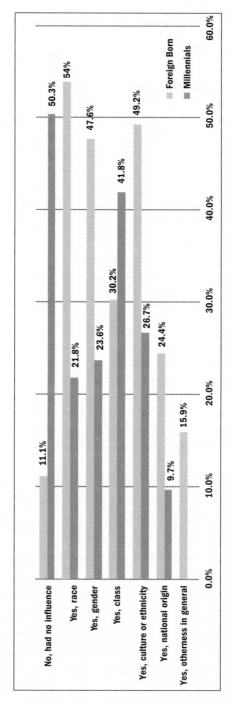

Figure 7.1. Did watching US TV influence views on race, class, gender, and national origin? Source: Rodríguez (2015).

also noted that US TV influenced their views on culture or ethnicity, but this high percentage was to be expected given that they were coming from abroad.[2]

The Influence of US TV on the Foreign Born

Race

As noted above, more than half of the foreign-born group said that US TV influenced their views on race. Suffice it to say that, for many, US TV presented "America" as a predominantly White, blond- or yellow-haired, middle-class society. For others, US TV was their first and sometimes only introduction to Black characters, people, or issues. Some said that US TV positively influenced their view of race and ethnicity. For example, one respondent from Spain said that it influenced him to think that "different people from different origins can work together and be successful." He also said, "[The] US is a good example of where someone from any class can move up if they work hard. Culture—[I have] never been in a country with so [many different cultures]. This is rich." Another respondent, a woman from Greece, was also positive but a bit more doubtful. She said her views on race, class, and national origin were very much influenced by US TV. "The presence of different racial groups within US TV has given me an image of a post-racial community, but yet one which is not smoothly realized in an egalitarian way." Some respondents, like Atsushi from Japan, were more negative. He summarized how he had been influenced by US TV by saying that he had picked up racial stereotypes, and added that US TV showed him "that people act within the guidelines of their gender, and that, in terms of class, the wealthy have the best life."

Gender

Close to half of the foreign-born sample said that their views on gender had been influenced by US TV. Many referred in their comments to the stronger role that women had on US TV. For example, Serbian native Milinka said: "Serbia is pretty patriarchal. Here genders share roles, and it is common to see that women are breadwinners—I also like that." Anna from Saint Petersburg, Russia, said that US TV influenced her view that "there were greater opportunities for women in the US." A student from China revealed that "*Sex and the City* [gave] me the idea that women can be as tough as [men]. They are independent and smart."

Males from both Asia and Europe agreed that US TV presented women, and the relations between men and women, differently from what they were familiar with in their own countries. For example, Nicolae from Moldova said that his views on gender were most influenced by watching US TV in his country. He said that men and women were seen differently in his country and that women weren't seen to have the same rights as men. Now in the United States, he saw that they had the same opportunities. He added that in the United States, he didn't see men giving up their chair for women on a bus, and he felt he had to be careful here and not to open doors for women, as this might be misunderstood as chauvinistic. Another male, from Kyrgyzstan, also said his views on gender were influenced by US TV. He said that US TV showed greater equality between the genders, and male and female relations were more open than they were in his country, where women were more dependent on men. He seemed to appreciate these more open views.

Same Sex

In speaking of gender, a number of the foreign-born respondents indicated that their views on same-sex relationships had also been very much influenced by US TV. For example, Narcisa from Romania said that US TV had the most influence on her views on gender and LGBTQ issues. Tong, who had indicated that he was in the United States because it was "difficult to be gay in China," said US TV had influenced his view of gender. He said, "In China there is one definition of masculinity only. In US TV [you] can see more options, directions."

Class

Only 30 percent of the foreign-born respondents stated that their views on class were influenced by US TV, but those who did mention this had a lot to say about it. For example, 24-year-old Eva, who had grown up in socialist Russia, said: "It gave me a certain stereotype of how [the] middle class should look like, how high class should look like, dress, what kind of cars and clothes and what kind of pleasures certain classes should have. And mostly I am talking about middle class and high class." Lena, a 29-year-old from Hungary, said simply: "You just sort of have an idea of what middle class should look like. It should look like what you see in the TV." Finally, an 18-year-old undergrad from the Philippines, who consumed a great deal of US TV, also affirmed *the strong middle-and upper-class bias of US TV*. Having gone to high school in Australia, she said:

> Class was not as significant [for me] as gender and race, because growing up in an upper-middle-class family in a third-world country, the differences were fairly stark. However, I still say that American media had an effect on me [and on my view of class] because I originally had no clue that poor people even existed when I first came to America [to visit] in 2006. Of course, by the time I moved to Australia four years later, I knew that, but I had no idea just how bad the problem could be.

For one respondent from India, this narrow portrayal of classes led her to think that "in the US, there are no classes; everyone is the same, [and this] influences ideas, for example, about freedom."

How do these responses compare with those given by the US millennial sample?

The Influence of US TV on US Millennials

We saw above that half of the US millennials responded that US TV had *not* influenced their views. But half said it had and provided comments showing how US TV had influenced their views; and the largest proportion (42 percent) indicated that US TV had influenced their views on class. Although the US millennials took their survey electronically, they were asked in this instance to provide an example of how US TV had influenced their views in one of the following areas: race, class, gender, culture or ethnicity, or national origin. Given that this item was placed at the end of the survey, when most students were heading for the door, I was very surprised that 56 respondents actually provided an example. What follows is a sampling of the examples they gave that pertained to the influence of US TV on the areas that they mentioned the most.

Comparing the US Millennials and the Foreign-Born Respondents

To sum up, given that they have lived in the United States and had exposure to a variety of influences, 50 percent of the US millennials said that US TV did *not* influence their views in any of these areas (see Figure 7.1). In the foreign-born sample, only 11 percent said that US TV did not influence their views, and a majority said their views about race were influenced by watching US TV—this is in contrast with the US millennials, a little more than one-fifth of whom acknowledged this influence. In addition, while a substantial portion of the foreign-born sample said their views on gender had been influenced by their viewing of US TV, fewer than one-quarter of the US millennials said the same. However, as noted above, proportionately more US millennials said US TV had influenced their views on class. This was the area millennials mentioned the most, followed by how US TV influenced their views on culture or ethnicity. Culture and ethnicity were also mentioned to a substantial degree by the foreign born, but they were coming from different cultures and different countries, so this was to be anticipated.

Responses are often better understood by examining what people actually said. We begin with how US millennials explained the ways that US TV influenced their views of class.[3]

Class

Like the foreign-born respondents, a number of US millennials referred to the *middle- and upper-class thrust* of much US TV. One said, "I can't give a specific example, but it seems like many of the shows on television today seem to give viewers a look only at the upper-middle-class life. They make it seem like the perfect family is one that is upper-middle class." Another said, "As a child I thought that a much larger percentage of the US population was wealthy or middle class than it is, based on television." However, another US millennial was quite metaphorical and somewhat cynical about the differences others noted in the portrayals of the rich and the poor. She said: "Rich people always seem to be portrayed as intelligent and laid-back, jetting about without a care in the world. Poor people are down-to-earth and full of hard-earned wisdom.

It's false and stereotypical. Some rich people are scheming jerks, greedy and frightened of losing their money and power. Some poor people are jerks too, fighting to keep others down, like the crabs in a bucket."

Some US undergrads felt that *class differences* were always on display. One US millennial put it this way: "Shows like *The O.C.* clearly depict the upper class while shows like *Friday Night Lights* depict [the] working class." Another said, "Shows are always comparing classes." Curiously, one millennial had a different perspective on class comparisons and said that they "helped me to identify with people of other socioeconomic classes." To what extent this particular response might have been influenced by the increasingly articulated concerns in academia and in the media over growing economic inequality in the United States is difficult to say. But there were a number of comments about class comparisons by others that suggested that US TV influenced their views on *inequality* more directly. For example, one student said that US TV accentuated "the power one social class has." Another said, "It made me realize the extent of wealth disparity in America." A third respondent, referring to a very popular HBO program, said, "In *Game of Thrones*, they focus primarily on the economic and social disparity caused by the established class system." One female middle-class student from North Dakota was actually turned off by the emphasis on wealth, saying: "The Kardashians, they live in so much luxury that's so unlike typical Americans. It's interesting to watch but would not make me want to live in this kind of splendor. It's over the top."

Other students were led to question how what they saw on TV was *not like what they experienced in real life*. For example, a middle-class female undergrad of Asian descent said the following with regard to class:

> [It] didn't really influence me the most, but [it] is the only one I can think of right now: *Gossip Girl* and class struggles. [It] brings to mind my parents' uphill struggle as immigrants to make more than enough money to support three children. We weren't like the families on *Gossip Girl* at all, but we grew up with frequent vacations, nice resorts, beach condo, nice clothing, nice furniture, extracurricular [activities], tutors, etc. But I was also taught to never have credit-card debt, and the importance of saving money and never spending more than you have. So while I am certainly not cheap, I could never be comfortable spending and living like the characters from *Gossip Girl*.

Another respondent, a middle-class White male from New York State, seemed to question "the ubiquitous assumption that characters or their families can afford smartphones, car, house, laptop, etc."

Class Styles

Still other US millennials admitted that US TV had *influenced their desire for certain class styles*, such as the desire to have a nice apartment, nice clothes, money to spend on alcohol, and so on. One White male US millennial from a working-class family specifically mentioned the show *Suits* and how it focused on showing the lifestyle of a lawyer in New York City. The implication appeared to be that this occupation carried with it a certain class style that he found desirable.[4]

Speaking to the *association of race, ethnicity, and class*, a number of respondents made comments like the following: "A lot of shows focus on the upper class and consist of primarily White people. This contributes to the stereotype that White people are the most wealthy." Another respondent referred to how ethnicity was usually obscured when wealth was on display. This millennial stated, "TV shows usually neglect people's national origin; many shows glorify the lifestyle of the wealthy." Still another referred to ethnicity at the opposite end of the social scale, and said, "The working class is not just meant to be full of ethnic races"— which, from this respondent's perspective, meant that TV shows should also include White characters as part of the working class.

In essence, these comments show that these US millennials think that US TV has influenced the way they see different classes. On US TV, they said, the classes are often compared, with the wealthy or upper classes generally projected as the desirable norm—often portrayed as White, with the working class projected as simply "full of ethnic races." A number of students realized that US TV influenced their desire to achieve the lifestyles associated with certain classes, and a few students saw beyond the projected images and posed critiques of what they saw.

Gender

Interestingly, even though the US millennials said their views on *class* were most strongly influenced as a result of watching US TV, they gave a larger number of examples of how their views on *gender* were influenced. A number of the examples given paralleled those given by the foreign-born sample, and they focused on how US TV showed images of empowered or empowering women. The following comments illustrate this view: "The shows are portraying more working women and more women working in high-power positions—[in] government, law, law enforcement, medicine." One student said simply, "a strong female protagonist" when giving an example of how TV influenced her views on gender. As in the interviews with the foreign-born respondents, the presence of strong female protagonists on TV shows provides models of roles that may not be available in the actual lives of US millennials, or that may be present but are not necessarily as encouraged, acknowledged, or celebrated as they may be on a TV show. Another spoke to how the presence of powerful or empowering women appealed to her. She said: "Seeing strong female characters on TV influenced the way I perceive my gender [and] gender role in society." Another millennial also liked the idea of strong female characters, but said they were too often the exception on US TV. She said: "The way that women are portrayed on TV is often not the way most women are. It can come off as offensive and extremely stereotypical. When I find a strong woman lead in a show, [however,] I think that that makes me like a show more."

Others were more critical of the gender images they saw and made comments such as this: "Gender differences [as shown on TV], like how women stay at home, but that's not true in society today." Or this: "Kids in shows about high school would treat other people in different classes differently. And other shows peg women as the stereotypical women that society has expected them to be—housewife, soccer mom, submissive . . . to [a] man, or a woman that needs or is searching for a man." One referred to the constraints of the gender roles that women played on US TV, saying, "I feel that gender is influenced the most because women are taught through television to act a certain way to be proper, but still be attractive."

A couple of students also referred to the constraints on gender roles, but included men as well as women, saying, for example, "Males and females are apparently supposed to follow their gender roles or they will be considered outliers." Still others echoed what some in the foreign-born group said and made reference to how US TV influenced their views on LGBTQ issues. For example, one student said: "I was conventional about gender, and I used to disagree [about] same-sex marriage. But after watching TV, I found that it's okay for same-gender marriage." Finally, some respondents spoke to the intersectionality they saw in US TV between gender and race. For example, one student said: "Specific races and genders are portrayed in a way that is prejudice[d]." Another said: "Shows like *SNL* would harken to societal woes in racism, gender inequality, et cetera." And a White middle-class male from rural Vermont said very directly that there was a "projection of stereotypes [of] race, and, gender relations." This more plainspoken view was also repeated by people in the foreign-born group.

Race

While the foreign-born respondents said that US TV influenced their views of race the most, the US millennials did not mention this area as much. However, the comments by the US millennials on race were formidable and compelling. One noted that TV portrayals of certain races are prejudiced. Another spoke to the linkage of certain themes with races and ethnicities, saying: "Shows like *Breaking Bad*, which includes a lot of reference[s] to the drug trade, presents many different races and ethnicities." Indeed, the main protagonists in this show were White, but the student appears to have remembered the association between drugs and "different races and ethnicities." This was stated more directly by another upper-middle-class millennial of Asian descent, who indicated that US TV mainly influenced his views on race and stereotypes. He said there were mainly racial stereotypes, and noted how, for example, "South American" generally "equals drug dealer and so on." Still another spoke to how rare it was to see non-White characters: "Rarely do we see TV shows on a main TV provider that [have] a cast that has main characters that are not Caucasian." Still another acknowledged, as did some in my foreign-born sample, that US TV showed "how people view certain races." (This comment was also made, almost verbatim, by a respondent in the foreign-born group.) These comments are extremely telling and informative, for they are telling us that viewers pick up on a group's general social status and position by how characters from that group are framed and treated by other members of the cast. However, one white upper-middle-class young male from Arizona, whose favorite form of music was rap and hip-hop, departed from this generalized view and suggested that negative racial representations had been present but were passé: "Any 'oldie' show . . . showed how bad African Americans and other minorities were treated."

Some foreign-born respondents mentioned the US TV show *The Wire* as a significant influence; this also surfaced in the US millennial sample. One upper-middle class male of Asian descent from suburban New Jersey said: "*The Wire* gives an in-depth look into the Black community." One wonders if this show influenced this student's view of the whole Black community in the United States—leaving aside the question of whether the show provides an accurate look at the Baltimore community in which it is set.

One very astute and perhaps slightly jaded millennial, an upper-middle-class White male who lived in the suburbs, said in response to the question of whether he thought that watching US TV had influenced his views: "I don't know what you mean by 'views.' It is obvious that pervasive stereotypes on television probably contributed to my subconscious biases. It is also possible these biases influenced my conscious opinions and policy preferences; however, I make a conscious effort not to let it." He also indicated that he watched less than an hour a week of TV but consumed "hours" of YouTube videos in a typical week.

Summary

In summary, a majority in both the foreign-born and US millennial groups agreed that watching US TV has influenced their views on race, class, gender, and ethnicity, with a much larger percentage of the foreign-born group acknowledging the influence. There was also a great deal of agreement on the direction of that influence, with the US millennials—as might be expected, given that they are from the United States—more critical of some areas like gender, race, and class portrayals. These findings raise questions about the extent to which our American brand—which many in our foreign-born sample said was very appealing to them and to others in their country—may be influencing views of race, class, and gender in other countries. Hopefully these findings will lead to further investigation in this area.

Given the strongly commercial bent of US TV, we turn in our next chapter to other questions that are also related to "degree of influence"— namely if and how US TV influences patterns of consumption. Do the two groups of respondents agree that US TV influences their consumption patterns and their views toward the consumption of ideas as well as their consumption of products and services? Are the patterns the same for both groups?

8

I Want That!

Consumption and Attitudes toward Sex, Smoking, and Drinking

We saw earlier that some authors were quite concerned with the dominance of US global and corporate media and their impact on other countries (Noam, 2009; Wu, 2010; González and Torres, 2011). Barber (2001), in particular, said that "the cultural wars were being won hands down by American television" (102). He added that it was the corporate sector that was the major beneficiary of global media and that it was universalizing markets and making national borders porous.[1] He made clear that it was not capitalism that he was opposed to in the world of media. In fact, he saw capitalism as an economic engine that drove change. Rather, his objection was with "unrestrained capitalism," an economic system that is not counterbalanced by a system of values; and this, he felt, endangered democracy. He was concerned about the "monopoly control over information," and he wished to "interdict that quiet, comfortable coercion through which television, advertising and entertainment can constrict real liberty of choice" (296). What concerned him and other authors was the power and control of the corporate media titans—which were no longer just US actors, but had now become consolidated *global* media companies—over pictures, information, and ideas that can influence people.

However, other scholars argued that the impact or influence of US TV, and US media more generally, is less significant than many assume and that such views do not take into account the "agency" that people naturally have to reject other countries' media, or the distance of the country from "the center" (Elasmar, 2003; Esser, 2010). In other words, the idea of the United States establishing a "cultural hegemony" via its media is overstated. Kuipers (2010) also highlighted the dynamics of transnational cultural diffusion and said that both the global and the local look different in different countries, and that local culture and intermediaries can block the import of new ideas. Regardless of where one stands on these debates, there is no doubt that US TV has, from its inception, been a commercial enterprise and that advertising and marketing have been important paths to these profits. The search for profits has also been an important driver in the US TV taken abroad. Many applaud this expansion of market for US goods. Others are concerned.

This volume cannot address the full extent of these concerns. It does, however, examine whether the foreign born and US millennials surveyed here felt that their consumption practices and their ideas about particular lifestyle issues were influenced by watching US TV—and, if so, how. Did they feel that watching US TV had influenced what they wanted and what they decided to buy? Were they swayed by product placement? And did US TV influence their attitudes toward lifestyle choices, such as their attitudes toward sex, birth control, gender roles, smoking, and alcohol consumption? Additionally, did the two groups agree or differ with regard to the influence of US TV on their consumption patterns and their attitudes toward lifestyle choices?

The answer to all these questions is largely "yes, but. . . ."

Majorities of both groups acknowledged the influence of US TV, but the foreign-born group reported slightly greater influence than the US millennials. Indeed, 74 percent of the foreign-born respondents said that watching US TV did influence their consumption views or habits. In the US millennial group, the proportion affirming some influence of US TV was 61 percent. In essence, in both groups, majorities acknowledged that US TV influenced some dimension of their consumption habits or lifestyle preferences. In addition, some said that they weren't sure if US TV had influenced their consumption or views, but they thought it might have influenced them unconsciously. For example, Nicolae from Moldova said, "No, I'm very pragmatic. There is more emphasis on sex in the US, and this influences people here [in the United States], but not me—at least not consciously." A US millennial also said TV had "no noticeable influence, [except] maybe subconsciously." Some in both groups were aware of the potential influence and consciously resisted it. For example, one US millennial said very directly, "No, I hate TV in general and watch it through a critical lens, and cynically." Another admitted some influence *and* some resistance

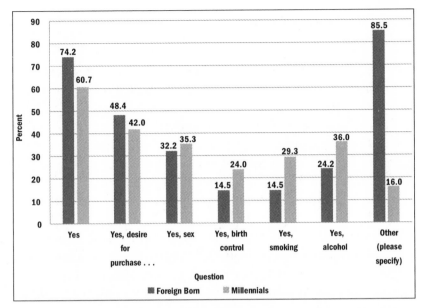

Figure 8.1. Do you think watching US TV influenced your consumption and views? Respondents could choose more than one category. Source: Rodríguez (2015).

to the influence, saying: "It probably desensitized me to violence as a kid, but it did not change any of my normative views, and I have made a conscious effort to reverse this."

Also, in both groups there were similarities with regard to which areas US TV influenced most. Both groups indicated that their "desire for, or purchase of, material goods" was the area most influenced by their viewing US TV—although the percentages in each group differed slightly. As Figure 8.1 indicates, 48 percent of the foreign born and 42 percent of the US millennials admitted that watching US TV influenced their "desire for, or purchase of, material goods." This was followed by slightly smaller percentages in both groups that indicated their "views toward sex" had been influenced by US TV—32 percent of the foreign born and 35 percent of the US millennials said this. The two groups differed more with regard to whether US TV had influenced their attitudes toward birth control, smoking, alcohol, and, as we will see, consumption of food and eating styles.[2] These differences will be discussed below.

The Influence of US TV on the Consumption of Goods and Services

In both groups, respondents were also asked to provide examples of how watching US TV had influenced their consumption habits and views. And both groups gave many examples of how watching US TV influenced "clothing choice" and "clothing preferences." Food consumption and "eating" were often mentioned among the foreign-born respondents, but few millennials referred to this. It was not too surprising that few in the millennial group mentioned the influence of US TV on food or eating. After all, they live in the United States and already consume US foods, while for the foreign born, the American foods they saw on US TV were different from what they had traditionally consumed in their home countries. The foreign born also noted a string of sometimes interconnected areas of influence as a result of watching US TV. For example, they would describe how watching US TV influenced not just their clothing styles and food consumption but also their views on what constituted "normative" gender roles and family relationships.[3]

Clothes and the Foreign Born

The influence of US TV on clothing and style was by far the area most mentioned by both groups. Margo, referring to the dominance of US TV in Canada, said: "[US TV] was the dominant media; to the extent that media influences, it had a large effect on lifestyle, style of clothing. Also it influenced how I saw the educational environment, what it meant to be a student, and it influenced [my views on] family relations, e.g., the roles played by characters in, for example, [the sitcoms] *Full House* [and] *Who's the Boss*. It normalized what was seen as traditional relations and interactions with siblings and parents." Adnan from Syria noted the generally heavy emphasis in US TV shows on consumption and said that he was "probably" influenced by that, "but on an unconscious level. In shows, they practice a way of life that is very consumer-focused. In *Friends*, they never wore the same clothes twice." Alicia from Brazil was somewhat embarrassed to admit the extent to which US TV influenced her clothing choices. She said, "[It] definitely influences who you want to look and dress like. [It] has more effect than you want to admit." Also referring to clothing preferences was a postdoctoral fellow from Greece who said, ruefully, that US TV influenced her "by making me look for clothes that were not available in my home market." By the time of the interview, she felt she had moved away from this influence, but she also acknowledged that now, having lived outside of Greece for a few years, she had easy access to such clothes.

Clothes and the US Millennials

The millennials also stated that watching US TV mostly influenced their purchase of clothing, but their responses were often brief.[4] For example, they said simply "clothes," "clothing item," "yes, clothing and accessories"—or they mentioned a specific item, such as Nike sneakers or "suits."[5] Other millennials referred to how seeing clothes on characters on TV shows influenced them, saying, for example: "I enjoy buying certain clothes I see in TV shows," "buying clothes to reproduce outfits as seen on actors," "buying what actresses had," "I want to buy a nice infinity scarf after I see the knitwear on *Outlander*," or "the clothing worn in some shows is luxurious." Another said, "If I saw clothes or something that I absolutely loved, I might try to find something similar." Still others mentioned how specific shows or characters influenced them to buy clothes. For example, one young woman, who had grown up in a northeastern US suburb, said, "*90210* encouraged me to buy clothes." A young male from a midwestern suburb said Olivia Pope, the main character in the highly popular show *Scandal*, "made me want a white hat."[6] Still another respondent, a young woman from a small town in New Jersey, mentioned that certain shows influenced her clothing choices. She said: "Love for certain designer brands and fashion in general (*The Devil Wears Prada, Gossip Girl*, etc.)." Last, one young woman from another small town in New Jersey succinctly summed up how she saw the relationship between influence and specific shows, saying, "Yes: when I see characters who dress very well, it inspires me to want to replicate those outfits." She added: "*Pretty Little Liars*: I can't tell you the plotline, but I can tell you where they got their clothes." Clearly, in a number of these instances, product placement had been very successful.

Eating and the Foreign Born

Somewhat surprising to me were the many references to food that surfaced among the foreign-born group when asked whether they felt that US TV had influenced their consumption habits. Some were stand-alone comments, and they illuminated for me the particular food products and styles that people from other countries took away from watching US TV—and what people in different countries saw as characteristically American. This was something that I had not really thought very much about before. For example, Leon from Indonesia said, "Watching what people ate made me want to try the foods like steak and what people ate for Thanksgiving. Generally we wouldn't eat those foods at home." Gretchen from Germany said, "Yes, go to a movie, have popcorn—cool. Had [a] milkshake. [I] get into US products." David from Colombia said, "Food, junk food and chain restaurant foods. Absolutely, you see a celebrity or role model, and you want to do what they do." Finally, Myriam from Peru said her diet had changed as a result of watching US TV, but she also alluded to other dimensions of globalization that contributed to her dietary changes. Her comments also touched on what she and many others in her country define as "American." She said, "Now I eat cornflakes! In America there are waffles and pancakes. More American restaurants have now arrived in Peru. In Peruvian culture, lunch is beans, rice, and salad, not sandwiches [like in the United States]. Now, we have Subway and pizza places. My father still says that's not lunch." These responses illustrate how in exporting US TV we also export what is seen by many as a particularly American and desirable lifestyle. Some may see this as soft power at work.

Interconnected Areas of Influence and the Foreign Born

As noted above, the foreign born, in contrast to the US millennials, mentioned more areas when discussing whether watching US TV had influenced their consumption habits. It is possible that this difference between groups may just be a reflection of the different ways in which the responses were gathered: the millennials responded to an electronically administered survey and the foreign born responded to the questions in personally administered interviews. Whatever the case may be, many of the foreign-born respondents noted the influence of a number of variables at the same time. Their responses give us a flavor of these multiple and often interconnected views, especially with regard to eating, clothes, sex, and gender roles: For example, Pablo from Peru mentioned that watching US TV influenced a multidimensional complex of clothes, food, lifestyles, and values. He said, "Maybe fashion, food choices, exercise, and how family values override other values." Others mentioned similar combinations. For example, a young woman from Kyrgyzstan said she "desired/bought short skirts, jeans, skinny pants," and that US TV "led me to think more about sex as [I] got older." Her "parents were strict," she added, so this was as far as she could go in rebelling from them. She noted that watching US TV also influenced her food consumption, for now she ate "pizza, pasta and sauce, [and] in Kyrgyzstan [you] had only noodles and meat." Nishi from Nagaland, India, said, "Yes," she began eating "pizza, Coca-Cola, burgers—[I] learned this from [watching The] Wonder Years, [seeing] kids doing this. [US TV also] influenced my desire for [and] purchase of bags, jewelry, clothes. Smoking was cool in college, but then [I] never liked it; [and TV] rarely influenced [my views on] sex."

Global Brands

US TV also influenced the spread of global brands and the coolness factor associated with them. Irina from Latvia said, "McDonald's at home was a big happening, the place to go—it was a treat. On sex and birth control, [it is] hard to say [if I was influenced], but probably yes to some extent. As a freshman I was very influenced with regard to clothes." Narcisa from Romania said:

Maybe in terms of [food and fashion]. I was watching, for instance, a fashion show. So obviously you are watching and you want clothes and shoes. And then I started eating peanut butter. . . . I love peanut butter, by the way, [and] that's not very common; nobody eats peanut butter in Romania. And actually, the first time I got to know that this thing exists is by watching TV shows and then the first time I eat it was in my third year in college that I could actually buy it there. I bought it. I like it. I've been eating it ever since.

The "coolness" variable also surfaced in these responses, often with references to American brands. A young woman from France said, "Brands, always cool! I didn't necessarily buy them but if I got them as a gift—this was cool." Just as McDonald's was big or cool at various points in different countries, so too was Starbucks. Lena from Hungary said, "Certain things seemed very cool. I remember the first Starbucks opened in Vienna and we were in Vienna and I was like 20, and we went to the Starbucks, and when you are 20 you know, okay, this is ridiculous, but on another level, this is where Meg Ryan had the coffee [in a scene in the 1998 movie *You've Got Mail*]. Brands seem cooler because they are American. I think as a girl it's probably clothes and fashion. . . . I think, well, many people think, the US is more [prudish]." Moving into the question about sex, she continued, "You can see more intense stuff in Hungarian movies."

Juliana from Mexico also referred to fashion and Starbucks when discussing how US TV influenced her consumption habits. She said, "In terms of fashion, wanting to go to Starbucks. Not so much about smoking, medication, sex, birth control—not in my case." Jose from the Philippines referred to how the "foreignness" of Starbucks (or perhaps its connection to the United States, a former colonial power in the Philippines and a world power today) actually helped it to be accepted in the Philippines. He said watching US TV influenced "what you wear, celebrities, food—coffee equals Starbucks. Filipinos are a conservative people, so if people from other countries are doing these things, it should be okay." Ju from China referred to this type of food-fashion-cool influence a bit more simply. She said, "Now I drink coffee. [It] influenced my style of dress; [I now pay] $100 for a single skirt. [It had] a little influence with regard to sex."

Watching US TV also carried over to the world of sports and there too influenced respondents' views of American brands. For example, Robert from London said: "There are a lot of American brands in the UK," and he "was attuned to [them]," particularly with regard to "sports clothing, Chicago Bulls, Dallas Cowboys." He also noted how US TV influenced his food consumption, saying: "I consume popcorn and a big drink." He also liked the fact that characters on US TV were "animated. The way they eat influenced me. Food would play a big role. There were food fights." When asked if his views on sex were influenced by watching

US TV, he said, "Oh, yeah," but he was not sure that his views on birth control had been influenced; he said, "I don't know, in a way," and, on smoking, he said, "maybe."

The Influence of US TV on Views about Sex and Gender

The Foreign-Born Respondents' Views

As noted above, similar proportions of both groups said their views toward sex were influenced by US TV. As Figure 8.1 indicates, just a slightly higher percentage, 35 percent, of the US millennials reported this, as compared with 32 percent of the foreign-born group. But how they said they were influenced differed quite a bit. Traditional or conventional practices in their home countries were an important determinant of how watching US TV influenced their views. Depending on their country of origin, either the foreign-born participants were *shocked* by the openness about sex and gender (relative to what existed in their country) or they *underscored how different* (or more restrictive) it was from their country.

A young woman from Kyrgyzstan spoke to the *gender differences* she observed on US TV and said that in US TV, people seemed

> more attractive—everything was shiny. Sex relations between genders were different from that in Kyrgyzstan. In the US, relations are easier; in Kyrgyzstan they are more closed and personal. Here [in the United States, people] choose partners in a reality show on TV. In Kyrgyzstan, your family has *a big* influence on that. In Russian shows [that I saw in Kyrgyzstan, they] also show smoking and alcohol, but male and female relations are shown more in US shows.

She implied in her latter comment that the relations between men and women were more the focus of US TV shows, and that they represented for her a broader set of possibilities between men and women than she saw in Russian programming or in her own country's programming. Others in my sample (both males and females) made reference, for example, to the various sexual and gender relationships that existed among the characters in shows like *Friends*. The fact that they could live together, and apart from their families, was a major departure from their own traditional patterns. The series of romantic relationships depicted in this program (and in others) also defied traditional norms in some cultures.

In other countries, like Finland or Germany, what respondents took from such programs was different, as such relationships were more common in their countries. For example, Milja from Finland became more conscious of the portrayal of women's bodies on US TV. She noticed, for example, that women who wore a size 4 or 6 seemed to be the norm on US TV, while women who wore a size 10 or larger were rarely shown (and, if they were shown, were depicted as being overweight or self-conscious about their weight). In her country, however, she felt people were generally less critical of people who wore a size 10 or larger. This also led to her becoming more body conscious when she gained weight in the United States. On sexual relations, she said that in her country, sex was very open and taken for granted; and so the media were less sexualized. She added that in her country, sex in US media was seen as "over the top, silly, trying too hard." Respondents from Germany said that watching US TV did not influence their views on sex, while Irina from Latvia was unsure, saying, "hard to say, maybe more freedom in sex [in the United States]." An interesting international perspective came from Carmen, who was raised by American parents in Paris. She said US shows "made it fun [but] also showed the downside." Atsushi from Japan also had an interesting perspective on sex: "Americans use it as a way to get to know people; they take it lightly."[7] In this case, his view that sex on US TV is "casual" corresponds, as we will see, with the views of many US millennials. Respondents from countries where sexual norms are more wide-ranging, for example, Brazil and Israel, either said it did not influence their views on sex or said they were unsure if it did.

Although foreign-born respondents expressed a variety of views on whether and how watching US TV influenced their views about sex, many of them made comments during the interviews suggesting that US TV, and more generally US media, did influence their views about gender and gender roles. (Gender roles refer to what could be expected from women and men in terms of jobs or education they could achieve, responsibilities they had with regard to families, both immediate and extended, and how and with whom they could have intimate relations.) The following story brought this home to me.

I spoke early on with a graduate student from South Korea who was studying the social sciences at a prestigious university in the northeastern United States. I was stunned at how impactful and unforgettable her early experiences were watching US media in her home country. In particular, I was struck by how much she took away with regard to gender relations from the US media that she saw early in her life. Making reference to one of the first US films that she had seen, when she was 7 years old, she said that what immediately struck her (and stayed with her) was how there were *men in the kitchen* with the women. This contrasted dramatically with her life in Korea at the time. The men were never in the kitchen with the women, and those who work in kitchens are generally of lower class status. She was also struck by the fact that the kitchen was not closed and separated from the dining area, as was the case in her home and the homes she had visited in her country. She volunteered this example because she was cognizant that both of these depictions (i.e., open kitchens and men helping in the kitchen) were common in US media and that they had introduced her, at a very early age, to the possibility that gender and class relations could be different from what she observed in her home country. Seeing this displayed in media that originated in the United States—an acknowledged world power—also made such gender and living arrangements more acceptable in her mind.

My foreign-born respondents had similar stories of how their watching US TV exposed them to alternative (and, for many, more acceptable) gender roles. Sandra from Abuja, Nigeria, was a 28-year-old graduate student pursuing a business degree when I interviewed her. Her first language was English, but she also spoke Ibu, Hausa, and Yoruba. She was married, had two small children, and had been living in the United States for two and a half years. Sandra said that watching US TV had a "100 percent influence on sex. [You] get to learn your rights and what you can stand up for. At home [in Nigeria], men just bring the money. [In US TV] you see that men also have to contribute [other things in a marriage]." She continued, "But men and white culture resist this. You get to see that earning is power for women—that is the message on US TV. In Nigeria, after college, women get married [and stay home.]" She said that she "wanted to be empowered" and that she told her mother she did not want her husband to "subjugate me and make me do what

I don't want." She also said that she "wanted to get a job so everyone would know you were valuable before you got married." She said, "In Africa, men have the purse strings and feel they can do what they want." But she added that she saw changes in Nigeria that suggested a new gender role for women and that "women are educated now and they know what they want." She added that you realize you "don't have to just be at home."

Although her views somewhat diverge from the basic thrust of this chapter, it is important to point out that Sandra's views on the impact of US TV were more complex than her comments on gender might imply. As might be gleaned from her comments, she had very positive views of US TV. Indeed, on the "Enjoyment of US TV Scale," where 10 is the highest value, she chose 8, but said that with particular programs, such as CNN news shows and soccer programming, it would be a 10. But she was also critical of what she called "imperial TV" and how it fed the country's appetite to see the United States as superior and homogenous. She was also critical of how US TV influenced everyone in her country to want to be "a big rap star" and how they would change their accents in order to strive for this. She was also critical of how in her country they saw the United States and Africa's problems through a US lens and that when you come here, the United States is different from how it is portrayed. In addition, she noted that when Africa was portrayed, all you saw were "naked, poor children with big bellies and flies." In essence, she said, it was depicted as a "poverty, debt- and a disease-ridden" continent. She said these portrayals have to be revisited. "People do not live in tents or have diseases."[8]

Sex, Technology, and Males

Some foreign-born males mentioned that watching US TV influenced their consumption of technical goods and also their views on gender/sex. For example, a male from Kyrgyzstan said that while watching US TV, he could see "how easy it was to talk about premarital sex, iPhones, notebooks, wireless, head phones, hamburgers, burritos, sodas, and alcohol a little." Tong from China said, "The first time I knew about the iPhone was from TV. Then I purchased it. That's the magic of advertising. . . . [I] don't know where I get it from; [I] just know [I] want it." He added that US TV "definitely influenced" his views on sex. Rafael from Venezuela said: "Could stay on top of new products in technology, e.g., new phone—had to get [it]," and he inadvertently referred to the "so-White" bias of US media when he added in response to this question, "Sex: [The] typical blond, blue-eyed girl became more desirable." The fact that adoption or consumption of new technology and references to sex surfaced at the same time among the foreign-born males was a particularly interesting finding, for this did not occur in the case of the foreign-born women or the US millennials.

The US Millennials: Sex and Gender

Many of the US millennials commented on how watching US TV made them see sex as more casual and acceptable. The following comments give a flavor of these responses: "Yes, I believe TV has caused me to view sex more liberally." "Yes, it made it more acceptable in my head." "Viewing sex on a TV show makes it more casual." "Yes—[it] makes casual sex more acceptable." "Sex is viewed more casually." There were also specific and positive references to particular shows; for example, "*Girl Code* made me much more comfortable with my sexuality." Some millennials even felt that ideas of casual sex were reinforced on shows that are considered more family-friendly, such as "*Friends*—makes sex seem more casual," and "Yes, sexually liberated characters on *Battlestar Galactica*." These comments were generally third-party or observer comments. But some spoke in the first person about how watching US TV influenced their own views about sex. For example, "Yes, [I am] more willing to [engage in sexual activity]." "*love it*." "It's okay to be promiscuous." "*Sex isn't that big of a deal*." "Yes: It has reinforced my views that casual sex is preferable to involving feelings."[9]

Others commented on how US TV has introduced, altered, or made more acceptable different sex/gender norms. For example, one millennial said, "Yes. Everyone does it." Another young woman from a large city in Pennsylvania articulated this view very explicitly when she said: "TV has given me a sense of what society thinks sex should or should not be." And another, referring to same-sex relationships, said, "Yes, *Modern Family* makes gay relationships more common." Two others spoke more generally to how societal norms had changed with regard to sex being out in the open. One said, "It is more open to discuss and talk about and not shaming." And another said, "Sex is a natural human action which should be respected."

However, a small number of US millennials said that watching US TV led them to be more critical of or more moralistic about what they saw. For example, one said, "Should be with the right person." Others spoke specifically to the portrayal of women, saying, "The double standards presented on TV are agitating," or, "Television is sexified and makes girls seem like their bodies aren't that important." Still another millennial repeated a sad but curious critique that I've heard from students before: "Women are perceived to have [sexual] 'skills' that aren't necessarily true, and if they don't possess those skills, they're considered worthless." Other millennials made comments that suggested that watching US TV left them with some reservations about the way sex is portrayed. For example, one young woman from a suburb in New Jersey suggested that portraying sex so casually robbed it of its significance. She said, "Yes, some shows make sex look like less of a big deal than it is." Another respondent said, "When I was younger, it made sex seem a lot more serious and glamorous than it really is, but then I actually had sex." And finally, one young millennial said, "It has made me conflicted about wanting to remain abstinent until marriage."[10]

Foreign-Born and Millennial Respondents' Views on Birth Control

As Figure 8.1 indicates, the groups diverged more on the extent to which they felt that watching US TV influenced their views on birth control. Only 15 percent of the foreign born said that it had influenced their views, as compared with 24 percent of the US millennials. But in both groups the comments in this area were few, and those who did comment said that US TV had made them think more positively about birth control.

Some comments made by those among the foreign-born group underscored interesting differences between cultures. For example, Kemi from Nigeria and London said that US TV did not influence her with regard to sex because she was taught sex education at an early age, 8, when she began to have her period. Because she had her period so early, this required her school to teach sex education to everyone, and that's when she learned about birth control. Mani from India mentioned that watching US TV influenced his desire for "fancy cars, clothes, accessories" and added that "in India, birth control is not considered good by society, but in the US it is preferred to getting pregnant" and that this influenced his views.

Those millennials who said US TV had influenced their views on birth control generally spoke of how teen pregnancies should be avoided, and some made reference to the "teen mom"–type shows. For example, a young working-class woman from New York City said, "I think birth control should be used effectively in order to subvert [avoid] teen pregnancy." Another young middle-class woman from a small town in New Jersey said, "Yes: Getting pregnant usually ruins these characters' lives, so it makes birth control even more desirable."

Influence of US TV on Smoking and Alcohol Consumption

The groups diverged in a similar way on the issue of whether watching US TV influenced their views on smoking, with more millennials (29 percent) than the foreign born (15 percent) being influenced in this regard. The groups also diverged on whether, and how much, US TV watching influenced their views on alcohol consumption, with both groups—but especially the millennials—more engaged on this issue. As Figure 8.1 indicates, 24 percent of the foreign born and 36 percent of the US millennials said that it had influenced their consumption of alcohol. To some degree, this is to be expected, for the millennials are young and in college, where drinking often occurs despite the legislation in some states prohibiting underage drinking. Below I present first the comments of the foreign born and then those of the millennials on smoking and drinking.

The Foreign Born and Their Multifaceted Views

Some of the foreign born did mention smoking, but in general few commented about smoking and alcohol consumption; and those who did were—in contrast to the US millennials—not particularly judgmental about either practice. Moreover, they also saw smoking and drinking as part of a general ambiance that was conveyed on US TV. The following comments suggest both the general contexts within which smoking and drinking were seen and the nonjudgmental attitudes of the respondents. Achilles from Greece said, "As a kid I really wanted to have things like a skateboard, a plane that hovered, clothes, Nike basketball shoes," but, he added, it was "difficult and expensive to get then; [I] saw smoking as a norm." Avis from Jamaica also admitted that watching US TV "influenced my desires," particularly food-related ads, including those for potato chips, which she said were "very expensive in Jamaica." She added that US TV "made smoking look cool; grandmother smoked too." Victoria from Paraguay was also less judgmental about smoking: "I used to think smoking was so cool. Today, I actually smoke socially, not every day, but I do smoke. Maybe it was influenced by my TV watching."

Western Media Enter the Soviet Sphere

Eva, who grew up in Russia, gave a more in-depth and multifaceted explanation of how her exposure to US TV, as an adult in a communist country, influenced her desires to want certain consumer goods and to emulate much of what she saw, including smoking and drinking. Russia had had very limited, if any, exposure to US programming when she was growing up. She said:

> Like for instance, in the shows' people, you want to be like them, and they all wear nice clothes of certain kinds and they always wear nice clothes; they have very nice hair and good skin and you want to be like them, of course. For instance, this show I mentioned before, *Gossip Girl*, it's about New York elite and a great deal of the show is devoted to how they are dressed. Smoking, no. I never smoked and I don't like smoking and I think that I don't see a lot of smoking in American shows. I think it's kind of banned from American shows. For drinking, I think yes, because drinking in the teenage shows and the shows for youth, it is portrayed as something rather positive. Socializing, like if you want to be in the popular circles you have to go to the drinking parties—red cups, red plastic cups[11]—and drink beer. I think it did influence alcohol consumption. Birth control, I never, I mean with *Teenage Mom*, I know the show influences birth control, but it didn't influence me personally because I watched it when I was already 23, and I had already my views

on birth control. And on sex I think it did. Because of the youth shows they portrayed that sex is a central part of, like, young adult's experience. And, cool kids did that, so I think it did influence.

In this response, Eva painted a fairly complex picture of how watching US TV, even as an adult, influenced her. But her comments perhaps require some contextualizing so that readers have a better sense of the world that existed in Russia, and in other Soviet satellite states before Western media arrived.

We begin with the following description of the impact of Latin American telenovelas in Russia, which conveys some of this context. Over the years, my students from the former Soviet Union have indicated to me that telenovelas from Latin America were allowed into Russia prior to US TV. When they arrived, the viewers marveled at the settings, that is, the colorful and often lavish homes in which the upper-class characters lived, the clothes these characters wore, the cars that they drove or were driven in, the technology (e.g., phones) that were so ever-present, and the freedom the characters seemed to have to travel. These were in stark contrast to the often regimented, colorless, ostensibly classless society within which Soviet citizens lived. However, perhaps because of the emphasis on a classless society, they also related to the often class-based plots that were typical of many telenovelas at the time, that is, where the poor but virtuous and kind heroine (often a Cinderella-type character who is taken in as a maid) marries the handsome, wealthy, romantic lead. Viewers avidly consumed these telenovelas because they presented a world that was so different from their own, and so desirable to many.[12]

While traveling in Budapest in 2016, I spoke with a young professional who dealt with US media companies. She said that in Eastern Europe, the entrance of US media was associated with the fall of the Soviet Union. Many in Eastern Europe had seen Soviet rule as a negative experience filled with deprivations. When US media entered the country, they introduced Pepsi, Coke, jeans, consumerism, ideas about fashion, and the sense that the United States was the "land of opportunity" and the best place to get an education. She felt that, despite the fact that the shows in Hungary were dubbed, US media were still influential, and this was evident from the volume and kinds of comments that some TV shows, like *Game of Thrones*, generated; these comments were more likely on Facebook than in person. She added that today it was more about "who to follow on Instagram," what you drink, what type of clothes you wear, and what types of electronics you want to get. She said the United States is still a place to look up to today. She also noted that there had been a shift, with more youths (17 to 20 years old) watching US TV in English; this trend, she said, had been aided by the availability of shows on the Internet and the growing number of youths who watched US TV on their computers and laptops.

US Millennials on Smoking and Drinking

In contrast to the limited comments on smoking and drinking by the foreign-born respondents, fully 32 percent of the US millennials volunteered comments on alcohol consumption, with another 26 percent commenting on smoking. On smoking, the millennials either expressed disgust toward smoking or spoke to how effective the antismoking commercials had been. Only a few praised the habit. Here is a sampling of what they said: "I think smoking is deliberately bad for you." "Don't do it." "It is bad." 'Smoking is bad. It's disgusting." "[TV] taught me it's bad." "Yes: Smoking now has a bad rap on television, for the most part, so I would say it has made it increasingly unappealing." Another added, "Most shows don't involve smoking." In a clear testament to the effectiveness of antismoking commercials, one said: "Yes, antismoking commercials are very effective." The few who were not so negative said, "I smoke sometimes" and "smoking is okay." Others spoke to how they felt US TV still portrayed smoking as "cool." They said, "It looks so cool," and "smoking looks cool even though I don't smoke."

Their general disparagement of smoking was in contrast to what they said when asked how watching US TV had influenced their consumption of alcohol. As in the case of sex described above, a number of millennials said, as one respondent put it, "Television made alcohol consumption seem very socially acceptable." Another said, "Yes—it's in every episode of HIMYM." (HIMYM is an abbreviation of How I Met Your Mother, another situation comedy like Friends.)[13] One young middle-class woman from the Bronx said that "some shows encourage drinking alcohol." Another said that drinking "alcohol seems like a normal weekend activity on TV." Still others said "it seems to be okay because of the way it is depicted in TV shows." One respondent noted, "People drink wine a lot."

Others spoke to how drinking is also associated on TV with becoming "better at life." For example, one millennial said that US TV conveyed the idea that "drinking is a way to be sociable." Another said it suggested that "drinking is a good way to unwind and is common behavior to indulge in when stressed or sad." Others spoke to how US TV made drinking look cool: "Yes, it made it look cooler." Another respondent said, "Drinking alcohol looks cool even though I don't drink alcohol." As with sex, some mentioned specific shows, for example, "*Mad Men* made me want to drink more." "Watching old movies, drinking was glamorous." And one young male millennial said somewhat facetiously: "Yup, Olivia Pope [the lead actress in the TV drama *Scandal*] put me on a diet of popcorn and red wine."[14]

Others spoke personally to how US TV influenced their consumption of alcohol, and some of the comments were disturbing.[15] For example, one young working-class woman from New York City said, "I started consuming alcohol by watching TV." Another respondent, a young middle-class woman from the suburbs, said, "Yes, the romanticizing of alcohol consumption affected my drinking." A gender-unidentified working-class respondent said: "I thought being drunk would be great thanks to TV, but when it actually happened, it wasn't all that."[16] A young upper-middle-class woman from California and Chicago said flatly: "Getting drunk does not solve your problems."

But others were more critical and wrote in comments that might be construed as lessons to others. It is unclear whether these were lessons gained from experience, but they are worth repeating here. They included admonitions, such as "WARNING: Don't overdrink." "Drink responsibly." "Drink to a limit." And, finally, "People on TV overdrink and can still function—not realistic." One young middle-class woman from a rural area in New Hampshire departed from the rest and said, "Taught me it's bad." But she did not indicate why.

Ads

Despite the influence of US TV on consumption purchases and practices, very few of the foreign-born respondents remembered any particular ads. The US millennials, in contrast, remembered quite a few. Indeed, while more than two-thirds of the US millennials recalled specific ads they saw on television, only 39.4 percent of the foreign-born respondents did—and only 6.6 percent recalled what country the ads were from. (One-fifth of the foreign-born group recalled seeing ads, but did not recall any ads in particular.) The foreign-born respondents who did recall ads accompanying US TV shows recalled them as local ads, such as for a local auto repair shop.

The clarity with which the ads were described by the US millennials and the vagueness of descriptions that accompanied the foreign-born respondents' comments on ads underscore the possibility that recall and memory played a role here. But the foreign-born group's responses here were clearly in contrast to their vivid recall of US TV programs and cast members described earlier. These differences in "recollection of ads" could also be due to the fact that many of the foreign born accessed their US TV programs via DVDs or the Internet, where ads were missing or less memorable. In any case, what is significant is that, according to the sample's responses, US TV programming nonetheless exerted a substantial influence on viewers' consumption purchases and practices, despite the fact that they did not recall many ads.

Summary

In summary, and returning to the concerns cited by scholars at the start of this chapter, what both the foreign born and the US millennials show in their responses is that US TV has been a generally effective commercial agent, selling material goods, lifestyle choices, and services, while at the same time assisting in creating or reinforcing very desirable American brands. Respondents in both groups said that watching US TV influenced their consumption patterns and views about sex/gender, birth control, smoking, and alcohol consumption. But it did not influence either group in a totally consistent way. There are clusters within each group that reject or are critical of the influence of US TV.

We have also seen that the ways in which the two groups were influenced (as a result of watching US TV) also differ. The foreign-born sample was especially influenced in their desire for and purchase of clothes, food, tech gadgets, and lifestyles featured on TV shows. The US millennials were also affected in their desires and decisions to purchase clothing styles and other goods, but watching US TV appears to have influenced their ideas on sex and alcohol consumption differently than those in the foreign-born sample. In short, many millennials reported that watching US TV influenced them to think about sex as a more casual and acceptable norm, while those in the foreign-born sample had more diverse reactions, depending on their country of origin.

But some in the millennial sample were also critical of this more casual, acceptable, or normative view of sex, and still others were critical of the representations of women on US TV. There were some in the foreign-born group who were similarly influenced with regard to how their views on sex and drinking had been influenced, but this seemed to be related to the customs followed in their home countries; for example, respondents who came from countries with more restrictive policies on drinking or sex were more influenced by US TV.

Finally, among the US millennials, watching US TV encouraged antismoking views among many, and the "teenage mom" shows appear to have engendered more positive views on birth control, while the foreign born were less disparaging about smoking and their views on birth control were not particularly affected. With regard to alcohol consumption, substantial minorities in both groups (24 percent foreign born, 36 percent US millennials) indicated that US TV had influenced their views. Both groups agreed that US TV presented drinking as a very acceptable (and sometimes romanticized) social practice, and some of the US millennials felt that it was portrayed as an aide to dealing with life's stresses—or as a "lubricant" for easier socializing or returning to a more balanced life. Some also addressed the dangers of overindulgence, which they said US TV downplayed.

Conclusion

As we have seen, the consumption of US TV in the United States and globally continues to be significant. This is despite changes in the way in which US TV content—especially entertainment programs—is accessed or viewed, such as through binge-watching, DVR programming, or subscription services, on tablets, or on cell phones. Despite the fact that the medium is shifting, research also continues to show patterns of under- and misrepresentation with regard to race, class, and gender in US TV programs. Therefore, the question driving this volume has been this: How has watching US TV programs influenced viewers both in the United States and in other countries with regard to their perceptions of race, class, and gender? Derivative questions included the following: Do these perceptions change once people come to the United States? How similar or different are the views of people from other countries when compared with the views held by US millennials?

In order to study these questions, I reviewed the literature in the United States and in other countries pertaining to these questions, and I developed two samples: one of foreign-born international students, faculty, researchers, and other professionals in the United States; and another of US millennials. (A description of my samples, method, and process can be found in the appendix.) The second part of this volume focused on my foreign-born sample, what they watched, how they saw the United States before they came, what surprised them the most when they first arrived, and whether—now that they were in the United States—they saw American TV as encouraging or discouraging of the integration of "Others." The third section in this volume compared the views of the foreign-born respondents and the US millennials with regard to the influence of US TV on their consumption patterns, their views on sex, drinking, smoking, and birth control, and whether they thought that US TV accurately reflected racial and ethnic relations in the United States. Below is a brief review of the major findings in these last two sections, as the first section was covered in previous chapters.

The Foreign-Born Group

When asked, "Do you recall when you watched your first American TV show? What was that show's name and how old were you when you watched it?," the foreign-born participants' recollections of their first exposure to American TV were vivid, lively, and warm. All but *one* respondent remembered the first show that they watched and how old they were when they watched it. Moreover, they were very aware of how much watching US TV had influenced their views of the United States. Indeed, all but four in the sample said that it had influenced them "a lot" or "more than a lot." (This surprised me, as I have found that most people in the United States are generally unaware of the influence of TV on their views of other countries, and on their views more generally.) Also intriguing to me were the many reasons given for how the foreign-born group knew that the shows they watched were "American" shows, especially given that some of the shows were dubbed. The reasons given included accents, well-known landmarks of the United States, the nature of personal relations between characters (e.g., the freedom that the female characters had on *Sex and the City* with regard to living arrangements and their sex lives), the marketing of the shows (e.g., direct advertising of the newest show), and discussions in other media (e.g., popular magazines) about "the new American show." Also of interest to me was how, for many, "watching American TV" appeared to reflect a certain class and cultural habitus in their home countries.

Many scholars, such as Stuart Hall (1990), have noted that how viewers are influenced can vary quite a bit depending on how the viewer decodes what is "encoded" or intended by the producers. This was evident in the responses of this foreign-born sample to questions about how they viewed the United States after having lived here. Many said they saw the United States in a more positive way *before* they came, especially in terms of American exceptionalism, easy living, more admirable gender relations, and a greater sense of "freedom." A few, however, were influenced to see the United States more critically before they came, and their views became even more critical after their arrival. Many respondents, from various countries, began to see the distinction between the easygoing youth culture they had seen portrayed on the screen and the actual work culture that they encountered in their real lives soon after they arrived. Others were more critical when they realized that the seemingly accessible accoutrements of an American middle-class lifestyle on-screen were not always so easy to attain in their experience. They had to come to terms with not being able to afford or acquire the kinds of homes, apartments, dinners, or cab rides they saw portrayed on-screen and which they had assumed would be easily accessible to them. Since this was a fairly elite group, this may have also been a major change from the lives they led before they came, where—because of their class positions—they may not have had as many financial or time restrictions.

The foreign-born respondents felt that watching US TV before they came to the United States greatly influenced their views of the country; this was evident when they responded to the questions "What surprised you the most about the United States when you first arrived? Why were you surprised?" Regardless of where they landed (e.g., in New York City or in a small town in Kansas), what surprised them the most was the bigness, the diversity, the economic divisions, and the differences—as compared with their home countries—in social norms and interpersonal relations. This is not to say that they were unaware of such economic divisions in their home countries; but they were expecting to experience the more sanitized America that is exported in US TV but which is not necessarily representative of the real United States. The TV programs consumed abroad may also not have included more recent, more diverse, and more inclusive offerings that have appeared since they left their home countries. Thus, the American TV they did consume did not lead them to expect the divisions of class and race that they experienced or witnessed when they came to the United States.

When asked whether they thought that watching US TV had influenced their views of race, class, and gender and their aspirations, they said yes and added that they now saw more of the reality as opposed to the media images. They mentioned that they now saw the United States as having more cultural and racial diversity, as well as greater class inequality than they had seen on US TV. But some said that they now saw that real people in the United States were "basically human," with all the blemishes and charms found among people in other parts of the world.

In addition, the majority now saw the United States as "more complex," and although their view of the American Dream was a bit tarnished, many still saw greater opportunity in the United States than in their home countries.

With regard to whether they *now* thought that US TV was encouraging or discouraging of "otherness," the picture was mixed. More (43 percent vs. 27 percent) saw US TV as encouraging versus discouraging of the integration of Others, while others saw it as improving in this regard, albeit slowly. However, a closer examination of why they saw US TV as encouraging of "otherness" indicated that they had a much more complex interpretation of what inclusiveness meant; for example, for some it meant that in contrast to their home country's own media, people of color were seen on US TV. Interestingly, when asked whether their own country's programming was inclusive of Others in their home country, all but five respondents (or 7.9 percent) acknowledged the existence of "Others" in their home country; and of these, only 10.5 percent said they were well portrayed, while another 73.7 percent said they were "rarely seen," "not portrayed well," or "not portrayed at all." There were also many comments given in response to this question that suggested that there are certain common characteristics that influence the designation of "otherness" across countries.[1] Curiously, some respondents totally missed the racial dimensions of some US media before coming to the United States, for example, interpreting Spike Lee's film *Do the Right Thing* as reflecting just class and not racial divisions.

Comparing the US Millennial and the Foreign-Born Groups

My global viewers watched a substantial amount of American TV before coming to the United States, with 81 percent watching American shows every day or a few times a week. Some engaged in nonlinear watching, accessing American TV shows via the Internet and viewing programs consecutively, that is, "bingeing on occasion." Despite the fact that the US millennials were full-time undergrads, they also watched a lot of TV. Close to half (49.1 percent) watched TV more than two hours per day, with one-fifth (21.6 percent) watching more than three hours a day (and of these, 9.9 percent watching more than four hours per day). Likewise, the US millennial group also watched American television shows online to a similar degree as did the foreign-born sample—62.5 percent as compared with 68.9 percent. In addition, like the foreign-born sample, but to a lesser degree, they also searched online for more information about the shows (such as plotlines, information on actors and actresses, or other hearsay).[2] They also looked for and downloaded music from the shows, but again to a lesser degree than the foreign-born group (i.e., 17.5 percent vs. 37.9 percent). Also, like the foreign-born sample, they read other people's discussions of the shows, still again to a lesser degree (i.e., 13.1 percent vs. 34.5 percent). In short, both groups watched a lot of US TV and utilized the Internet to complement their viewing, with the foreign born making more use of the Internet.

How Much Did the Two Groups Enjoy US TV?

The foreign-born group enjoyed American TV very much, registering an 8.76 on a scale from 1 to 10, and with more than half rating their enjoyment a 9 or a 10. They were very clear and expressive about *why* they liked American TV, citing, in order of significance, excellent production values, the opportunity/experience of seeing a different lifestyle or culture, the entertaining or funny qualities of American TV, and the ability to gain knowledge (e.g., more knowledge of the English language). However, a few said that they watched US TV because it was all they really had access to. Although the groups are not directly comparable because of different scales and because they are somewhat younger, the US millennial group also said that they enjoyed US TV very much, with 73.7 percent saying "very much" or "more than somewhat" and only 3.5 percent saying they did not enjoy it at all. Clearly both groups liked US TV a lot.

How Did the Foreign-Born and the US Millennial Respondents Compare with Regard to Whether They Thought That US TV Accurately Reflected Racial and Ethnic Relations in the United States?

To a surprising degree, the views of the foreign born were consistent with the findings of scholars who have found a great deal of racial and ethnic under- and misrepresentation on US TV. As Figure C.1 indicates,

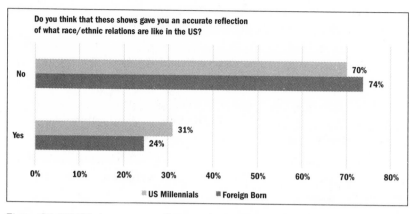

Figure C.1. US TV: An accurate reflection of race/ethnic relations in the United States?

the majority of the foreign-born sample (74 percent) said US TV had *not* given them an accurate picture. Additionally, some (13 percent) of those who said the representation was *not* accurate said this was because racial and ethnic relations were worse than shown on TV, or that the shows had a narrow focus (16 percent) and that other types of diversity were not shown, including religious and intraethnic diversity (10 percent). Finally, 5 percent felt it was not an accurate picture because it didn't show the positive side of diversity.

Those (24 percent) who felt the shows *did* give an accurate reflection of what racial and ethnic relations were like did not comment much, but those who did provided varied responses. For example, of these, 7 percent said that the shows gave them an accurate picture, but they noted that this was because they depicted racial and ethnic distances (or distancing) in the United States. However, another 3 percent said US TV was their initial exposure to diversity, and so they didn't know what to expect. All in all, although the reasons varied, few in the foreign-born sample felt that US TV had given them an accurate reflection of racial and ethnic relations in the United States.[3]

A similar proportion of the US millennials (70 percent) said that US TV did *not* give them an accurate reflection of what racial and ethnic relations were like in the United States. The reasons given by the US millennials for why the shows did not give an accurate picture were similar to those noted by the foreign-born group—although they were articulated somewhat differently. Many agreed that the shows they watched had a narrow focus and lacked diversity, but they used sharper language, such as "white-washed," "overexaggerated," and "stereotyped."

Did the Foreign-Born and US Millennial Groups Think That Watching US TV Had Influenced Their Views of Race, Ethnicity, Class, and Gender?

Both groups agreed that US TV influenced their views on race, ethnicity, class, and gender, but proportionately more in the foreign-born group indicated that their views on these topics were influenced by US TV. Since the responses to each of the variables, that is, race, gender, ethnicity, and class, varied and have been described in an earlier chapter, suffice it to say here that only 11 percent of the foreign-born respondents said that watching US TV had *no* influence on their views in these areas, compared with 50 percent of the US millennials. To some degree, this stands to reason, as the US millennials have lived in the United States and have had many more, longer-term sources of influence over their lifetimes (e.g., schools, friendships, teachers, athletics, etc.) on how they view race, class, ethnicity, and gender. More interesting, however, were the areas that each group agreed had been influenced by watching US TV. While in the foreign-born group it was their views on race, ethnicity, and gender that were most influenced, among the US millennials perspectives on class and gender were most affected (see Figure 7.1).

The examples given in each group illustrate the type of influence. For example, among the foreign-born group, watching US TV strengthened their view of the United States as a predominantly White, "yellow-haired" country, with greater gender equality and with more liberal views toward gender roles and identities. Among the US millennial group, the examples given on gender were similar to those given by the foreign-born group, but the examples given on class were quite different. They ranged, for example, from those who felt that US TV mainly focused on the middle and upper classes as the desirable norm to those who felt US TV always had class differences and inequality on display. Respondents in the US millennial group varied with regard to these two views on class, with some wanting to achieve the privileged class styles they saw on TV and others wanting to change the inequalities they saw.

Last, some respondents in this group stated that US TV influenced them to view, or to associate, non-Whites with the working or poorer classes.

Consumption of Products and Styles

The question posed to both groups was whether watching US TV "influenced their desire to purchase material goods and, if so, how." Substantial proportions of both groups said yes (i.e., 48.4 percent of the foreign-born group and 42 percent of the millennials), and only 26 percent and 39 percent of the respective groups said no. However, there were many who had mixed answers, such as not answering yes or no but giving other responses.[4] For example, in both groups there were some who acknowledged the influence, but also rejected or were critical of how US TV sought to influence purchasing and lifestyle decisions. Others said that they were not consciously influenced to purchase certain goods but may have been unconsciously influenced. Among those who acknowledged the influence, the foreign-born sample was especially affected in their desire for and purchase of clothes, food, tech gadgets, and lifestyles featured on TV shows.[5] Very briefly, the US millennials who recognized that they were influenced also mentioned their "desire to purchase" or their actual purchase of clothing styles and other goods they saw on US TV. In sum, watching US TV does appear to influence both groups' consumption of (or their desire to consume) goods and services associated with the programming they view. This may warm the hearts of the commercial interests that make US TV possible—even though specific ads, or product placement, were not noted by many in the foreign-born group and were noted by only some in the US millennial group.

Influence of US TV on Views toward Sex, Birth Control, Smoking, and Alcohol Consumption

Both groups were similarly influenced to desire and purchase material goods. But did watching US TV influence the groups' views on sex, birth control, smoking, and drinking? In these samples, watching US TV appears to have influenced the US millennials' ideas on sex and alcohol consumption differently than those in the foreign-born sample. Many US millennials reported that watching US TV influenced them to think about sex as a more casual and acceptable norm. But some in the US millennial sample were critical of this projection of sex as nonchalant. Still others were critical of the representations of women on US TV.[6] Those in the foreign-born sample had more diverse reactions, and this depended on their country of origin. For example, those from countries with more restrictive sex codes felt US TV influenced them to have more liberal views with regard to sex (and gender roles with respect to sex). But those from countries with more liberal views in these areas did not feel that watching US TV influenced their views about sex. For example, as stated previously, Milja from Finland said that sex on US TV and US media more generally was "over the top," "silly," and "trying too hard." She said that in Finland, sex was "open" and "taken for granted," and therefore "less sexualized."

Among the US millennials, watching US TV has encouraged antismoking views among many, and the "teenage mom" shows appear to have influenced more positive views toward birth control; that is, respondents saw it as an important practice to follow so as to avoid problems teenagers may experience with unwanted pregnancies. The foreign-born respondents, on the other hand, were less disparaging about smoking and seldom mentioned birth control. Finally, with regard to drinking, substantial minorities in both groups indicated that US TV presented drinking as a very acceptable (and sometimes romanticized) social practice. Some of the US millennials felt that it was portrayed as an aide to dealing with life's stresses, and a few spoke to the dangers of overindulgence.

Wrap-Up

Obviously, whether accessed traditionally or via the Internet, US TV has powerful effects on the people who watch it in the United States or in their home country or in other countries. It is a powerful medium, and it projects US values, lifestyles, and soft power around the world. It also influences the attitudes and viewpoints of global viewers in many dimensions. These include adopting more US-like attitudes (as portrayed on US TV) about consumption (of clothes, fast foods, technologies, etc.), gender relations, attitudes toward sex, and even occupational choices. But being in the United States altered the views that respondents in the foreign-born group had developed of the United States in their home countries. After arriving, many respondents said that the US TV they watched seemed to portray a more positive, perhaps more sanitized, view of the United States than that they had developed after living here. Practically all were initially struck by the "bigness" of the United States—regardless of whether they landed in a large city or a small town. They also indicated that attitudes toward "Others" were portrayed differently on US TV than they were experienced in reality.

As these findings show, the soft power of US TV in other countries is strong, but not absolute. Some respondents—especially those from more economically advanced countries—were more critical of the United States and its media before they came; others became more critical after being in the United States, for example, because of the extent of poverty and the inadequate health care poor people received. The US millennial sample was younger and had been raised with these media, yet they too were not brainwashed. Indeed, they were more critical in some regards of US TV than the foreign-born respondents. Moreover, robust majorities in both groups said that US TV did *not* accurately reflect racial and ethnic relations in the United States. However, the US millennial group was more taken by US TV's slanted representations of class than were the foreign-born respondents. This may reflect the fact that in the United States, class is (1) not often openly discussed and (2) undergoing major social changes as inequality has been increasing considerably in the United States and many US millennials are concerned about social mobility and whether they will be able to improve or even retain their current class positions. It seems that for both groups, increased exposure to US TV, combined with the reality of living in the United States, weakens US TV's influence.

But perhaps the most significant finding for this study is that substantial majorities of both groups—74 percent of the foreign-born respondents and 70 percent of the US millennial group—echoed what scholars have found but is seldom discussed in traditional media, in policy circles, in corporate boardrooms, or even in many of the households watching television content. This is that US TV does *not* accurately represent or reflect racial and ethnic relations in the United States—as the #oscarsowhite and #hollywoodsowhite movements have also contended. Moreover, as noted above, even some of the foreign born who responded that shows did give an accurate picture of racial and ethnic relations said this was because they depicted actual racial and ethnic distances (or distancing) in the United States. Others added that the representation was not accurate because racial and ethnic relations *were worse* than shown on TV, or that the shows had a narrow focus and did not show other types of diversity, such as religious or intraethnic diversity, or did not show the positive side of diversity. The younger US millennials also offered similar, often more strongly worded comments about the narrow focus and lack of diversity.

Moreover, majorities of both groups acknowledged that US TV did influence how they viewed race, class, ethnicity, and gender—with a higher proportion of the foreign born than the US millennials reporting being affected. The fact that majorities in both groups *acknowledged* the influence of US TV on their views is somewhat surprising to me, for, as I have said elsewhere in this volume, until researching this issue, I wasn't very aware of how much my own views were influenced by what I saw on US TV. Most interesting, however, was that the US millennial group felt that it was their views on class and gender that were most influenced, while the foreign-born group said it was their views on race, ethnicity, and gender that had been most influenced by watching US TV. This suggests that gender may be a more global concept, while race, ethnicity, and class may be more context- or nation-dependent.

Acknowledging the power of the economic and commercial engine that accompanies US TV, both groups noted that US TV influenced their consumption of material products (especially clothing and technology), services, and other goods that reflect particular lifestyles. But the groups differed on whether they felt that US TV influenced their views toward sex, birth control, and alcohol and tobacco consumption. As was noted earlier, these differences in views reflect the distinct cultural, social, and political milieus of the two groups and of the diverse foreign-born respondents in particular. These differences suggest that although both groups can wear the same American brands, use the same American technology, and assume similar lifestyles, their views are still influenced differently depending on what they bring to the viewing screen, for example, their own cultural views, their lived race, and their personal experiences and preferences.

For viewers who can compare depictions on US TV shows with their experiences living in the United States for a while, the power of US TV is limited. But my interviews with the foreign-born participants indicate that the countless numbers of people who watch US TV in their home countries and never get to the United States may continue to absorb a slanted view of the United States, and this may, in turn, contribute to people in most of the world adopting, or reacting against, increasing amounts of US culture and its worldviews.

The Future: What's Next?

As of this writing, the future is uncertain. TV is a medium in flux; it has changed greatly in the past decade, and the only thing we can be certain about is that it will continue to change. Will there be more international-ization of the market for TV, or will the United States always dominate? On the supply side, the questions include the following: What about immigrant producers of media—will these increase, and, if so, will new voices dominate and change the landscape? Will new forms of media consumption become more available and more dominant—for example, YouTube viewing or alternative-, simulated-, or parallel-reality products? How will such shifts influence projections of race, ethnicity, class, and gender? On the demand side, two forces in particular—increasing glo-balization and viewership throughout the world, and changes in racial and ethnic demographics among the viewers in the United States—are fundamentally impacting *who* is viewing US TV (Chavez, 2013). Will changes in viewership affect the racial, ethnic, and gender patterns we have seen in US TV programming? If so, how?

Also, what role will "new media" play in effecting changes along these lines in traditional television programming?[7] Fleming and Mor-ris (2015) provide an interesting example of the impact of social media in their analysis of social media sites, such as Black Twitter, Facebook, and hashtags. They show how social media have been used to raise con-sciousness about the Black Lives Matter movement. For example, by juxtaposing the mainstream media's negative media images of Michael Brown, who was shot dead by police in Ferguson, Missouri, against "re-spectable" images of Brown (e.g., in a graduation cap and gown), the Black Lives Matter movement reframed and globalized this incident and the larger issue of police brutality against people of color. This raises the question of "to what extent efforts to raise awareness about racism in one national setting affect anti-racist discourse across the globe" (115) and whether "ethnoracial movements interpenetrate globally, sharing ideas, visions, and strategies that affect their trajectories" (120). In addition, have the #oscarsowhite and #hollywoodsowhite Twitter protest movements created a similar global consciousness about racial patterns in the US media that have been and are increasingly consumed globally? The attempts at the 2016 Academy Awards ceremony on February 28, 2016, to mollify these "so white" charges only added legitimacy, in the eyes of many, to the criticisms being made in the Twitterverse.[8]

Social media allow people to represent themselves the way they want to be seen. This means that, from the marketing perspective, they create their own content. Consequently, it is often in these sites that we see content that more often affirms values like "it's cool to be bicultural" or "to be Chinese" or "racially mixed" or any of the "other" lived realities (or subaltern voices) that are not mentioned, downplayed, subordinated, or exoticized on more mainstream media and television. As of this writing, it appears that social media are, in many instances, used as an adjunct, or a supplement, to television programming. People still comment on shows, as they did in the past, with friends, on social media, and in person—no matter if those shows were watched on terrestrial TV, cable, or Internet TV, including via Netflix or Apple TV. However, as of this writing, it appears the television industry is still trying to figure out how best to use Twitter, Snapchat, and others; and the question still remains as to whether social media, and the Internet more generally, will continue to be a talent-finding machine or a content-generating machine, or both. Moreover, the question of how much new media will change how people view diversity is still to be answered. For new media to lead us to greater inclusivity, as Smith, Choueiti, and Pieper (2016:17) point out, "requires creating an ecosystem in which different perspectives hold value and stories represent the world[s] in which we live."

ACKNOWLEDGMENTS

There are so many people to acknowledge and to thank for helping me to write this book that I quote again a now deceased New York Puerto Rican poet, Tato Laviera, who once said "with every word I write I give thanks to 50 people." This book has been a long time in the making and there have been so many, many people who have helped along the way. But perhaps it is best to begin by acknowledging some of the first people who contributed to my thinking, but who I haven't acknowledged in other works. These would include both my English professor/teacher at Morris High School, Ms. Avis Hanson, one of the first African American women to teach at Morris High School in the South Bronx, and Miss Clara Wurman, head of the Math Department there. Both believed in my abilities and potential in these areas—when I had no clue, or no sense of what my interest in these areas might mean for my future. Both also helped me—in ways I am just beginning to understand—to follow the paths that I have pursued throughout my academic career.

I have to also acknowledge that the crazy family that I was born into was also instrumental in helping me—not that they could provide a road map, but that somehow I always knew that I had their support, which often amounted to their just not setting up barriers for me. But, I begin by acknowledging these folks because somehow in that history is where my interests in race/ethnicity, class, and gender began. As Ms. Hanson was often fond of saying, humankind has accomplished so much (e.g., we have gone to the moon and back, we have developed technology and systems we couldn't even imagine before), "but one thing that we can't seem to figure out is how to get along with each other." In writing this book her words often came back to me as we witnessed, via our respective media outlets, the continuing tides and struggles of refugees throughout the world, and the backlashes against immigrants and (often) their children.

I would also like to acknowledge my amazing crew, who were so important to having it move along effectively. Organized alphabetically, they are Burk, Chase, Dalia, Danni, Gelvin, Gelvina, Jimmy, Jose A., Linda, Martha, Minnie, and Rosa. They may not have realized it, but they were my local support group at a particularly crucial time. My research assistants and scholarly associates were also invaluable, supportive, and critical to the completion of this work. I include just a few here: Christina LaBruno, Lia Isono, Aigerim Askarova, Jennifer Kang, Grace Liu, Tom Wang, Fan (Zoe) Zhang, and Katherine Richardson. In addition, I want to thank Arianna Futerfas, Gianna Sciangula, and Sydney Thornell for their invaluable transcription assistance. And, it could not have been written without the vital and inestimable assistance of Ryan Stellabotte, whose astonishing skills never cease to impress me. I would also like to thank Fordham University for providing me with a Faculty Fellowship, which allowed me to begin this work, and with a Faculty Research Grant, which allowed me to finish it. And thanks to Dean Michael X. Delli Carpini, Sharon Black, Head Librarian, and their staffs at the University of Pennsylvania, Annenberg School of Communications for assisting me in my research and facilitating my immersion in the global communications literature and in faculty and student discussions there. I am also grateful to Columbia University's Department of Sociology, in particular Alondra Nelson and the then Chair of the Department, Yinon Cohen, for extending a visiting position so that I could make use of their resources while beginning this project. I am particularly indebted to the following individuals at these and other universities who early on helped to make this project a reality: Klaus Krippendorff, Grace Kao, Shena Ashley, Amy Jordan, Nadia Kim, Kate Zambon, Alexandra Sastre, Michael Schudson, Carmen López Santana, Marwan Kraidy, Dan Romer, Monroe Price, Steve Wildman, Robert G. Picard, Roger Goebel, Sal Longarino, Chris Toulouse, Erica Chito Childs, Crystal Fleming, and Fran Blumberg. Many others should be included here—too many to name—but I thank them all for their contributions—especially those who helped at the very beginning when the project was not yet fully formed.

I also want to thank and acknowledge the staff at the press, in particular Caelyn Cobb, Maryam Arain, and Ilene R. Kalish, for their support and assistance throughout. These thanks include the anonymous reviewers for their spot-on suggestions and for all of the others at New York University Press whose hard work and enthusiasm for this project made it all possible. Finally, I would like to thank all of those who participated as respondents to my questionnaires for helping me to make this project a reality.

APPENDIX

My Research Questions and My Methods

The Research Questions

As noted in the Introduction, in order to get a better sense of how US TV influences people's views of race, ethnicity, class, and gender, I conducted, over a three-year period (2013–15), personal and in-depth interviews with 71 respondents from different countries. I used a semi-structured questionnaire that consisted of 95 questions that covered general background information and their viewing habits in their home country and in the United States. The interviews generally lasted an hour to an hour and a half, and took place throughout the Northeast of the United States. They were all conducted in English, although the questionnaire and the Informed Consent Form were translated into the Russian language and the Russian alphabet for a few respondents in the sample.[1] My questionnaire borrowed from earlier work that I had done (Rodríguez, 1997) and from work by Gao (2013).

Initially my basic research question was this: Given the patterning of race, ethnicity, class, and gender in US TV scripted programs, and given the extent to which people in the United States and in other countries watch US TV, how does US TV influence the ways in which people in other countries think about race, class, gender, and ethnicity? A number of other related questions also surfaced as I began to review the literature. These included the following: How do our exported US-TV entertainment programs affect the views of people in (or from) other countries about "otherness," immigrants, gender, and racial and ethnic minority groups in the United States, and also in their countries? Does watching US TV programs influence their consumption habits or views on birth control, sex, drinking, or smoking? And do these views change (or not?) once these global viewers come to the United States?

To answer these questions, I interviewed international students, faculty, and professionals who were fairly recent arrivals. The mean length of time in the United States was 3.37 years, and the median was 2 years. I was interested in fairly recent arrivals because I wanted to manage, to some degree, the problems of recall and "retrospective data." Undoubtedly, these are issues that may still affect the data collected, but I was pleasantly surprised at how crystal-clear respondents' recollections were during my interviews. Their recollections of watching American television shows were quite vivid, even for those who had been here for a bit more than six years. Many also began viewing US TV in their countries early in their lifetime and, for many, US TV seemed to have played a very important role in their decisions to come to the United States.

The Sample of Foreign-Born Young Adults

My sample of the foreign born was derived mainly as a result of posting, emailing, and personally distributing flyers that had been approved by my university's Institutional Review Board (IRB). The flyer indicated that I was seeking persons born and/or raised in other countries for a research study of television viewing in other countries. The flyer asked if prospective participants had been born and/or raised in another country, if they were at least 18 years old, if they currently resided in the United States, and if they had watched US TV in their home country. It then indicated that, if so, they would be eligible to participate in a research study that I was conducting on the television viewing habits of people in other countries. The flyer also indicated that the study would examine how much people born and/or raised in other countries had been exposed to US television and what their reactions to US television had been. In addition, the flyer indicated that all information collected would be confidential and that the interview would take about one hour at a location that was convenient to them. Respondents came from a variety of countries, and a few claimed two countries of origin. The 37 countries noted were Australia, Austria, Azerbaijan, Brazil, Canada, China, Colombia, England, Finland, France, Germany, Greece, Hungary, India, Indonesia, Ireland, Israel, Italy, Jamaica, Japan, Kyrgyzstan, Latvia, Mexico, Moldova, Nigeria, Paraguay, Peru, Philippines, Poland, Romania, Russia, Saudi Arabia, Serbia, Singapore, Spain, Syria, and Turkey.

The largest group of respondents (37 percent) hailed from European countries, and the next largest group was from countries in Asia (25 per-

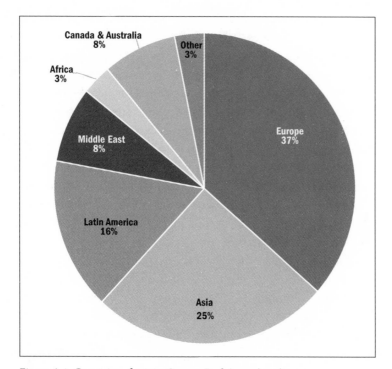

Figure A.1. Countries of origin. Source: Rodríguez (2015).

cent). Latin America accounted for 16 percent of the sample, the Middle East for 8 percent, Canada and Australia for another 8 percent, and Africa, the English-speaking Caribbean, and more than one country of origin for the remaining 6 percent (see Figure A.1).[2]

Finally, the flyer indicated that participants would not be compensated but that they would be invited—but not required—to attend a reception with other participants at the conclusion of the study, where they would have the opportunity to discuss the study with other participants. Some in my sample volunteered as a result of this flyer, and others contacted me because they were referred by others. So this was by no means a representative or random sample, and it is impossible to generalize findings. However, the interviews do provide important insights into the role of media, especially among this seldom-studied but important and growing group.

These insights became especially evident to me when I analyzed the results of my group of 171 US undergrads (sample described below), who it can be argued more closely represent undergraduate millennials in the northeastern United States. I should note that it was only because I was able to conduct the personal interviews with the foreign-born group that I was able to better understand some of the results in the electronically derived sample of 171. The personal interviews made me more aware of what is missed when using only survey data. They also reminded me that when we use only quantitative methods, much of the context gets lost; we may miss alternative interpretations and not go beyond the ones that we bring to our research. As Amanda Turner has noted, often we don't have a strong sense of how "these images and storylines are interpreted" (Turner, 2015). Although she was speaking here of images in video games, this can also be applied to the reception or interpretation of television images by viewers.

Data collection on the foreign-born group occurred throughout the Northeast, at a variety of physical locations, depending on individual availability and preference. Although semistructured, each interview began with general background information, and then I asked about participants' viewing habits in their home country and in the United States. I asked at the end of each interview whether they had additional comments they wanted to make, and if the interview had made them think about anything in particular. Interviews lasted between 60 and 90 minutes, and were digitally recorded and transcribed. I also made notes on the paper questionnaires I used during and after the interviews. After each interview, I reviewed my notes. All of this was subsequently entered into the Survey Monkey (SM) computer program. This was an unusual use of SM, as this program is generally used to "gather" and not to enter data. This presented a few challenges, but the benefits were that comparisons could more easily be made between the samples, for the 171 undergrads had taken their survey on Survey Monkey.

I should note that although I personally conducted 71 in-depth, personal interviews, 8 were lost because I had to shift my work space or because of the changeover shifts of research assistants inputting the data—yes, this happens. So the data presented are limited to the 63 remaining interviews, but I make some reference to some of the interviews that were lost, as I had made separate notes on these prior to their disappearance. What is the lesson here? Always have a backup of your questionnaires—and make it quickly. In terms of the response rate, I was very lucky in that only one person who initially agreed to be interviewed did not come and was not interested in rescheduling. My impression is that those who participated in the interviews enjoyed them and often said so. I take this as further indication of the fact that they enjoyed discussing US TV.

As per the usual IRB protocols, the names of all of the respondents have been changed, as has any other identifying material. To the extent possible, I tried to keep the comments that respondents made in their own voice, so in some instances the phrasing may sound stilted, or not like standard American English. I also used brackets to distinguish between respondents' comments and my insertions for clarification or to indicate where I probed further.

A General Description of the Foreign-Born Sample

In my foreign-born sample, slightly more than two-thirds of respondents were women, and close to one-third were men; one identified as gay. All had watched US TV prior to coming to the United States. The majority of the sample was single, and only two had children. The mean age was 29. As Figure A.1 indicates, they are a very diverse group in terms of their countries of origin. Interestingly, it is a fairly urban sample; more than two-thirds had been raised in large cities and only a few in small towns or rural areas. The remainder had been raised in a combination of areas, such as in a military compound and then in a large city. A simple majority described the neighborhood that they had primarily grown up in as "mostly White," with the second largest grouping or almost a quarter of the sample indicating that their neighborhoods had been mostly Asian. Only a few reported that their neighborhoods had been mixed racially and ethnically—or religiously.

A large majority (76 percent) indicated that their parents were of the same racial and ethnic backgrounds, but, in some instances, other variables, such as religion or tribe, were viewed as important distinguishing characteristics. All had some college education, with the largest group having earned graduate degrees. Interestingly, many had degrees in the social sciences, mainly in economics, public policy, or administration, while others had graduate degrees in business or in the health professions, natural sciences, or engineering. Only a few had earned degrees in the humanities or fine arts areas. A large proportion (68 percent) consisted of students, manly graduate students, but the remaining 32 percent of the group was working—mainly in professional or management positions, including as software engineers, administrators, visiting faculty, or postdoctoral researchers, or in business or social media.

Somewhat surprising to me, but consistent with the idea that many of those who come to study or work in the United States often came from privileged or middle-class backgrounds, was the fact that their parents were also highly educated and employed at the top tiers of their country's occupational scales. Fully 60 percent of the mothers and 67 percent of the fathers of respondents had earned bachelor's or graduate degrees. The mothers were also employed in a wide variety of upper-level occupations—as professors, chemists, physicists, and psychologists, for example, and in fields such as mechanical engineering, medicine, nursing, and business—with 60 percent being in managerial and professional occupations. A higher proportion of fathers (73 percent) were in this same category, and they too held a wide variety of high-status occupations, with engineers, lawyers, medical doctors, and businessmen being the most prominent.

Consequently, it is not surprising that when asked how they would describe the social class background of their immediate family, 6 percent of my respondents chose wealthy, 21 percent said upper middle class, and 46 percent said middle class—for a total of 73 percent who said their family's class status was middle class or higher. Although a number, especially from former Soviet Republics, indicated that their family's class position changed while they were growing up, no one said their family had been poor, and only four in the whole sample indicated that their families had working-class origins.

My foreign-born respondents also had received an excellent education in their respective countries of origin, an education that often had been in American schools abroad or English-language-oriented schools—which is why I was able to conduct the interviews in English.[3] Thus, with few exceptions, this is a fairly elite sample, skewing to middle- and upper-class backgrounds. Perhaps the exclusivity of this group should not be surprising, for there is a consensus within cross-cultural media consumption research that compared with other social demographics, educated, cosmopolitan-oriented youths are particularly drawn to global media in general and Hollywood storytelling in particular (Gao, 2016). Given that US TV was so predominant in so many countries for such a long time, and given that many came from families that had the resources to access US TV content even when the respondents were young, many did consume a considerable amount of US TV.

Consequently, in addition to the human and cultural capital that is evident in their descriptions of themselves and their families, many also acquired transnational cultural views and a certain cosmopolitan, global perspective. With regard to television's role in creating cosmopolitans, Vertovec and Cohen (2002:6) note that other authors have observed that "routine exposure to global cultural difference through television creates the possibility of people becoming cosmopolitans in their own living rooms." Since little has been written about this relatively new but rapidly growing group of global transnationals,[4] I provide a description of two of my respondents that indicates how their cosmopolitan and transcultural views were acquired.[5]

Global Cosmopolitans, with Transnational Cultural Views

Carmen was a 24-year-old law assistant I approached at a global event, in part because I understood, from both her first and last names, that she might be Latin American or from Spain. As it turned out, she was not quite either, but she reflected, in many ways, the transnational flows of intellectual and cultural capital, images, and ideas that many authors in the literature refer to. She had grown up in Paris, and as she indicated her father was American but had a Spanish surname because his parents were Catholic and from Albuquerque, New Mexico; her mother, who was Protestant, was Asian and German—the German part was by way of upstate New York, where her mother's family had settled. Her parents had met at a university in the United States where one was a lab engineer and the other was pursuing a doctorate in neurobiology. They both worked in Paris: her father was a research scientist, and her mother monitored the economies of other countries. She did not speak Spanish (nor had she spent much time in a Spanish-speaking country), but she was fluent in Italian and had watched movies in Arabic and Hebrew, and, like many others in my sample, she had watched "lots of" US TV shows. She specifically mentioned as favorites Grey's Anatomy, Gossip

Girl, and 24, among others; and she indicated that she watched American shows every day, often downloaded from the Internet or on DVDs she rented. She had been in the United States for four years. Her parents spoke English at their home in Paris and were part of a larger expat community. She classified herself as Other, saying she was a mixture of Asian, Hispanic, and Caucasian in the United States, and that often others in the United States did not know how to classify her and sometimes asked if she was Asian, Afghan, or Hispanic.

Jose provides another example of a global cosmopolitan, but he was originally from Asia. Jose was a 19-year-old undergraduate who had been born and raised in Jakarta, Indonesia, in a mostly Islamic, Asian neighborhood. Both his parents were professionals from the Philippines, and he described his family as being upper middle class. At home they spoke English, but in Indonesia the nannies spoke Indonesian, and he had learned some Spanish and Tagalog while in the Philippines. (Despite his being raised in Indonesia, he had never watched programs from Indonesia because he did not speak the language well enough.) But he was an avid US TV viewer. He attended an international school in Indonesia, where he said his teachers were a mix of US-born and those who had studied in the United States. When he was young, his parents would go back to the Philippines to visit. He said his parents considered themselves Filipino, but "nationality was not important to him." When asked how he would classify himself racially or ethnically, he said "Asian" but added that in the United States people often guessed wrong and took him to be "Hispanic." Part of this may also have been influenced by the fact that his first name was of Spanish origin, as is the case with many Filipinos of the upper classes because of the Philippines' history as a Spanish colony.

These examples also suggest how diverse the backgrounds of my respondents were and what they brought to the common experience they shared of watching US TV. It is also useful to keep in mind that, given their original class backgrounds and their high levels of education, often at selective educational institutions in their home countries and in the United States, my respondents, and others like them, will likely take on significant roles in the future—either in their home countries, if they return, or in the United States, if they stay. Therefore, it is important to know how they view the United States and their countries of origin, and how the long-term and, in some cases, ever-present exposure to US TV content has influenced their views of both the United States and their home countries, especially with regard to race, ethnicity, class, gender, and immigrants.[6] It is important to note that these interviews were conducted before the 2016 US presidential election and the president's executive action temporarily closing US borders to citizens of seven predominantly Muslim countries; and before his plan to build a wall at the Mexican border.

The Sample of US Millennials

I also administered electronically a shorter version of my semistructured questionnaire to 171 US undergraduates, also based in the northeastern United States, in order to see what differences or similarities might exist between the foreign-born group and the US undergraduate group. The undergrads were part of a research participant lab at a medium-sized private university in the Northeast. As part of this research pool, they participated in a battery of IRB-approved surveys and experiments. Data were collected at three points in time during the fall 2014 semester.

This sample differed from the foreign-born sample in a number of ways. In terms of gender, they were more evenly represented, with 51.8 percent female and 48.2 percent male. More (59.2 percent) were from suburban areas, as contrasted with the large-city emphasis of people in the foreign-born sample; and, reflecting their status as undergrads, they were younger, that is, between 19 and 21 years of age (the mean age of those in the foreign-born sample was 29). Interestingly, however, their class backgrounds were not dramatically different, except that the US undergrads reported slightly more class diversity, with more reporting their families as poor (1.2 percent) or working class (18.7 percent), but also with more indicating they were upper middle class (43.9 percent) or wealthy (8.2 percent). In addition, as compared with the foreign-born sample, fewer undergrads described their family's class as middle class (28.1 percent vs. 46 percent in the foreign-born sample). But in both samples more than 73 percent came from families that were predominantly middle class and above (see Figure A.2).

The samples differed somewhat with regard to racial/ethnic self-classification. In the US undergraduate sample, 70.9 percent (117) re-

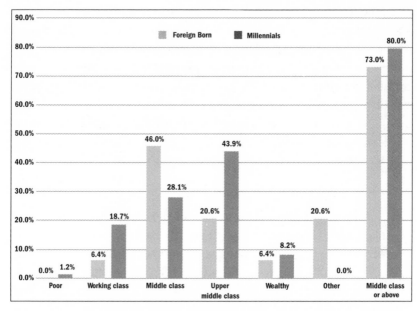

Figure A.2. Social class. Source: Rodríguez (2015).

sponded that they were White, 3 percent Black or African American, 18 percent Asian/Pacific Islander, 16 percent Hispanic/Latino, and 0.6 percent Native American Indian; 2.9 percent (5) chose the "Other, specify" category. In contrast, only 34.9 percent (22) of the foreign-born sample said they were White. Another 11.1 percent said they were Asian/Pacific Islander, 7.5 percent said Hispanic/Latino, and 1.6 percent said Black; none said they were Native American Indian. Fully 77.8 percent (or 49) of the foreign born chose the "Other" category. This is not too surprising given that they came from many different countries with different racial, ethnic, tribal, and religious classification systems.[7]

How I Analyzed the Data: Traditional Data Analysis and Computerized Analysis

Having taught research methods and statistics for a number of years, I was curious to see how the more traditional, textual analysis of qualitative data would match up with a more computerized analysis. In other words, would another researcher, in this case a computer program—Survey Monkey—arrive at the same categories, using the same methodology? So, for each question I did my own traditional, textual data analysis on the qualitative comments provided, and I conducted a "text analysis" of the comments made on each question using the Survey Monkey program. I found that, in some cases, the analyses were similar, but in others they were not. One example of where both analyses arrived at similar categories is with the question about what respondents enjoyed about watching US TV. The categories that I had uncovered with my traditional data analysis were as follows: Production Values, Seeing a Different Lifestyle and/or Culture, Entertaining and/or Funny, To Gain Knowledge, and Access and Limited Options.

The computerized analysis produced similar categories, but they were organized and labeled somewhat differently. For example, in analyzing my sample's responses to the question of why they enjoyed US TV, the computerized analysis produced the following categories: Best of Available Options; Funny: Comedies; Format Light, i.e., Easy to See and Follow; and "A Different World," which meant a way of coming to learn about American culture, people, and landscapes. These categories were similar to what I had arrived at via my more traditional text analysis. However, what was underscored in the computerized analysis were the high number of positive adjectives used to describe why they watched US TV, such as "exciting," "realistic," "authentic," "interesting," and "cool." These upbeat comments accounted for one-third of all responses. Also positive—but this was not so labeled by the computer program—was another 30 percent of comments that cited "superior quality, i.e., well-made, professional quality, money behind them," and "story and character development [were] well-written; could identify with them," which accounted for another 25 percent of the comments and was equivalent to my "Production Values" category. The other categories that the computerized text analysis detected paralleled those I had also uncovered.

Making this comparison between both types of analyses gave me more confidence in both my own analytical abilities and the computer program's ability to find important themes in the qualitative data gathered. In essence, when reviewing and summarizing each analysis, we could see a similar picture. In essence, both analyses showed that the sample's responses reflected a group that had a very positive view of US TV—for a variety of reasons, some of which involved self-interest (i.e., learning a language or a different culture), but many of which celebrated entertainment and "production values."

However I also saw instances of where the computerized analysis did not yield similar or significant categories. For example, in response to the question "Do you think that American television is encouraging or discouraging of the integration of 'Others'?" one of the categories it identified was "television shows," which was rather meaningless; most respondents mentioned that term in answering a question like this, but that term didn't provide any insight into the respondents' views. The computerized text analysis simply counted the number of times a word or phrase was used, and if it was repeated a sufficient number of times, it became a category or a theme. So, I realized that it was important to review each computerized analysis carefully and see if it was a dumb analysis or one that had picked up a significant theme or finding. In analyzing the results of the surveys, I compared and used both approaches, but I was also careful to evaluate the degree to which the computerized analysis was useful.

My Voice and My Approach

In reviewing both the data and the literature, I departed from the approach that some traditional social scientists take in that I inserted or made clear what my own experiences, background, and reactions were, or had been, to what I was reviewing. For example, in reviewing the literature, I discussed my own journey *to* and *through* the media literature. I did this purposely for a number of reasons. One was to make the material more accessible to readers; another was to make clear what my own perspectives and possible biases might be. A third reason was to enliven what can sometimes be a simply boring analysis of the literature or analysis data. This explains to some degree why, when I analyze the data, I may speak in terms of being "surprised" at one result or another, as opposed to speaking in terms of having a hypothesis supported or not. However, in constructing the questionnaire, I was clearly aware of the fact that I was seeking support for, or against, a particular hypothesis, and exploring specific questions.

This study is in many ways quite exploratory; there are very few studies that have examined this area in this way. Moreover, although I did attempt to control for education and age, the study is based on sample data that cannot be generalized to larger populations. Nevertheless, it does provide a number of fascinating insights into the perspectives of both youthful undergrads in the United States and foreign-born, professional young adults who are relatively recent arrivals to the United States, about how watching US TV has influenced their views of the United States, their countries, and issues of race, ethnicity, class, and gender.

Some Definitions

I've clarified that I use the terms "US TV" and "American TV" somewhat interchangeably. However, it should be noted that the terms have a somewhat different resonance for different people. US TV is generally understood to be "American TV" or "American shows" by those in most other countries. Indeed, when I clarified in my interviews that US TV meant American TV, respondents would often light up as if now they really knew what we would be talking about, and they began talking about what I understand US TV to be. I used the term "US TV" because it (1) seemed to be a simple, shorthand way of describing entertainment programming, and (2) it avoided the issue of referring to US television as if it encompassed both South and Central America, and the parts of North America to our north. However, many of the respondents still thought and spoke in terms of "American TV." It should also be noted that even though US TV may be technically more correct, most *US residents* do not think in terms of US TV; to them, it is just TV—and, of course, it is "American." Some people, however, may debate this issue and question the extent to which US TV is not strictly US TV but more global and transnational TV these days.

Since this volume focuses on groups and their representation in the media, I capitalize Whites, Blacks, and Others. And, as per the *Chicago Manual of Style*, I also capitalize Hispanics, Latinas and Latinos, Asians, and other recognized or national origin groups. In terms of who were the "Others," I asked respondents if there were "Others" in their country, and I defined "Others" as groups in their countries who were not recent immigrants to their country but who were seen as different from the general, mainstream population. In other words, the definition was "those who are seen as other than the mainstream population" in any

country. The overwhelming majority (92 percent) of foreign-born respondents said yes and gave examples of "Others" in their countries.

Watching Television versus "Content" on Television

There is sometimes confusion over what is meant when we talk about
TV or television. Some assume that it refers only to watching television
as people did prior to the invention of the Internet and the use of mobile
phones, tablets, and laptops to stream content—in other words, watching scheduled TV programs, often with family members, in one's living
room on a piece of furniture called a TV. This is the way that television
was watched in earlier times, with families gathered around the TV. In
this book, "watching television" refers to watching the *content* in televised, often serialized programs, regardless of whether the content is
accessed via the Internet, DVDs, satellite, or terrestrial television.

Transnationals, Immigrants, Foreign Nationals, or Foreign Born

I considered how to refer to my foreign-born sample. They were not
immigrants because they had not decided to immigrate and stay in the
United States. They were not all transnationals because they were not in
a constant or consistent situation of traveling back and forth from their
home countries to the United States. They could be considered foreign
nationals, but the term "foreign nationals" implies that they or members of their family are working in the United States, but while some in
the sample were full-time professionals working in the United States,
many were full-time students. In addition, the sample is defined by the
number of years they have been in the United States and whether they
watched US TV in their home countries. But referring to the group as
"people who were born elsewhere but have lived in the United States for
six years or less" is a bit cumbersome. So, I settled on the term "foreign
born" as being the most comprehensive, straightforward, and accurate.
In a few cases, when it is applicable to particular respondents, I use the
term "transnational."

Theoretical Perspectives

There are numerous theories in the media literature. Indeed, Graves (1999) notes at least five major theoretical perspectives that seek to explain how or why television influences viewers. I did not follow one particular theoretical orientation or attempt to replicate other works with a particular theoretical perspective. Rather I took an inductive approach to analyzing the data to see what generalizations could be derived. And when applicable, I did discuss the findings in relation to relevant theoretical perspectives. Some of the theoretical frameworks most relevant to this work were the following: Gerbner's Cultivation Theory, the Drench Hypothesis, and the Uses and Gratifications Model.

Gerbner's Cultivation Theory argues that the more people watch TV, the more likely they are to believe that what they see on TV and what is portrayed on television is an accurate reflection of social reality. Consequently, within this perspective, television exercises a significant influence on viewers' attitudes, beliefs about society, and ideas and perceptions of everyday life. A few authors have also argued that television viewing does influence people's biases toward others and toward themselves, especially if they have limited personal experiences with such groups (see, for example, Graves, 1999; Alexandrin, 2009; Persson and Musher-Eizenman, 2003; and Holtzman and Sharpe, 2014). However, the Drench Hypothesis maintains that when you have *both* positive and negative portrayals, the negative portrayals are diminished. Each of these perspectives was helpful in explaining much of the data.

Then there is the Uses and Gratifications Model, according to which viewers exercise preferences when viewing television. According to some scholars, this is currently the most prevalent theory, for it focuses on the motivations viewers have to seek particular media. A number of authors cited in this volume subscribe to this theory, and I used this framework on occasion.

Constructivism, which reasons that viewers bring something to what they view, is yet another theoretical approach. This perspective underlies the discussions in this volume that address how respondents' prior experiences in their home countries influence what they take away from US TV in terms of race, class, and gender. A final theoretical approach that's relevant to this work is Social Cognitive Theory, which claims that viewers imitate what they see on TV. This perspective is useful in explaining why people in other countries imitate and desire the American brand, especially as that brand is projected on US TV.

A Final Note

Good interviews are two-way streets, with respondents and interviewers both learning, and this was the case in all of the interviews that I conducted—even among those interviews that seemed uneventful. No matter how routine, repetitive, or unremarkable the interview might have seemed at the time, upon reflection and review, I always felt that I had gained some knowledge or insight. Sometimes I realized my lack of knowledge at the start of the interview. This happened when I interviewed my first African interviewee. My experience reflected how little I knew about Africa—and how much I, too, was a captive of media representations. For example, I did not know that Abuja was the capital of Nigeria. I knew that many Nigerians I had met spoke English, but I did not really appreciate that English was one of several languages commonly spoken in the country. I also knew there were different groups in Nigeria, for example, the Ibu and Yoruba, but I did not think about how they interacted with each other, where they lived, what religions they practiced, or how this might influence their interactions. At other times, the interviews took me on a discovery trip, for example, to better understand the history, geography, and languages of the Baltics, Moldova, the former Soviet Republics, and a few areas that I had never heard of before. I take this moment to thank all of those who participated in these amazing interviews and who taught me so much.

NOTES

INTRODUCTION

1 *The Eye* is the magazine of the *Columbia Daily Spectator*. The article was written by Wilfred Chan and titled "The China Game" (February 21, 2013). Columbia University is located on the Upper West Side of Manhattan.

2 In conducting my study, I expressly used the term "US TV" as a way of acknowledging that the United States is just one part of the "Americas"—there being both South and Central America to the south and Canada to the north. However, much of the literature and most of my respondents consistently referred to what I called US TV as "American TV." So I use both terms in this volume.

3 See, for example, Beltrán (2002, 2004, 2005), Children Now (1998, 2001, 2004), Cortés (2000), Entman (2006), Garcia Berumen (1995), Hall (1981), Hoffman and Noriega (2004), Hunt and Ramon (2015), Kennedy (2011), Lichter and Amundson (1994), Lopez (1991), Mastro and Behm-Morawitz (2005), Mastro and Robinson (2000), Mastro and Tukachinsky (2011), Mendible (2007), Merskin (2011), Montalvo and Torres (2006), National Hispanic Foundation for the Arts (2001), Navarrete and Kamasaki (1994), Negrón-Muntaner et al. (2014), Noriega (1992, 1997), Ramírez Berg (1997, 2002), Rodríguez (1997, 2004, 2008a), Shohat and Stam (1994), Siegemund-Broka (2015), Signorielli, Milke, and Katzman (1985), US Kerner Commission (1968), Valdivia (2000), Williams (1997), Wilson and Gutierrez (1985, 1995).

   Indeed, the recent study by Smith, Choueiti, and Pieper (2016) continued to find that "Hollywood has a diversity problem." Their analysis included 10 major media companies and prime-time first-run scripted series and digital offerings airing from September 2014 to August 2015. Reviewing the prevalence on-screen of racial and ethnic characters who have speaking roles, series regulars, and leads ($N = 10,444$ characters) on film, broadcast, cable, and streaming platforms, they concluded: "No platform presents a profile of race/ethnicity that matches proportional representation in the US" (16). Moreover, despite the many gains of women in various fields, women are still not equally represented with men on US television or film.

4 For an analysis of similar patterns in US films, see Smith, Choueiti, and Pieper (2013), who find in their review of the top 100 grossing films between 2007 and 2012 that only 10 percent of the characters in these most popular films were Black, Hispanic, Asian, and Other or Mixed. Yet between 2000 and 2010, these groups

together composed between 32 and 36 percent of the US population, with much larger percentages in large urban areas, like New York City and Los Angeles, where many films were set. In addition, 75 percent of the speaking characters in these films were White. Females were underrepresented in every group, with Hispanic females "more likely to be depicted in sexy attire and partially naked than Black or White females," while Asian females were less likely to be sexualized. They also found little deviation over the five-year period that they studied.

A similar pattern was found for cable news programs. A 2014 analysis of these programs also found White male guests to dominate across CNN, Fox, and MSNBC, with some groups particularly underrepresented. For example, Latinos, who made up 16 percent of the US population at the time, accounted for just 3 percent of the sources; and women of color, who made up 18 percent of the US population, accounted for just 5 percent of sources across the networks. Even on the more liberal show *Democracy Now*, sources were 79 percent White and 60 percent male. See FAIR (2014) and Zorita-Sierra and Sanchez (2012).

There was, however, some good news about women in television. There was an increase in the percentage of female producers and directors on network television shows (Gibson, 2014). It was also found that when more women are on the creative team, more women appear in TV and film ("When Women Are on the Creative Team," 2014).

5 When we say that race and gender are socially constructed or invented, we are saying that the importance of race and gender has less to do with physical attributes and more to do with "society's interpretation of what it means to be a member of a particular gender or racial/ethnic group" (Ryan, 2010:54, quoting Lind, 2010:6). Increasingly many in the social sciences prefer viewing others through an intersectionality perspective. This means seeing others not just as Black or White, or as male and female, but as the result of a combination of many additional experiences—some of which we share with them—for example, class background, age, religious beliefs, music, sports, literary preferences, etc.

6 The Minuteman Project is an activist organization started in August 2004 by a group of private individuals in the United States to monitor the US-Mexico border's flow of illegal immigrants.

7 In some cases, employers who hire undocumented workers net higher profits and incur fewer expenses for labor costs.

8 See, however, Wayne (2015), who investigates the diverse ways in which US middle-class adults continue to watch TV content while inventing linguistic devices (e.g., attaching, conveying, or manipulating class inflections) to distinguish their watching of post-network television content from that of mass watching of "Boob Tube" programming.

9 They also therefore brought the greatest amount in ad revenues, with advertising costs still higher for TV than for any other media. As the *Economist* ("Hollywood: Split Screens," 2013:61) points out, "TV networks earn money from advertising

and from the fees that cable and satellite operators pay to carry their programs. These fees amount to some $32 billion a year in America, and are growing by about 7% annually. People love watching TV, and, per hour, it is one of the cheapest forms of entertainment." See also *Adweek* ("Hottest Broadcast Network: CBS," 2011:30–34), which describes actual ad rates for different programs.

10 Nielsen's ranking of the top 25 cable programs for the week ending June 10, 2012, showed that the highest rated non-sports, non-reality show, *Rizzoli & Isles* on TNT, was number 8, netting only 5,620,000 viewers. *True Blood* at number 10 (HBO) netted 5,201,000. Data from "Nielsen Television, TV Ratings for Primetime, 2011–12 Season to Date" (data in the author's possession). Nielsen ratings for a random week ending March 22, 2015, showed a decline across the board, but the top network shows, including *Empire, Dancing with the Stars, The Voice, 60 Minutes,* and *Madam Secretary,* still showed audiences ranging from 10.8 million to 17.6 million viewers (Levin, 2015:2D).

11 However, there is still a debate as to whether TV viewing is diminishing or just changing as viewer demographics change. As youths switch to nontraditional outlets for content, older demographics are consuming more TV on their sets. As the *Economist* ("Media's Ageing Audiences," 2011) noted, the median age of viewers of *CSI, Desperate Housewives,* and *American Idol* got older from 2001 to 2011; *American Idol* had the lowest median age of the three shows, *CSI* the oldest. Advertisers were not concerned about this trend, the article noted, because older fans have more money and tend not to download content illegally, either because they have scruples or because they see it as "too much work." There is also the issue of "Peak TV," a point at which there are more television program options than people can consume, which may influence viewers to watch what is most popular or accessible (see "Winner Takes All," 2017).

12 This also includes the use of YouTube and various forms of social media.

13 Some individuals also tune in to TV programs to see what people are tweeting about.

14 In this book, I use both terms interchangeably, and I am referring to the *content,* not the method of delivery. So *Madam Secretary* and *Scandal* are both television shows, whether they are seen on a television set or via the Internet. Some assume that programs on the Internet are not television, but that is not the case in this volume.

15 See, for example, the study conducted by the Associated Press and the NORC Center for Public Affairs Research (2014) with a nationally representative telephone survey of 1,492 adults from January 9 to February 16, 2014, which found that 87 percent of Americans utilize television to follow the news. However, this is changing rapidly and varies from country to country. In 2015, the Reuters Institute for the Study of Journalism (2016) survey used weighted online samples (of more than 1,500) in each of 10 countries and found that those in the United States mainly used online sources for their news. Additionally, this latter survey found that respondents in France, Germany, Italy, Japan, Spain, and the United

Kingdom still relied on television for their news, while those in Australia, Brazil, Denmark, Finland, and Ireland relied more on online sources for their news. This latter study also found substantial generational differences, with younger people using online sources more frequently than TV to access the news (Reuters Institute, 2016). To some degree, the differences between the two studies cited here might also be explained by the nature of the samples, i.e., a telephone sample versus an online sample.

16 The "digital divide" refers to the division between those who have ready access to computers and the Internet, and those who do not. On one side of this divide are those individuals or countries with greater income, education, and access to the tools and infrastructure supporting new technology, and on the other side are those with less access, income, and education.

17 Although the debate revolves around the rate at which Internet viewing will grow, many agree that Netflix has transformed how television is made and how we consume it.

18 See Kim (2016) for an interesting analysis of the stereotypical representation of Asian characters on the popular, and some say progressive, show *Orange Is the New Black*. As Kim notes, the show "is no different from other shows, as it fails to challenge stereotypical images of racial minorities" (10).

19 To some degree this may also be influenced by the lack of gender and racial and ethnic diversity at the top tech companies. For example, in 2015, the proportion of Blacks *and* Hispanics was 6 percent or less of total employees at Google, Facebook, Twitter, and Pinterest. Other companies fared a bit better, but none reflected population proportions. Asians were overrepresented at all of the companies. With regard to women, Twitter was only 30 percent female in 2014, as was Google in 2015. Intel had an even lower percentage of women, i.e., 24 percent, in 2015. Pinterest had the highest proportion of women, with 42 percent. The other companies fell somewhere in between this high and the Intel low. The proportion of women was as follows: Apple, 31 percent; Facebook, 32 percent; and Amazon, 37 percent (in 2014). The numbers cited come from the chart "By the Numbers: How Diversity Adds Up at Some of the Top Tech Companies" cited in Vara (2015). The data in that chart come from the companies themselves—all of them have publicly reported on the diversity of their workforces.

20 In September 2015, Nielsen, the major TV ratings company, tracked viewers who watched a single TV episode "live, as well as those who used DVRs, video-on-demand services, connected TVs, and computers and mobile devices" for 35 days and found that "across all demographics, 45% of viewers caught the show live." However, it was the youngest viewers (18–24) who were more likely to watch the episode live. Only the young adults (25–34) were more likely to watch on a computer or mobile device (Laporte, 2016a:28).

21 Source: Graham (2002). What effect might such intense devotion to TV have? An interesting study of general TV use in 25 European societies confirmed the Putnam hypothesis: that increased TV time consumption had substantial nega-

tive effects on individual social trust. However, high market shares of public TV increased social trust. The study was based on data from the 2002 and 2004 waves of the European Social Survey (ESS) in combination with aggregate data from telemetric audience research (Schmitt-Beck and Wolsing, 2010).

22 These data are based on a poll of 15,551 adults in 20 countries conducted by Ipsos, a market and public opinion research firm (Ipsos, 2014).

23 The EU was created by treaty in 1992, but it evolved from the Council of the European Community and other organizations, such as the European Economic Community (ECC) (Jones, 1997; see also European Commission, 2008). Of particular concern was the imbalance of trade in this sphere.

24 According to Arango (2008), in 2000 major European networks broadcast about 214,000 hours of American programming per year. By 2006, this had increased by nearly 50,000 hours to more than 266,000 hours per year. It should be noted, however, that despite the general increase in US TV viewing, the member countries vary considerably with regard to the amount of television airtime that is occupied by European and non-European production. For example, in 2006, European productions accounted for 80.9 percent of total airtime in Denmark, 73.3 percent in France, but only 53 percent in the United Kingdom and 45.4 percent in Sweden (European Audiovisual Observatory, 2011).

25 European Audiovisual Observatory (2011: band 2, 169). The Council of Europe is part of the executive branch of the European Union.

26 See also Gibbons and Humphreys (2012) on the impact of government regulation, new media technology, and globalization on the television sectors in France, Germany, the United Kingdom, and Canada. They also cover the impact of nonregulation in the United States and the development of "quota quickies," i.e., programs produced quickly and cheaply in some countries "without much (if any) regard for their content and broadcast merely to fulfil quota obligations" (143).

27 In the literature there are also concerns regarding television's effects on its passive recipients—especially among the young, both in the United States and abroad. As Breitschaft (2009:292) notes, "Once the consumer has actively selected a video, he or she becomes passive again and potentially captured by the influencing moving images."

28 In all, 79 percent believed this—although only 30 percent completely agreed with this view, and 66 percent said they liked the pace of modern life. These interviews were conducted from April 15 to May 27, 2015, by the Pew Research Center (see Wike and Parker, 2015). An earlier study by the Pew Research Global Attitudes Study found that among the 20 countries surveyed, only 4 had majorities that said they did not like American movies, music, and TV. These were Pakistan, Turkey, Egypt, and Jordan. However, not all predominantly Islamic countries are the same. In Lebanon, 6 in 10 Sunni Muslims were positive about US media, as were almost half of Lebanon's Shia Muslims (Wike, 2013).

29 "Diasporic programming" refers to the creation of programs in the receiving country that are based on the home countries of immigrants. For example, Univi-

sion, Telemundo, and others create or show programs in Spanish or in Spanglish for people in the United States from Spanish-speaking countries.

30 See Wike (2013), who, speaking more generally of Hollywood film, argues that "Tinseltown is actually pretty effective at nudging America's international image in a positive direction."

31 Other programs that may be seen as quintessentially "American" were actually birthed elsewhere, e.g., *Shark Tank*, *American Idol*, *Antiques Roadshow*, *Weakest Link*, *Wife Swap*, *Supernanny*, and *Being Human*. See Michalski (2013).

32 There is also public programming in the United States, but American TV is overwhelmingly commercial.

33 And, as Wolff (2015) has noted, despite the changes in electronic technologies, television is still about making money, and it is still making money.

34 It should be noted that Nye (2004) defined soft power as the ability to attract and persuade; he identified three broad categories of soft power: culture, political values, and policies. For him, and for many others, soft power can also imply intentionality on the part of the state. But in my work, the term "soft power" refers more to the effect that watching US TV has had on my respondents than to intentional state policies oriented toward a political goal. Because US TV is such a commercial medium, its "soft power" is more the result of business/corporate interests, not political goals or intent.

35 On the extent to which different countries have become more globalized, see KOF (2015), which has a list of countries in terms of where they rank on this globalization scale.

36 This growth in international students at US educational institutions is part of a global "mass trend," as "[m]ore university and college students than ever are studying outside their home countries" ("Brains without Borders," 2016:51).

37 The Trump administration's policies on immigration, refugees, and the building of a wall at the Mexican border may affect future trends regarding the growing number of international students, faculty, researchers, and other professionals who visit or collaborate with US colleagues. On the impact of such policies, see the February 2, 2017, letter sent to President Trump, drafted by the presidents of Princeton University and the University of Pennsylvania and signed by 46 other presidents of American colleges and universities (including all of the Ivy League schools), which urges him "to rectify or rescind the recent executive order closing our country's borders." On the value of "law-abiding students and scholars from the affected regions," they add:

> Their innovations and scholarship have enhanced American learning, added to our prosperity, and enriched our culture. Many who have returned to their own countries have taken with them the values that are the lifeblood of our democracy. America's educational, scientific, economic, and artistic leadership depends upon our continued ability to attract the extraordinary people who for many generations have come to this country in search of freedom and a better life. ("Eisgruber, Other University Presidents," 2017)

38 This report is published annually by the Institute of International Education in partnership with the US Department of State's Bureau of Educational and Cultural Affairs. The two entities have been producing the report together since 1972. Contributing to the growth potential is that many foreign students are seen by some universities as an increasingly lucrative market, for about two-thirds pay their own way, and most aren't eligible for US government aid programs. In addition, many colleges charge them additional fees (Porter and Belkin, 2013; see also Brown et al., 2014).

39 According to the *Wall Street Journal*, the top four US universities enrolling the most international students—the University of Southern California, the University of Illinois at Urbana-Champaign, Purdue University, and New York University—each drew more than 9,000 foreign students in 2012–13. California for the second year in a row hosted more than 100,000 international students, the most of any state, followed by New York, with both New York University and Columbia showing large numbers of international students. Texas, Massachusetts, and Illinois also had large numbers, and the University of Pennsylvania and the University of California, Berkeley entered the top 20 list in 2012–13 (Porter and Belkin, 2013).

40 India was ranked second, with 96,754; South Korea third, with 70,627; Saudi Arabia fourth, with 44,566; and Canada fifth, with 27,357 (Institute of International Education, 2013). According to Porter and Belkin (2013), in 2012 there were 235,597 Chinese students in the United States. Although there are 4,000 accredited colleges in the United States, nearly 70 percent of international students are concentrated in 200 schools (Institute of International Education, 2013).

CHAPTER 1. THE GLOBAL TELEVISION LANDSCAPE LITERATURE

1 Although this quote is often attributed to Marshall McLuhan, some dispute this and say that it was actually written by Father John Culkin, SJ, a professor of communication at Fordham University in New York and friend of McLuhan's ("We Shape Our Tools," 2013).

2 McLuhan's work was dismissed by many then and is still dismissed today; however, it did succeed in drawing attention to the issue and in making many think about how what he said applied to them.

3 See "What We Can Do" in Rodríguez (1997:261–69) for a listing of possible strategies to make changes.

4 Fordham has always attracted a lot of students interested in the media—in part because it is located in the middle of the New York City media world. It is surrounded by the corporate offices of major US TV networks and other media conglomerates.

5 See here Ang (1985), Bielby and Harrington (2008), De Bens, Kelly, and Bakke (1992), De Bens and de Smaele (2001), Elasmar (2003), Hertsgaard (2002), Liebes and Katz (1990). Other authors also wrote about these issues but gave more attention to issues of race and difference. These include Hall (1981), Shohat and Stam (1994), and Signorielli, Milke, and Katzman (1985).

6 He never formally studied any Asian culture and did not speak their languages. He had spent eight months a year at a boarding school in England and four months at a home in California—in an Indian household. That was the extent of his international/intercultural experience when he embarked upon the book.

7 It was one of the last languages that the Bible had not been translated into. As Suskind (2001) notes, he was sent "to advance the mandate of the Wycliffe Bible Translators, also known as SIL International (derived from its original name, Summer Institute of Linguistics)." The organization sent missionaries trained in linguistics to the most remote corners of the world, places that did not yet have written language; their mission was to construct a written language from an ancient spoken tongue, teach the indigenous population to read, translate the entire New Testament (and portions of the Old) into the people's "mother tongue," and then give copies of their translation to one and all. They maintained that this was the best way to spread God's word.

8 See the following for a variety of views—from historians to anthropologists to journalists and poets—speaking to this same experience: Higham (1994), Kalam (2003), Robles (1972), Smedley (2007), and Takaki (1994).

9 Much of the work done, particularly on patterns with regard to race, class, and gender in US TV, was covered earlier. But it should be noted that at the same time that the more recent works being reviewed here were being conducted, the two major theoretical media perspectives, i.e., Social Learning Theory and Cultivation Theory, were also being reexamined in terms of how the Internet had affected these theories. For example, the concept of multiple identities was introduced because of the rapid increase in the social relations that people acquire because new and various groups and individuals are now part of their worlds (see Jeffres et al., 2011:103–6). For a broader view of the history of television studies, see Gray and Lotz (2012).

10 As noted earlier, this was part of the concern that led to the passage of the Television without Frontiers Directive by the European Union in 1989.

11 Dallas (1978–91) was an American prime-time television drama about a wealthy, feuding family in Dallas, Texas, who owned an oil company and a cattle ranch.

12 Ugochukwu (2008) also reviewed studies testing the cultural imperialism thesis in various countries and found "inconclusive results." This included studies conducted in Greece, Korea, northern Belize, and Israel. He concluded that this was, in part, due to researchers using different variables to assess the impact of US media. His own experimental study of 482 high school students in Nigeria, which sought to isolate and examine the impact of such variables as knowledge, beliefs, attitudes, behaviors, and values, also did not find strong support for the cultural imperialism thesis. He found limited effects, with acquisition of knowledge about the United States being the main influence.

13 Straubhaar (2007) also looked at the creation of global media firms (chap. 4) and how national or local producers have worked within cultural industries to pro-

duce TV (chap. 6). In addition, he interviewed viewers who often described the multilayered areas of interest and identity to which he alluded (see chaps. 8 and 9). Finally, he examined the roles and impacts of technology (chap. 5); however, when he was writing, mobile phones had not yet affected media viewing.

14 The period of review was 1962 to 2001. The countries that Straubhaar reviewed were Brazil, Chile, Columbia, Mexico, and Venezuela in Latin America; Australia, Canada, Ireland, New Zealand, the United Kingdom, and the United States in the Anglophone world; China, Hong Kong, India, Japan, South Korea, and Taiwan in East Asia; France and Italy in Europe; Israel and Lebanon in the Middle East; and Cameroon and Nigeria in Africa. He also included French Canadian programming as part of Europe and Hispanic (Latino) programming in the United States as part of Latin America (see Straubhaar, 2007:259–66).

15 Other authors have also focused on international media markets. For example, Havens (2006) and Kuipers (2012) both focused on the relationships between buyers and sellers in the international program market. Both studies are well worth reading to gather insight into how and why particular programs are picked up in different countries. However, since this volume is concerned more with consumers of international television rather than with the players in the markets, I will focus on Straubhaar, whose work concentrates on issues of consumption.

16 This is how I understand his use of the term "cultural proximity." However, in using this term to refer to television in Eastern Europe, Štětka (2012a:159) defines it as "the common attraction audiences feel for cultural products . . . that are close in cultural content & style to the audience's own cultures."

17 Interestingly, Univision, the huge Spanish-language television network that operates in the United States, the Caribbean, and Latin America, used a similar concept when they conducted their study of the viewing habits and preferences of Hispanics (18–34) in the United States. However, they called it the "cultural connection" and created the Cultural Connection Index (CCI) to measure and evaluate viewers' responses. They found that 62 percent of the group surveyed scored high or in the middle range on the index. The study's authors argued that their results showed how culture deeply influences those millennials across social interactions, attitudes, purchasing behaviors, technological usage, and media consumption (Univision Communications, 2012).

18 See, for example, Kraidy (2005), who describes what often emerges as a strongly localized/hybridized adaptation of global patterns.

19 As noted previously, "diasporic media" refers to the creation of media based on the home countries of immigrants.

20 See, for example, Malik (2010).

21 See Straubhaar's (2007:6ff.) discussion of the media viewed by Mexican immigrant families.

22 For excellent analyses of these various sources, see Dávila (2012), Dávila and Rivero (2014), and Rojas and Piñón (2014).

23 He uses the Islamic term "Jihad" to refer to a generic form of fundamentalist opposition to modernity that can be found not only among Muslims but also in many world religions (Barber, 2001:205).

CHAPTER 2. BUILDING ON PREVIOUS STUDIES IN THE UNITED STATES AND OTHER COUNTRIES

1 See chapter 6, "Mutual Aid in the Decoding of Dallas," of Liebes and Katz (1990).
2 Gender differences in viewing preferences also increased with age among many of my respondents.
3 See Liebes and Katz (1990: chap. 7).
4 See Liebes and Katz (1990: chap. 8).
5 See Liebes and Katz (1990: chap. 9).
6 This may have also been the case with Brazil, but it was not part of their study.
7 As Gao (2016) demonstrates, this is a concept that is still alive and well today among urban, educated Chinese youths viewing TV.
8 Another issue that was addressed in this study was how dubbing and subtitles change the meaning and reception of the programs watched. I did not specifically ask my respondents about this, but the issue did surface in some of the interviews with my foreign-born respondents.
9 Although some authors studied the impact of international TV coverage, Ward, O'Regan, and Goldsmith (2010) analyzed the reverse question, i.e., why Australian soaps continued to be successful in Australia despite the onslaught of US or global TV.
10 See, for example, Eisend (2010), Steinhagen, Eisend, and Knoll (2010), Franco (2008), and Kavka (2003). On immigrants and otherness, see Aalberg and Strabac (2010), Olmos and Garrido (2012), Ardizzoni (2005), Hargreaves and Perotti (1993), Igartua, Barrios, and Ortega (2012), and Jacobs, Claes, and Hooghe (2015). On policies and practices in Canada, the Netherlands, and Switzerland, see D'Haenens (2011:375); on newscasts on TV and radio in the German-speaking part of Switzerland in 2007, see Signer, Puppis, and Piga (2011); on the representation of minority groups in the main newspapers and television news broadcasts of *all member states* in the EU, see ter Wal (2004). Finally, Davis and Sosnovskaya (2009) focused on Russian newspapers and found evidence of group hierarches.
11 For analyses of gender, race, and otherness in reality shows in New Zealand, see Kavka (2003), and for an analysis of the US reality show *The Biggest Loser*, see Folsom and Castro (2015).
12 See, for example, European Commission (2009) and Frachon, Vargaftig, and Briot (1994), who surveyed 15 countries in Europe on differing national responses to issues of ethnicity, cultural diversity, and migration, and the media's handling of such matters. See also ter Wal (2002), who presented an overview of research and examples of good practice in 6 EU countries from 1995 to 2000.
13 For work on the identity of the children of immigrants, see Crul, Schneider, and Lelie (2012) and Kesler and Schwartzman (2015).

14 For me, the underresearched question is, how possible or useful are such "multiple identities" for *visible* minority populations in these countries? And does this imply the need to discard those features that can be altered, e.g., wearing hijabs?

15 The German commercial was backed and coordinated by private companies and leading economic professionals. It was shown on most public German TV stations in 2005 and 2006 (Haag, 2010:339).

16 This issue has been covered extensively, but for an overview of European and non-European countries, see the *Economist*, April 27 ("Social Policies," 2013), March 9 ("How Other Minorities Cope," 2013), August 10 ("Hungary's Roma," 2013), and August 31 ("Racism in Italy," 2013:44), and German Marshall Fund (2013), which highlights the issue as one of continuing concern.

17 He cites here German Chancellor Angela Merkel, British Prime Minister David Cameron, and French President Nicolas Sarkozy, who had all taken turns attacking state multiculturalism in 2010 and 2011 (Prey, 2011:110).

18 See, for example, Aalberg and Strabac (2010) and the German Marshall Fund (2013), which randomly sampled 1,000 respondents (18 and over) in each of 13 countries (in 2011 and 2013) on their views of immigration. In addition to the EU as a whole, the countries sampled were France, Germany, Italy, the Netherlands, Poland, Portugal, Romania, Slovakia, Spain, Sweden, Turkey, the United Kingdom, and the United States.

19 For my foreign-born sample, I asked before and after questions, e.g., how much US TV they watched before they came to the United States and how much they watched after they came to the country.

CHAPTER 3. ENJOYING AMERICAN TV BEFORE COMING TO AMERICA

1 These categories are not too dissimilar from those noted earlier by Marghalani, Palmgreen, and Boyd (1998), when they surveyed 495 people in Saudi Arabia about why they had chosen to watch satellite TV. They found that they had traditional motives, such as entertainment, relaxation, and social utility. They noted the 24-hour-a-day availability of satellite TV, greater choice with regard to content, and greater control over when they accessed the TV. They also noted that some respondents had what they termed an "intercultural information motive," which involved a "need to know" something. Another motive, they wrote, was the ability to see women on TV—women were banned from appearing on government TV.

A study by James (2003) also noted similar reasons for the popularity and abundance of (cheaper) US media in Hungary, where television was the major source of entertainment and relaxation. However, she also cautioned against assuming that this meant wholescale Americanization of Hungarians and the displacement of their traditional values and local traditions. In particular, she noted that, perhaps for geographic and historical reasons, cultural synthesis is viewed as an "inevitable process," but it is not without Hungarians' cultural or critical assessment of what is being imported.

2 The other categories were mentioned at about the same rate, i.e., the degree to which they were mentioned did not vary greatly.

3 US TV is not the only TV with good production values. TV in South Korea is also highly developed, as is British TV. Indeed, like the United Kingdom, South Korea exports its programs to other countries, including Spanish-speaking countries, and this programming is also popular there (see one entertainment marketing website's coverage of this phenomenon: "With Korean Dramas Booming," 2014).

However, Garcia (2007) notes that many South Koreans have also become fans of American dramas, and these shows have become so popular that the term "midjob," which combines the Korean words for "American drama" and "clan," is used to describe the craze. Garcia, in accounting for this craze, notes features and reasons similar to those that were mentioned by respondents in my foreign-born sample, e.g., dissatisfaction with homegrown dramas because of tired story lines and seeing American shows as having better story lines and scripts. Also, people liked the shows because they were unpredictable, were large in scale, and covered different regions and topics. In addition, South Koreans felt "they pulled you in, demand your entire attention." For some, the shows were a way to improve their English. And, like some in my sample, some accessed the shows from the Internet, where there were also "fan cafes" and online communities dedicated to American shows, with more than 100,000 members. Some also watched the shows from pirated DVDs.

4 An article in the *Economist* ("Film and Television," 2015) indicated that in China in 2015, "All films and TV shows are vetted by a government committee." *Prison Break* is a US TV show.

5 The multilingual nature of the sample was impressive. Not only did they speak English well, they had also mastered other languages.

6 Habitus as used here refers to people's social and class environment and how their milieu influences the way they perceive the social worlds to which they are connected—either personally or via the Internet. Their habitus also influences and reflects the way they are socialized (i.e., their individual and social experiences), and their objective opportunities.

7 For example, a couple of respondents noted that professors teaching English in their home countries would often use US TV programs in the classroom. They were "a teaching tool/material," one male undergrad from China said, "to show the way real people talk and students understand American humor."

CHAPTER 4. THE IMPACT OF AMERICAN TELEVISION

1 When respondents referred to having gone to an American school, they meant that many of the teachers were American and that they taught American English and also utilized American literature and materials. They did not indicate whether the schools were affiliated with larger US institutions. Respondents referred to "American schools" often, and I came to see them as "academies" that were

acknowledged by the middle and upper classes as the "best places" to prepare students for higher education and perhaps life in the United States.

2 David later admitted that he watched more US TV than many of his fellow Colombians; only a small percentage (less than 10 percent) of the Colombian population watched US TV content according to David. He also indicated that he did watch some Colombian programming, in particular the telenovelas, but he watched them with his family, and did so mainly as a way of being with his family, not because he preferred watching those shows. See Barrera and Bielby (2001) on the role that "novelas" play in structuring family time.

3 He noted, in particular, the ads for Red Lobster, the restaurant chain, which displayed fresh, appetizing, delicious-looking lobsters.

4 Others include *Rugrats, Garfield, Popeye, Captain Planet, Powerpuff Girls, Gummi Bears, Mister Rogers' Neighborhood, Flash Gordon, Lassie, Teenage Mutant Ninja Turtles, Tarzan, The Bad News Bears, The Simpsons, Rescue 911, Gilligan's Island,* and *Knight Rider* (known in Spanish as *El Auto Frantástico*).

5 Other shows mentioned include *Friends, Sex and the City, Heroes, The Young and the Restless, The Phil Donahue Show, Full House, The Bold and the Beautiful, Baywatch, Fame, Family Matters, Dallas, Melrose Place, The X-Files,* and *Prison Break*.

6 Some US TV programs were viewed in English, but with subtitles in another language. An interesting example of how different generations dealt with the use of subtitles in exported US TV is found in the response to this question by a female grad student from Peru. She said that while watching *Dawson's Creek*, she and her sister listened to shows in English, "and my mother read the Spanish subtitles."

7 It should also be noted that most of these interviews took place in the BT period, i.e., before the Twitter protests of #oscarsowhite or #hollywoodsowhite.

8 The median was 4.00, with a standard deviation of 1.20.

CHAPTER 5. NO WAY!

1 Non-Hispanic Whites constituted 62.2 percent of the total US population in 2014 (Colby and Ortman, 2015).

2 As noted earlier, according to Holtzman and Sharpe (2014:xvi), this is "regardless of the platform, time of day, network, or program selected."

3 I am indebted to one of my anonymous reviewers for these vivid descriptions.

4 There were 95 questions, but I say *more* than 90 as I often added probes to my questions.

5 This last media category included comments about how the racial and ethnic variations in lifestyles and residential areas they observed upon arrival had not been evident in the US TV or US films they had seen.

6 Some respondents gave more than one response to this question.

7 According to the *New York Times*, as of January 9, 2017, "all New York City subway stations had cellphone service and free Wi-Fi connectivity." See "Wi-Fi and Cellphone Service" (2017).

8 According to Sam Roberts (2010:A1), "while there is no precise count, some experts believe New York is home to as many as 800 languages—far more than the 176 spoken by students in the city's public schools or the 138 that residents of Queens, New York's most diverse borough, listed on their 2000 census forms."

9 She did not indicate who had told her this.

10 The hashtag #oscarsowhite represented a movement, which included celebrities, that protested and lamented the fact that so few African Americans had been nominated. See Blades (2016), who expanded on this and pointed out that Black people were not the only ones "being snubbed," as members of other racial and ethnic groups were overlooked as well.

11 The remainder (19.3 percent) articulated other views or had no opinion on the matter, but close to 80 percent had a comment to make on this question.

CHAPTER 6. SAY WHAT?

1 There were a number of respondents who included more than one reason. To some degree, responses in categories 2 and 3 overlapped, so in terms of the category that netted the greatest number of responses, this "combined category" of "too narrow or too exclusionary" would have been the one most often mentioned.

2 The respondent may have been making a comparative statement here, saying perhaps that the American Dream was still more possible in the United States than in Brazil at that time. For she also alluded to the issue of language and who is American when she responded to this question. She said that in Brazil, everyone referred to the United States as America, even though Brazilians were aware they were part of the Americas too. She seemed to suggest, albeit somewhat sadly, that the idea of achieving the American Dream could be conceptualized and implemented outside of US borders, but perhaps not at this point in time.

3 Her father was Slovenian and Catholic, from an upper middle-class family, and her mother was mostly Serbian and from a working-class background.

4 Macau is somewhat like the city of Hong Kong in that it functioned as a somewhat independent country, but it was handed back to China in 1999 under the same "one country, two systems" policy that saw Hong Kong gifted back to China in 1997. Under the agreement signed by Portugal and China, Macau is guaranteed its own monetary system, immigration controls, and legal system.

5 The issue of how to racially classify oneself within the US biracial context, i.e., the White and non-White schema, came up a few times with Latin American respondents. For more on this issue, see Rodríguez, López, and Argeros (2015), Rodríguez, Miyawaki, and Argeros (2013), and Rodríguez (2000).

6 Social psychologist Deaux (2006) also finds that although race plays a limited role in the West Indies, it becomes more relevant to migrants in the United States, where they are primarily identified by others as Black, rather than Guyanese or Jamaican.

CHAPTER 7. TV MATTERS

1 Because millennials have been described as being different from previous generations with regard to their relationship to the media, in this chapter I refer to the
US undergraduate group as millennials, so as to underscore this dimension.

2 The "otherness in general" category did not appear in the millennials' survey instrument. I did not include it in my survey instrument for US millennials as it was
a category that surfaced only in some of the personal interviews that I conducted
with the foreign born. Also, I wasn't sure whether these young respondents
(probably 17–19) would know or respond well to a question asking them about
otherness in general. It is not a concept or phrase that is often heard in the United
States.

3 I had expected the race, class, and gender of the US millennial respondents to be
correlated with how they responded to the question of whether watching US TV
had influenced their views of race, class, or gender. But on further analysis, I did
not find statistically significant relationships. Therefore, I omit mention of these
variables in these sections, except when they help to contextualize a particular
comment.

4 However, reflecting the increasing diversity of US millennials today, a young male
working-class student who grew up in New York City volunteered: "[My] parents
are from China, and we live very differently from the White Americans from the
suburbs."

CHAPTER 8. I WANT THAT!

1 He also acknowledged, however, that technological changes had ushered in
greater global diversity and changes in content, e.g., global rap.

2 The large number of Other responses by the foreign-born participants reflects
some areas, such as food preferences, but it also reflects the fact that explanations
or examples given were coded in the Other category. For example, if they indicated that US TV influenced their clothing choices, and then specified what type
of clothing or brands they now consumed, their answers were also included in the
Other category.

3 The responses of the foreign-born participants may have been influenced by the
person-to-person style of the interview, which allowed them time to reflect and
make more connections in their mind than if they had been taking the survey
electronically.

4 This, again, may have been the result of their taking an electronic survey as
opposed to having in-person interviews. Indeed, it was surprising to me that
the millennials gave the number of examples that they did; it suggested to me
more than a passing interest on their part in the question of how watching US
TV influenced their views, especially with regard to their views on sex, alcohol
consumption, and smoking—areas that may be more in transition, or emotionally
in development, for this younger age group.

5 Some other specific items mentioned included cars, jewelry, cell phones, "sports equipment that I don't need," the iPad mini, and Mountain Dew.

6 He added that watching Olivia Pope also influenced his views toward sex, saying, "Yes, Olivia Pope made me want to do her husband."

7 He had also become critical of US TV and said, "Yes, I buy less material things now. I'm fascinated about the idea of how industries control and manipulate the consumer."

8 I asked her about Nigerian media. (See "Lights, Camera, Africa" [2010], which argues that Nigerian media production is hard to avoid in Africa: it is the world's second most prolific film industry after India's Bollywood, and Nollywood, as it is called, produces about 50 full-length features per week.) She said that "90 percent of television viewing in Nigeria was US TV" and that there were very few African channels. She added that other African countries consumed Nigeria media, but that "a king is not recognized in their own country." She was educated in a Christian school, but said that Islamic values also permeated the country. As an example, she commented, "In Nigeria when you go to the beach, you see everyone fully dressed," and there is no public nudity.

9 Females constituted 52 percent of the US millennial sample, males 48 percent. In general, more females than males made comments about how US TV influenced their views on sex. But there did not appear to be clear patterns that distinguished how the females were influenced as compared to the males. For example, in the preceding paragraph, all but three of the comments (noted in italics) were made by males.

10 Gender was not reported.

11 Red plastic cups were mentioned more than once during the interviews, and I had never realized that they too had a kind of "American" brand status associated with them because they were for a time so plentiful in shows and not available in other countries.

12 As many have noted, the actors in these telenovelas, in particular the leads, all conformed to European prototypes of the time, i.e., they were light-skinned, and the fact that telenovelas were also dubbed (albeit sometimes crudely) added to their very positive reception at the time. Russia was not the only country that received Spanish-language telenovelas; other countries in the Middle East and Africa also received these programs.

13 These two shows were also hugely popular with the foreign-born sample.

14 Reading this comment made me reflect on how often this character, played by Kerry Washington in the Shonda Rhimes production of *Scandal*, is seen drinking wine by herself or with others. I also reflected on how often main characters in other popular shows, often women, end up with friends at a bar trying to decompress or pull themselves together after a particularly dramatic day dealing with, for example, legal issues in *The Good Wife* or medical disasters in *Grey's Anatomy*.

15 Because their comments were disturbing, I decided to look more carefully at their gender and class background to see if these might have influenced their com-

ments. Beyond the fact that all but one of these comments was made by a female, I did not find any clear relationship between comments about getting drunk and the class, residence, or race of the people who made the comments. I thought it important to include this information, however, in the event others might want to investigate these relationships further with larger sample sizes.

16 This respondent did not answer the question about gender.

CONCLUSION

1 The most common "othering" characteristics mentioned were (in the order from most to least cited) the following: language spoken, color or physical type, religion, lower education and income, rural residence, illicit behavior or activities, and indigeneity. Often associated with "language spoken" was the ethnicity or immigrant status of the group designated as "Others."

2 Of the US millennial group, 37.5 percent did this, as compared with 65.5 percent of the foreign-born sample.

3 Of the foreign-born sample, 1.6 percent gave mixed responses, e.g., they said that US TV did accurately reflect racial and ethnic relations in some ways, but not in other ways.

4 It must be recognized that in today's globalized, shopping-mall world, US media were probably not the only influence on their consumption patterns.

5 Specific foods and places or ways to eat food were often mentioned by respondents in the foreign-born group, but these topics seldom came up among those in the US millennial group.

6 Some in the foreign-born sample were also critical of how women were represented on US TV; this too was related to how free or constrictive gender relations were in their home countries.

7 The impact of social media on traditional media is not limited to the United States. As Xiaochang Li notes in a web essay about East Asian television and new media, "these emergent and developing circulation practices [i.e., new social media] destabilize established paradigms of power and control by intervening in the traditional flow of media texts" (Li, 2015). By this, the author means that by quite publicly circulating media content for social rather than market-driven purposes, these viewers are asserting a tangible influence on the commercial media industry, which now seeks to see what is trending to help determine the stories they will cover or incorporate into television programming.

8 My respondents related to social media to greater and lesser degrees. However, a particularly thought-provoking response among some of my non-White respondents was how, with regard to race, they were now influenced more by what they read on their social media than by what they saw on television.

APPENDIX

1 The translated questionnaire was also reviewed for accuracy by a professor of Russian literature. A volunteer Russian-speaking translator was also present dur-

ing these interviews and was able to translate any questions or responses that may have been unclear to the respondent or to me. However, many of the Russian-speaking respondents were sufficiently competent in English and did not rely on or utilize the translated questionnaire.

2 Despite the geographic distance between these two countries, Canada and Australia are combined in this study because the respondents in this sample were all English speakers and their viewing of US TV, as well as their relationship to US TV programs, was very similar. Within the framework presented by Straubhaar (2007), they can be seen to constitute a cultural-linguistic market, although they do not form a regional market.

3 It should be borne in mind that, while the majority of this sample was very proficient in English and many likely watched US TV programs in English, different countries receive US TV programming differently. How US programs are received also changes over time. In general, and for example, Germany, France, Spain, and the Czech Republic have historically chosen dubbing over subtitling. Juxta reading (this is where the volume of the original program's voice track is lowered and a voiceover artist or lecturer reads the translation in a bland tone) is popular in some Eastern European countries, e.g., Poland and former Soviet Republics. In the Netherlands, the Scandinavian countries, Indonesia, and the Balkan countries, subtitles are the preferred method. But children's programs are dubbed in European countries that generally use subtitles. Some countries have mixed approaches, e.g., Singapore. Last, in the Philippines, US programs are shown in English, but other foreign programs are dubbed.

4 However, see the presentations at the panel discussion on "Global Culture and Aesthetic Cosmopolitanism" at the International Sociological Association's Third Annual Forum held in Vienna, Austria, on July 11, 2016.

5 As Vertovec and Cohen (2002:1–22) document, "cosmopolitanism" is a term that has been much debated. I use it here descriptively to refer to individual behaviors, values, or dispositions that manifest a capacity to engage in cultural multiplicity. My global cosmopolitans also reflect Stuart Hall's use of the term. He says: "It means the ability to stand outside of having one's life written and scripted by any one community, whether that is a faith or tradition or religion or culture—whatever it might be—and to draw selectively on a variety of discursive meanings" (cited in Vertovec and Cohen, 2002:3).

6 I did not include responses to the question of how their views of their home countries had changed since coming to the United States because of space limitations.

7 Respondents in both samples could choose more than one category, so the figures do not sum to 100.

BIBLIOGRAPHY

Aalberg, Toril, and Zan Strabac. 2010. "Media Use and Misperceptions: Does TV View-ing Improve Our Knowledge about Immigration?" *NORDICOM Review* 31, no. 1: 35–52.

Adorno, Theodor W., Else Frenkel-Brunswick, Daniel J. Levinson, and Sanford Nevitt. 1950. *The Authoritarian Personality*. New York: Harper & Row.

Alba, Richard D., and Victor Nee. 2003. *Remaking the American Mainstream: Assimila-tion and Contemporary Immigration*. Cambridge, MA: Harvard University Press.

Alexandrin, Julie R. 2009. "Television Images: Exploring How They Affect People's View of Self and Others." *Multicultural Perspectives* 11, no. 3: 150–54.

"Americans Love TV but Are Also on the Web." 2011. *Adweek*, September 12.

Ang, Ien. 1985. *Watching Dallas: Soap Opera and the Melodramatic Imagination*. Lon-don: Methuen.

———. 2003. "Together-in-Difference: Beyond Diaspora, into Hybridity." *Asian Studies Review* 27, no. 2: 141–54.

Arango, Tim. 2008. "World Falls for American Media, Even as It Sours on America." *New York Times*, December 1.

Ardizzoni, M. 2005. "Redrawing the Boundaries of Italianness: Televised Identities in the Age of Globalisation." *Social Identities* 11, no. 5: 509–30.

Artz, Lee, and Yahya R. Kamalipour. 2007. *The Media Globe: Trends in International Mass Media*. Lanham, MD: Rowman & Littlefield.

Associated Press and the NORC Center for Public Affairs Research. 2014. "How Americans Get Their News." March 17. http://mediainsight.org.

Awad, Isabel, and Andrea Roth. 2011. "From Minority to Cross-Cultural Programmes: Dutch Media Policy and the Politics of Integration." *International Communication Gazette* 73, no. 5: 400–418.

Barber, Benjamin R. 2001. *Jihad vs. McWorld: Terrorism's Challenge to Democracy*. New York: Ballantine Books.

Barrera, Vivian, and Denise D. Bielby. 2001. "Places, Faces, and Other Familiar Things: The Cultural Experience of Telenovela Viewing among Latinos in the United States." *Journal of Popular Culture* 34, no. 4: 1–18.

Beltrán, Mary C. 2002. "The Hollywood Latina Body as Site of Social Struggle: Media Constructions of Stardom and Jennifer Lopez's 'Cross-over Butt.'" *Quarterly Review of Film & Video* 19, no. 1: 71–86.

———. 2004. *Más Macha: The New Latina Action Hero*. New York: Routledge.

———. 2005. "The New Hollywood Racelessness: Only the Fast, Furious, (and Multiracial) Will Survive." *Cinema Journal* 44, no. 2: 50–67.

———. 2009. *Latina/o Stars in U.S. Eyes: The Making and Meanings of Film and TV Stardom.* Urbana: University of Illinois Press.

Bielby, Denise D., and C. Lee Harrington. 2008. *Global TV: Exporting Television and Culture in the World Market.* New York: New York University Press.

———. 2015. "Video Cultures: Television." *International Encyclopedia of the Social & Behavioral Sciences* 25: 80–86.

Blades, Ruben. 2016. "Will Smith y Su Boycott a Los Oscars: A Black Motion Picture Superstar Complaining about Exclusion?" January 22. www.rubenblades.com.

"Brains without Borders." 2016. *Economist*, January 30, 51.

Breitschaft, Andreas. 2009. "Evaluating the Linear/Non-linear Divide: Are There Any Better Factors for the Future Regulation of Audiovisual Media Content?" *Entertainment Law Review* 20, no. 8: 291–95.

Brown, Jane E., Erinn Kehoe, Bryce Loo, Katya Musacchio, and Dimitri Nessas. 2014. *One to World: Building Intercultural Competence.* New York: One to World.

Browne, Don R. 1967. "Problems in International Television." *Journal of Communication* 17, no. 3: 198–210.

Bureau of Labor Statistics. 2016. "American Time Use Survey." www.bls.gov.

Campbell, Kurt. 2014. "Why China's Leaders Love to Watch 'House of Cards.'" *Financial Times*, March 9.

"Canadian Multiculturalism: The More the Merrier." 2014. *Economist*, January 18, 38.

Carroll, Marnie Enos. 2001. "American Television in Europe: Problematizing the Notion of Pop Culture Hegemony." *Bad Subjects*, October. http://bad.eserver.org.

Carter, Bill. 2012. "The Case of the Disappearing Viewers." *New York Times*, June 28.

"A Census in Myanmar: Too Much Information." 2014. *Economist*, March 28, 44.

Chan, Wilfred. 2013. "The China Game." *Columbia Daily Spectator*, February 21. http://columbiaspectator.com.

Chavez, Leo R. 2013. *The Latino Threat: Constructing Immigrants, Citizens, and the Nation.* 2nd ed. Stanford, CA: Stanford University Press.

Children Now. 1998. "A Different World: Children's Perceptions of Race and Class in the Media. A Series of Focus Groups and a National Poll of Children." Oakland, CA: Children Now.

———. 2001. "Prime Time Diversity Report, 2000–01." Oakland, CA: Children Now.

———. 2004. "Fall Colors, 2003–04 Prime Time Diversity Report." Oakland, CA: Children Now.

Childress, C. Clayton. 2012. "All Media Are Social." *Contexts* 11, no. 1: 55–57.

Cohen, Adam. 2009. "How Europe Sees America: Our Survey on Attitudes about U.S. Cultural and Political Influence." *Wall Street Journal*, June 19. http://online.wsj.com.

Colby, Sandra L., and Jennifer M. Ortman. 2015. "Projections of the Size and Composition of the U.S. Population: 2014 to 2060." Population Estimates and Projections, Current Population Reports, P25–1143. www.census.gov.

Cortés, Carlos E. 2000. *The Children Are Watching: How the Media Teach about Diversity*. New York: Teachers College Press.

"Countries Compared by Media > Television Viewing." 2002. *NationMaster*. www.nationmaster.com.

Crul, Maurice, Jens Schneider, and Frans Lelie. 2012. *The European Second Generation Compared: Does the Integration Context Matter?* Amsterdam: Amsterdam University Press.

Crul, Maurice, and Hans Vermeulen. 2003. "The Second Generation in Europe." *International Migration Review* 37, no. 4: 965–86.

Dailey, Dharma, Amelia Bryne, Alison Powell, Joe Karaganis, and Jaewon Chung. 2010. "Broadband Adoption in Low-Income Communities." Social Science Research Council. www.ssrc.org.

Dalisay, Francis, and Alexis Tan. 2009. "Assimilation and Contrast Effects in the Priming of Asian American and African American Stereotypes through TV Exposure." *Journalism & Mass Communication Quarterly* 86, no. 1: 7–22.

"Data Points: A Nation of Multitaskers." 2011. *Adweek*, September 12, 18.

Dávila, Arlene. 2012. *Latinos, Inc.: The Marketing and Making of a People*. Berkeley: University of California Press.

Dávila, Arlene, and Yeidy M. Rivero, eds. 2014. *Contemporary Latina/o Media: Production, Circulation, Politics*. New York: New York University Press.

Davis, Howard, and Anna Sosnovskaya. 2009. "Representations of Otherness in Russian Newspapers: The Theme of Migration as a Counterpoint to Russian National Identity." *Journal of Intercultural Communication*, no. 21: 19–36.

Deaux, Kay. 2006. *To Be an Immigrant*. New York: Russell Sage Foundation.

De Bens, Els, and Hedwig de Smaele. 2001. "The Inflow of American Television Fiction on European Broadcasting Channels Revisited." *European Journal of Communication* 16, no. 1: 51–76.

De Bens, Elsa, Mary Kelly, and Marit Bakke. 1992. "Television Content: Dallasification of Culture." In *Dynamics of Media Politics*, edited by Karen Siune and Wolfgang Truetzschler, 75–150. London: Sage.

"Destination Europe." 2012. *National Geographic*, March: 148–49.

D'Haenens, Leen. 2011. "Prospects for Transformative Media in a Transcultural Society: Drivers and Barriers in Media Policy, Production and Research." *International Communication Gazette* 73, no. 5: 375–79.

Diaz, Johnny. 2011. "Network TV Is Picking up a Little Espanol." *Boston Globe*, May 15.

Dowling, Julie A. 2014. *Mexican Americans and the Question of Race*. Austin: University of Texas Press.

Downey, John, and Sabina Mihelj, eds. 2012. *Central and Eastern European Media in Comparative Perspective: Politics, Economy and Culture*. Farnham, UK: Ashgate.

Downey, Maureen. 2013. "More International Students Studying in US and More American Kids Going Abroad." *Atlanta Journal Constitution*, November 11. www.ajc.com.

Dudrah, Rajinder Kumar. 2002. "Zee TV–Europe and the Construction of a Pan-European South Asian Identity." *Contemporary South Asia* 11, no. 2: 163–81.

Edgerton, Gary R. 2007. *The Columbia History of American Television*. New York: Columbia University Press.

Eisend, Martin. 2010. "A Meta-Analysis of Gender Roles in Advertising." *Journal of the Academy of Marketing Science* 38, no. 4: 418–40.

"Eisgruber, Other University Presidents Ask President Trump to 'Rectify or Recind' Immigration Order." 2017. *News at Princeton*, February 2.

Elasmar, Michael G. 2003. *The Impact of International Television: A Paradigm Shift*. Mahwah, NJ: Erlbaum.

El Sghiar, Hatim. 2011. "Debating Diversity and Conceptual Purity: Reflections on Identification as Meaningful Concept for Diasporic Minority Research." *International Communication Gazette* 75, no. 3: 440–58.

"The Entertainment Industry and Online Media: Pennies Streaming from Heaven." 2013. *Economist*, August 17, 14.

Entman, Robert M. 2006. "Young Men of Color in the Media: Images and Impacts." Washington, DC: Joint Center for Political and Economic Studies, Health Policy Institute.

Erigha, Maryann. 2015. "Shonda Rhimes, *Scandal*, and the Politics of Crossing Over." *Black Scholar* 45, no. 1: 10–15.

Esser, Andrea. 2010. "Television Formats: Primetime Staple, Global Market." *Popular Communication* 8, no. 4: 273–92.

"Ethnic Minorities: Into the Melting Pot." 2014. *Economist*, February 10, 55.

European Audiovisual Observatory. 2011. "Film, Television and Video in Europe. Vol. 2: Television and On-Demand Audiovisual Services in Europe." Strasbourg: Council of Europe.

European Commission. 2008. "Eighth Communication on the Application of Articles 4 and 5 of Directive 89/552/EEC 'Television without Frontiers,' as Amended by Directive 97/36/EC, for the Period 2005–2006." Commission Staff Working Document Accompanying the Communication. Sec (2008) 2310 Final, July 22, 2008. Brussels: European Commission.

———. 2009. "Media4diversity: Taking the Pulse of Diversity in the Media." Directorate-General for Employment, Social Affairs and Equal Opportunities, Unit G.4. Brussels: European Commission.

FAIR. 2014. "Who Gets to Speak on Cable News?" July 1. www.fair.org.

"Film and Television: Blood and Cuts." 2015. *Economist*, December 12.

Fleming, Crystal M., and Aldon Morris. 2015. "Theorizing Ethnic and Racial Movements in the Global Age: Lessons from the Civil Rights Movement." *Sociology of Race and Ethnicity* 1, no. 1: 105–26.

Folsom, Jenny, and Alma Castro. 2015. "The Lies, Damn Lies, and Statistics of Reality Television: A Novel Look at *the Biggest Loser*." Paper presented at the American Sociological Association Annual Meeting, Chicago, August 24.

Frachon, Claire, Marion Vargaftig, and Laurence Briot, eds. 1994. *European Television: Immigrants and Ethnic Minorities.* London: John Libby.

Franco, Judith. 2008. "Extreme Makeover: The Politics of Gender, Class, and Cultural Identity." *Television & New Media* 9, no. 6: 471–86.

Freedman, Des, and Daya Kishan Thussu. 2011. *Media and Terrorism: Global Perspectives.* London: Sage.

Gao, Yang. 2013. "TV Talk: American Television, Chinese Audiences, and the Pursuit of an Authentic Self." Doctoral dissertation, Vanderbilt University.

———. 2016. "Fiction as Reality: Chinese Youths Watching American Television." *Poetics* 54: 1–13.

Garcia, Cathy Rose. 2007. "Addicted to American Dramas." *Korea Times*, May 31. www.koreatimes.co.kr.

Garcia Berumen, Frank Javier. 1995. *The Chicano/Hispanic Image in American Film.* New York: Vantage Press.

Georgiou, Myria. 2012. "Watching Soap Opera in the Diaspora: Cultural Proximity or Critical Proximity?" *Ethnic and Racial Studies* 35, no. 5: 868–87.

Gerbner, George. 1998. "Cultivation Analysis: An Overview." *Mass Communication & Society* 1, nos. 3/4: 175–94.

German Marshall Fund of the United States. 2013. "Transatlantic Trends: Key Findings." http://trends.gmfus.org.

Gibbons, Thomas, and Peter Humphreys. 2012. *Audiovisual Regulation under Pressure: Comparative Cases from North America and Europe.* New York: Routledge.

Gibson, Megan. 2014. "Here's a Sliver of Good News about Women in Television." *Time*, September 16.

"Global Culture and Aesthetic Cosmopolitanism." 2016. Panel discussion at the International Sociological Association's Third Annual Forum, Vienna, July 11. http://isaconf.confex.com.

González, Juan. 2011. *Harvest of Empire: A History of Latinos in America.* London: Penguin.

———. 2014. "On History and Strategies for Activism." In Dávila and Rivero, *Contemporary Latina/o Media*, 337–48.

González, Juan, and Joseph Torres. 2011. *News for All the People: The Epic Story of Race and the American Media.* New York: Verso.

Goren, Erkan. 2013. "Pew Research Center's Global Attitudes Project." University of Oldenberg.

Graham, Ian. 2002. "Countries Compared by Media > Television Viewing. International Statistics at NationMaster.com." www.nationmaster.com.

Graves, Sherryl Browne. 1999. "Television and Prejudice Reduction: When Does Television as a Vicarious Experience Make a Difference?" *Journal of Social Issues* 55, no. 4: 707–27.

Gray, Jonathan, and Amanda D. Lotz. 2012. *Television Studies.* Cambridge: Polity Press.

Grazian, David. 2010. "Neoliberalism and the Realities of Reality Television." *Contexts* 9, no. 2: 68–71.

Haag, Oliver. 2010. "'You Are Germany'—'I Am Australian': The Construction of National Unity through Diversity in Select Examples from Australia and Germany." *National Identities* 12, no. 4: 333–49.

Hall, Stuart. 1981. "The Whites of Their Eyes: Racist Ideologies and the Media." In *Silver Linings: Some Strategies for the Eighties*, edited by George Bridges and Rosalind Brunt, 28–39. London: Lawrence and Wishart.

———. 1982. "The Rediscovery of 'Ideology': Return of the Repressed in Media Studies." In *Culture, Society and the Media*, edited by Tony Bennett, Michael Gurevitch, James Curran, and Janet Woollacott, 56–90. London: Metheun.

———. 1990. "Encoding, Decoding." In *Culture, Media and Language*, edited by Stuart Hall, Dorothy Hobson, Andrew Lowe, and Paul Willis, 90–103. London: Unwin Hyman.

Hammarberg, Thomas. 2011. "Promotion of Pluralism in New Media." Paper presented at the OSCE Supplementary Human Dimension Meeting, Vienna.

Hargreaves, Alec G., and Antonio Perotti. 1993. "The Representation on French Television of Immigrants and Ethnic Minorities of Third World Origin." *Journal of Ethnic & Migration Studies* 19, no. 2: 251–61.

Havens, Timothy. 2006. *Global Television Marketplace*. London: British Film Institute.

———. 2013. *Black Television Travels: African American Media around the Globe*. New York: New York University Press.

Havens, Timothy, Anikó Imre, and Kati Lustyik. 2012. *Popular Television in Eastern Europe During and Since Socialism*. New York: Taylor & Francis.

Hertsgaard, Mark. 2002. *The Eagle's Shadow: Why America Fascinates and Infuriates the World*. New York: Farrar, Straus and Giroux.

Higham, John. 1994. "Strangers in the Land." In Takaki, *From Different Shores*, 78–82.

Hoffman, Allison R., and Chon A. Noriega. 2004. "Looking for Latino Regulars on Prime-Time Television: The Fall 2004 Season." Los Angeles: UCLA Chicano Studies Research Center.

"Hollywood: Split Screens." 2013. *Economist*, February 23, 61.

Holtzman, Linda, and Leon Sharpe. 2014. *Media Messages: What Film, Television, and Popular Music Teach Us about Race, Class, Gender, and Sexual Orientation*. Armonk, NY: M.E. Sharpe.

Horsti, Karina. 2009. "Antiracist and Multicultural Discourses in European Public Service Broadcasting: Celebrating Consumable Differences in the Prix Europa Iris Media Prize." *Communication, Culture & Critique* 2, no. 3: 339–60.

"Hottest Broadcast Network: CBS." 2011. *Adweek*, December 5, 30–34.

"How Americans Get Their News." 2014. American Press Institute, March 17. www.americanpressinstitute.org.

"How Other Minorities Cope: Never Say Dai." 2013. *Economist*, March 9, 55.

"Hungary's Roma: How to Get Out of a Vicious Circle." 2013. *Economist*, August 10, 47.

Hunt, Darnell, and Ana-Christina Ramon. 2015. "The 2015 Hollywood Diversity Report: Flipping the Script." Los Angeles: UCLA Ralph J. Bunche Center for African American Studies.

Ibold, Hans. 2010. "Disjuncture 2.0: Youth, Internet Use and Cultural Identity in Bishkek." *Central Asian Survey* 29, no. 4: 521–35.

Igartua, Juan-José, Isabel M. Barrios, and Félix Ortega. 2012. "Analysis of the Image of Immigration in Prime Time Television Fiction." *Comunicación y Sociedad* 25, no. 2: 5–28.

Imre, Anikó. 2009. "Gender and Quality Television." *Feminist Media Studies* 9, no. 4: 391–407.

Institute of International Education. 2013. "Open Doors 2013: More International Students in the US, Most Growth from China." New York: US Department of State, Bureau of Education and Cultural Affairs, Institute of International Education. www.iie.org.

Ipsos. 2014. "Most (86%) Global TV Watchers Use 'Live TV' but Other Modes Increasingly Popular: Computers (27%), Streaming from Internet to TV (16%), Recording Device (16%) and Mobile (11%)." April 15. www.ipsos-na.com.

Iyer, Pico. 1988. *Video Night in Kathmandu: And Other Reports from the Not-So-Far East*. New York: Vintage Departures.

Jacobs, Laura, Ellen Claes, and Marc Hooghe. 2015. "The Occupational Roles of Women and Ethnic Minorities on Primetime Television in Belgium: An Analysis of Occupational Status Measurements." *Mass Communication & Society* 18, no. 4: 498–521.

James, Beverly. 2003. "Two Cheers for the Red, White, and Blue: Hungarian Assessments of American Popular Culture." In Ramet and Crnković, *Kazaaam! Splat! Ploof!*, 148–57.

Jamieson, Patrick, and Daniel Romer. 2008. *The Changing Portrayal of Adolescents in the Media since 1950*. Oxford: Oxford University Press.

Jeffres, Leo W., David J. Atkin, Jae-Won Lee, and Kimberly Neuendorf. 2011. "Media Influences on Public Perceptions of Ethnic Groups, Generations, and Individuals." *Howard Journal of Communications* 22, no. 1: 101–21.

Jenkins, Henry, Sam Ford, and Joshua Green. 2013. *Spreadable Media: Creating Value and Meaning in a Networked Culture*. New York: New York University Press.

Jones, Clifford A. 1997. "European Union: Television Policy." In *Museum of Broadcasting Communications Encyclopedia of Television*, edited by Horace Newcomb, 572–73. Chicago: Fitzroy Dearborn.

Kaiser Family Foundation. 2010. "Generation M2: Media in the Lives of 8- to 18-Year-Olds." Menlo, CA: Henry J. Kaiser Family Foundation.

Kalam, Murad. 2003. "Egyptian Like Me." *New York Times Magazine*, November 16, 116.

Kanellos, Nicolas. 1998. *Thirty Million Strong: Reclaiming the Hispanic Image in American Culture*. Golden, CO: Fulcrum.

Karppinen, Kari. 2013. *Rethinking Media Pluralism*. New York: Fordham University Press.

Kasinitz, Philip, John H. Mollenkopf, Mary C. Waters, and Jennifer Holdaway. 2008. *Inheriting the City: The Children of Immigrants Come of Age*. New York: Russell Sage Foundation.

Kavka, Misha. 2003. "A Different Kind of Paradise: Reality Television in New Zealand." *Metro*, no. 136: 68.

Kennedy, Channing. 2011. "Batman's Latino Nemesis, Bane, Gets Airbent in New Nolan Film." *Colorlines*, January 21. www.colorlines.com.

Kesler, Christel, and Luisa Farah Schwartzman. 2015. "From Multiracial Subjects to Multicultural Citizens: Social Stratification and Ethnic and Racial Classification among Children of Immigrants in the United Kingdom." *International Migration Review* 49, no. 3: 790–836.

Kim, Minjeong. 2016. "'You Don't Look Full . . . Asia': The Invisible and Ambiguous Bodies of Chang and Soso." In *Feminist Perspectives on* Orange Is the New Black, edited by April Kalogeropoulos Householder and Adrienne Trier-Bieniek, 61–76. Jefferson, NC: McFarland.

Kim, Nadia Y. 2008. *Imperial Citizens: Koreans and Face from Seoul to LA*. Stanford, CA: Stanford University Press.

KOF. 2015. "Index of Globalization." Zurich: Swiss Federal Institute of Technology, ETH.

Kosnick, Kira. 2004. "'Speaking in One's Own Voice': Representational Strategies of Alevi Turkish Migrants on Open-Access Television in Berlin." *Journal of Ethnic & Migration Studies* 30, no. 5: 979–94.

———. 2005. "The Gap between Culture and Cultures: Cultural Policy in Berlin and Its Implications for Immigrant Cultural Production." Fiesole, Italy: European University Institute, Robert Schuman Centre for Advanced Studies, Mediterranean Programme Series.

Kraidy, Marwan. 2005. *Hybridity, or the Cultural Logic of Globalization*. Philadelphia: Temple University Press.

———. 2008. "Reality TV, Nationalism, and Gender: Superstar and the Lebanon-Syria Media War." Paper presented at the meeting of the International Communication Association, Quebec.

Kuipers, Giselinde. 2010. "*South Park* Boys and *Sex and the City* Women: Television Trade, Narrowcasting and the Export of Gender Categories." *Interactions: Studies in Communication & Culture* 2, no. 3: 179–96.

———. 2012. "The Cosmopolitan Tribe of Television Buyers: Professional Ethos, Personal Taste and Cosmopolitan Capital in Transnational Cultural Mediation." *European Journal of Cultural Studies* 15, no. 5: 581–603.

Kuipers, Giselinde, and Jeroen de Kloet. 2009. "Banal Cosmopolitanism and *the Lord of the Rings*: The Limited Role of National Differences in Global Media Consumption." *Poetics* 37: 99–118.

Kydd, Elspeth. 2001. "Differences: *The X Files*, Race and the White Norm." *Journal of Film and Video*, no. 4: 72–82.

Laporte, Nicole. 2016a. "The Audience Puzzle: What's Measured Is What Matters." *Fast Company*, April, 25–28.

———. 2016b. "How Apple, Facebook and Google Are Infiltrating Movies & TV." *Fast Company*, May, 68–76, 94–96.

Levin, Gary. 2015. "Prime-Time Nielsen Ratings: Beyond the Numbers." *USA Today,* March 25. http://usatoday.com.

Levitt, Peggy. 2001. *The Transnational Villagers.* Berkeley: University of California Press.

Lewis, Tania, and Fran Martin. 2010. "Learning Modernity: Lifestyle Advice Television in Australia, Taiwan and Singapore." *Asian Journal of Communication* 20, no. 3: 318–36.

Li, Xiaochang. 2015. "Transnational Audiences and East Asian Television." *Spreadable Media.* http://spreadablemedia.org.

Lichter, S. Robert, and Daniel R. Amundson. 1994. *Distorted Reality: Hispanic Characters in TV Entertainment.* Washington, DC: Center for Media and Public Affairs.

Liebes, Tamar, and Elihu Katz. 1990. *The Export of Meaning: Cross-Cultural Readings of Dallas.* New York: Oxford University Press.

"Lights, Camera, Africa." 2010. *Economist,* December 18, 85.

Lim, Merlyna. 2012. "Clicks, Cabs, and Coffee Houses: Social Media and Oppositional Movements in Egypt, 2004–2011." *Journal of Communication* 62, no. 2: 231–48.

Lind, R. A. 2010. "Laying a Foundation for Studying Race, Gender, and the Media." In *Race/Gender/Media: Considering Diversity across Audiences, Content, and Producers,* edited by R. A. Lind, 1–11. Boston: Allyn & Bacon.

Livingston, Gretchen. 2011. "Latinos and Digital Technology, 2010." Washington, DC: Pew Hispanic Center.

Lopez, Ana M. 1991. "Are All Latins from Manhattan? Hollywood, Ethnography, and Cultural Colonialism." In *Unspeakable Images: Ethnicity and the American Cinema,* edited by Lester D. Friedman, 404–24. Urbana: University of Illinois Press.

Lopez, M. Nakamura. 2016. "A Blackanese Beauty Queen." *Contexts* 15, no. 1: 73–75.

López, Nancy. 2013. "Contextualizing Lived Race-Gender and the Racialized-Gendered Social Determinants of Health." In *Mapping "Race": Critical Approaches to Health Disparities Research,* edited by Laura Gómez and Nancy López, 179–211. New Brunswick, NJ: Rutgers University Press.

Lotz, Amanda D. 2013. "Book Review Essay: Television 2013." *Cinema Journal* 52, no. 3: 190–97.

Malik, Sarita. 2010. "From Multicultural Programming to Diasporic Television: Situating the UK in a European Context." *Media History* 16, no. 1: 123–28.

Marghalani, Khalid, Philip Palmgreen, and Douglas A. Boyd. 1998. "The Utilization of Direct Satellite Broadcasting (DBS) in Saudi Arabia." *Journal of Broadcasting & Electronic Media* 42, no. 3: 297–314.

"Marketing in the Digital Age: A Brand New Game." 2015. *Economist,* August 27.

Mastro, Dana E., and Elizabeth Behm-Morawitz. 2005. "Latino Representation on Primetime Television." *Journalism & Mass Communication Quarterly* 82, no. 1: 110–30.

Mastro, Dana E., and Amanda L. Robinson. 2000. "Cops and Crooks Images of Minorities on Primetime Television." *Journal of Criminal Justice* 28, no. 5: 385–96.

Mastro, Dana E., and Riva Tukachinsky. 2011. "The Influence of Exemplar versus Prototype-Based Media Primes on Racial/Ethnic Evaluations." *Journal of Communication* 61, no. 5: 916–37.

McLuhan, Marshall, and Quentin Fiore. 1967. *The Medium Is the Massage: An Inventory of Effects*. New York: Random House.

"Media's Ageing Audiences: Peggy Sue Got Old." 2011. *Economist*, April 9, 79.

Mendible, Myra, ed. 2007. *From Bananas to Buttocks: The Latina Body in Popular Film and Culture*. Austin: University of Texas Press.

Merskin, Debra. 2007. "Three Faces of Eva: Perpetuation of the Hot-Latina Stereotype in *Desperate Housewives*." *Howard Journal of Communications* 18, no. 2: 133–51.

——. 2011. *Media, Minorities, and Meaning: A Critical Introduction*. New York: Peter Lang.

Michalski, Jennifer. 2013. "17 American TV Shows That Started in Other Countries." *Business Insider*, November 17. www.businessinsider.com.

Montalvo, Daniela A., and Joseph Torres. 2006. "Network Brownout Report." Washington, DC: National Association of Hispanic Journalists.

Moran, Albert. 2009. *New Flows in Global TV*. Chicago: Intellect Books.

Morgan, Michael, and Nancy Signiorelli, eds. 1990. *Cultivation Analysis: New Directions in Media Effect Research*. NewburyPark, CA: Sage.

Muñiz, Carlos, Alma Rosa Saldierna, Felipe de Jesús Marañón, and Alba Belinda Rodríguez. 2013. "Screens to See the World. Television Stereotypes of the Mexican Indigenous Population and the Generation of Prejudice." *Revista Latina de Comunicación Social* 16, no. 68: 290–308.

National Hispanic Foundation for the Arts. 2001. "Prime Time for Latinos: 2000–2001, Prime Time Television Season. Report II." Washington, DC: National Hispanic Foundation for the Arts.

Navarrete, Lisa, and Charles Kamasaki. 1994. *Out of the Picture: Hispanics in the Media*. Washington, DC: Policy Analysis Center, Office of Research Advocacy and Legislation, National Council of La Raza.

Negrón-Muntaner, Frances, Chelsea Abbas, Luis Figueroa, and Samuel Robson. 2014. "The Latino Media Gap: A Report on the State of Latinos in the U.S. Media." New York: Columbia University, Center for the Study of Race and Ethnicity.

Niessen, Jan, and Thomas Huddleston. 2009. *Handbook on Integration: For Policy-Makers and Practitioners*. 3rd ed. Brussels: European Commission, Directorate General for Justice, Freedom and Security.

Noam, Eli M. 2009. *Media Ownership and Concentration in America*. New York: Oxford University Press.

Noriega, Chon A. 1992. *Chicanos and Film: Essays on Chicano Representation and Resistance*. New York: Garland.

——. 1997. "Citizen Chicano: The Trials and Titillations of Ethnicity in the American Cinema, 1935–1962." In Rodríguez, *Latin Looks*, 85–103.

Norris, Pippa, and Ronald Inglehart. 2009. *Cosmopolitan Communications: Cultural Diversity in a Globalized World*. New York: Cambridge University Press.

Nye, Joseph S. 2004. *Soft Power: The Means to Success in World Politics*. New York: Public Affairs.

Ogan, Christine. 2011. "'Why Can't We Just All Get Along?' The Concepts That Divide Academics, Policymakers and Citizens Related to the Muslim Ethnic Minorities in Europe." *International Communication Gazette* 73, no. 5: 459–72.

Olmos, Juan Carlos Checa, and Ángeles Arjona Garrido. 2012. "Anti-immigrant Feeling in Spain." *Polish Sociological Review*, no. 177: 39–53.

Persson, Anna, and Dara R. Musher-Eizenman. 2003. "The Impact of a Prejudice-Prevention Television Program on Young Children's Ideas about Race." *Early Childhood Research Quarterly* 18: 530–46.

Pew Global Attitudes Project. 2012. "Global Opinion of Obama Slips, International Policies Faulted." www.pewglobal.org.

Picard, Robert G. 2011. *The Economics and Financing of Media Companies*. New York: Fordham University Press.

Piñón, Juan. 2014. "Corporate Transnationalism: The US Hispanic and Latin American Television Industries." In Dávila and Rivero, *Contemporary Latina/o Media*, 21–43.

Poiger, Uta G. 2003. "Afterword." In Ramet and Crnković, *Kazaaam! Splat! Ploof!*, 55–68.

Porter, Caroline, and Douglas Belkin. 2013. "Record Number of Foreign Students Flocking to U.S." *Wall Street Journal*, November 11. www.wsj.com.

Prey, Robert. 2011. "Different Takes: Migrant World Television and Multiculturalism in South Korea." *Global Media Journal: Canadian Edition* 4, no. 1: 109–25.

"Racism in Italy: Educating Cecile." 2013. *Economist*, August 31, 44.

Ramet, Sabrina P., and Gordana Crnković, eds. 2003. *Kazaaam! Splat! Ploof! The American Impact on European Popular Culture since 1945*. Lanham, MD: Rowman & Littlefield.

Ramírez Berg, Charles. 1997. "Stereotyping in Films in General and of the Hispanic in Particular." In Rodríguez, *Latin Looks*, 104–20.

———. 2002. *Latino Images in Film: Stereotypes, Subversion, and Resistance*. Austin: University of Texas Press.

Rentfrow, Peter J., Lewis R. Goldberg, and Ron Zilca. 2011. "Listening, Watching, and Reading: The Structure and Correlates of Entertainment Preferences." *Journal of Personality* 79, no. 2: 223–58.

Reuters Institute. 2016. "Executive Summary and Key Findings of the 2015 Report." Oxford: University of Oxford, Reuters Institute for the Study of Journalism. www.digitalnewsreport.org.

Revers, Matthias, Casey Brienza, and Andrew Lidner. 2013. "Section Proposal: Media Sociology, American Sociological Association." Paper presented at the American Sociological Association annual meeting, New York.

Rivero, Yeidy M. 2014. "Anatomy of a Protest: *Grey's Anatomy*, Colombia's *A Corazon Abierto*, and the Politicization of a Format." In Dávila and Rivero, *Contemporary Latina/o Media*, 149–68.

Roberts, Sam. 2010. "Mamuju? Vlashki? Garifuna? In New York, You Hear It All." *New York Times*, April 29, A1.

Robles, Alfred A. 1972. "It Was a Warm Summer Day." In *Asian-American Authors*, edited by Kai-yu Hsu and Helen Palubinskas, 135–38. Boston: Houghton Mifflin.

Rodríguez, Clara E., ed. 1997. *Latin Looks: Images of Latinas and Latinos in the U.S. Media*. Boulder, CO: Westview.

———. 2000. *Changing Race: Latinos, the Census, and the History of Ethnicity in the United States*. New York: New York University Press.

———. 2004. "Diversifying Hollywood: Hispanic Representation in the Media." Forum Report. Washington, DC: Congressional Hispanic Caucus, Joint Forum of Task Forces on Corporate America, Technology, Telecommunications, and Arts & Entertainment.

———. 2007. "Film Viewing in Latino Communities, 1896–1934: Puerto Rico as Microcosm." In Mendible, *From Bananas to Buttocks*, 31–50.

———. 2008a. "Census Realities vs. Media Distortions: U.S. Latinos." In *Hybrid Americas: Contacts, Contrasts, and Confluences in New World Literatures and Cultures*, vol. 2, edited by Josef Raab and Martin Butler, 229–47. Münster, Germany: LIT-Verlag.

———. 2008b. *Heroes, Lovers, and Others: The Story of Latinos in Hollywood*. Washington, DC: Smithsonian Books.

———. 2015. "Sample of Foreign Born, Gathered 2013–2015 and Sample of Millennials, Gathered in 2014." Unpublished data.

Rodríguez, Clara E., Nancy López, and Grigoris Argeros. 2015. "Latinos and the Color Line." In *Emerging Trends in the Social and Behavioral Sciences*, edited by Robert Scott and Stephan Kosslyn, 1–11. New York: John Wiley.

Rodríguez, Clara E., Michael H. Miyawaki, and Grigoris Argeros. 2013. "Latino Racial Reporting in the US: To Be or Not to Be." *Sociology Compass* 7, no. 5: 390–403.

Rojas, Viviana, and Juan Piñón. 2014. "Spanish, English or Spanglish? Media Strategies and Corporate Struggles to Reach the Second and Later Generations of Latinos." *International Journal of Hispanic Marketing* 7: 28–42.

Ryan, Erin L. 2010. "Dora the Explorer: Empowering Preschoolers, Girls, and Latinas." *Journal of Broadcasting & Electronic Media* 54, no. 1: 54–68.

Schiefer, David, Anna Möllering, Ella Daniel, Maya Benish-Weisman, and Klaus Boehnke. 2010. "Cultural Values and Outgroup Negativity: A Cross-Cultural Analysis of Early and Late Adolescents." *European Journal of Social Psychology* 40, no. 4: 635–51.

Schlesinger, Arthur M., Jr. 1992. *The Disuniting of America*. New York: Norton.

Schmitt-Beck, Rudiger, and Ansgar Wolsing. 2010. "European TV Environments and Citizens' Social Trust: Evidence from Multilevel Analyses." *Communications: The European Journal of Communication Research* 35, no. 4: 461–83.

Shohat, Ella, and Robert Stam. 1994. *Unthinking Eurocentrism: Multiculturalism and the Media*. London: Routledge.

Shome, Raka. 2012. "Mapping the Limits of Multiculturalism in the Context of Globalization." *International Journal of Communication* 6: 144–65.

Siegemund-Broka, Austin. 2015. "Audiences Want More Ethnic Representation, a New UCLA Study Shows." *Hollywood Reporter*, March 6.

Signer, Sara, Manuel Puppis, and Andrea Piga. 2011. "Minorities, Integration and the Media: Media Regulation and Media Performance in Multicultural and Multilingual Switzerland." *International Communication Gazette* 73, no. 5: 419–39.

Signorielli, Nancy, Elizabeth Milke, and Carol Katzman. 1985. *Role Portrayal and Stereotyping on Television: An Annotated Bibliography of Studies Relating to Women, Minorities, Aging, Sexual Behavior, Health, and Handicaps*. Westport, CT: Greenwood.

Smedley, Audrey. 2007. *Race in North America: Origin and Evolution of a Worldview*. Boulder, CO: Westview.

Smith, Stacy L., Marc Choueiti, and Katherine Pieper. 2013. "Race/Ethnicity in 500 Popular Films: Is the Key to Diversifying Cinematic Content Held in the Hand of the Black Director?" Los Angeles: University of Southern California, Media Diversity and Social Change Initiative.

———. 2016. "Inclusion or Invisibility? Comprehensive Annenberg Report on Diversity in Entertainment." Los Angeles: University of Southern California, Annenberg School for Communication & Journalism, Institute for Diversity and Empowerment at Annenberg.

Smith, Stacy L., Marc Choueiti, Elizabeth Scofield, and Katherine Pieper. 2013. "Gender Inequality in 500 Popular Films: Examining On-Screen Portrayals and Behind-the-Scenes Employment Patterns in Motion Pictures Released between 2007–2012." Los Angeles: University of Southern California, Annenberg School for Communication & Journalism.

"Social Policies: Time to Scrap Affirmative Action." 2013. *Economist*, April 27, 11.

Sontag, Deborah. 2005. "I Want My Hyphenated-Identity MTV." *New York Times*, June 19, 1.

Sotomayor, Sonia. 2013. *My Beloved World*. New York: Knopf.

Steinhagen, Josefine, Martin Eisend, and Silke Knoll. 2010. "Gender Stereotyping in Advertising on Public and Private TV Channels in Germany." *Advances in Advertising Research* 1: 285–95.

Štětka, Václav. 2012a. *Back to the Local? Transnational Media Flows and Audience Consumption Patterns in Central and Eastern Europe*. Farnham, UK: Ashgate.

———. 2012b. "From Global to (G)Local: Changing Patterns of Television Program Flows and Audience Preferences in Central and Eastern Europe." *Journal of Popular Film and Television* 40, no. 3: 109–18.

Steven, Peter. 2003. *The No-Nonsense Guide to Global Media*. Oxford: New Internationalist Publications.

Stoute, Steve. 2011. *The Tanning of America: How Hip-Hop Created a Culture That Rewrote the Rules of the New Economy*. London: Gotham Books.

Straubhaar, Joseph D. 2007. *World Television: From Global to Local*. Thousand Oaks, CA: Sage.

Suich, Alexandra. 2013. "The Internet Is Changing Television Habits." *Economist*, November 18.

Suskind, Ron. 2001. "A Plunge into the Present." *New York Times Magazine* 151, no. 51955: 84.

Takaki, Ronald T., ed. 1994. *From Different Shores: Perspectives on Race and Ethnicity in America*. New York: Oxford University Press.

Tan, Alexis. 2012. "Stereotypes of White-Americans and American Media Use among High School Students in South Korea: A Test of a Cognitive Processing Model." Unpublished manuscript.

Tan, Alexis, Francis Dalisay, Yunying Zhang, Eun-Jeong Han, and Mariyah M. Merchant. 2010. "A Cognitive Processing Model of Information Source Use and Stereotyping: African-American Stereotypes in South Korea." *Journal of Broadcasting & Electronic Media* 54, no. 4: 569–87.

Taylor, Paul. 2016. "The Demographic Trends Shaping American Politics in 2016 and Beyond." Pew Research Center, January 27. www.pewresearch.org.

ter Wal, Jessika. 2002. "Racism and Cultural Diversity in the Mass Media. An Overview of Research and Examples of Good Practice in the 15 EU Member States." Vienna: European Monitoring Centre on Racism and Xenophobia.

———. 2004. "European Day of Media Monitoring: Quantitative Analysis of Daily Press and TV Contents in the 15 EU Member States." Utrecht: European Research Centre on Migration and Ethnic Relations, Utrecht University.

Thompson, Kenneth. 2002. "Border Crossings and Diasporic Identities: Media Use and Leisure Practices of an Ethnic Minority." *Qualitative Sociology* 25, no. 3: 409–18.

Titcomb, James. 2015. "Which Country Watches the Most TV in the World?" *Telegraph*, December 10. www.telegraph.co.uk.

Tomascikova, Slavka. 2010. "British Situation Comedy and the Consciousness of New Class Differences in Slovakia." *European Journal of English Studies* 14, no. 3: 207–20.

Triandafyllidoub, Anna, and Iryna Ulasiuk. 2011. "Studying and Evaluating the Role of the Media in Migrant Integration: Introductory Remarks for the Mediva Project." Fiesole, Italy: European University Institute, Robert Schuman Centre for Advanced Studies.

Turner, Amanda. 2015. "Understanding the Gender and Sexuality Game: A Qualitative Textual Analysis of Two Console Games." Paper presented at the American Sociological Association annual meeting, Chicago, August 24.

Ugochukwu, Chioma. 2008. "Cultural Resistance and Resilience amid Imported TV Programming in Nigeria." *Africa Today* 55, no. 1: 35–58.

Univision Communications. 2012. "Univision Study on Hispanic Millennials Reveals How Culture Influences Behavior and Purchasing Decisions." http://hispaniccmo.wordpress.com.

US Census Bureau. 2015. "New Census Bureau Report Analyzes U.S. Population Projections." CB15-TPS.16. March 3. www.census.gov.

US Kerner Commission. 1968. *Report of the National Advisory Commission on Civil Disorders*. New York: Dutton.

Valdivia, Angharad N. 2000. *A Latina in the Land of Hollywood: And Other Essays on Media Culture*. Tucson: University of Arizona Press.

Vara, Vauhini. 2015. "Pintrest's Great Expectations." *Fast Company*, November, 33–36. www.fastcompany.com.

Vertovec, Steven, and Robin Cohen. 2002. "Introduction: Conceiving Cosmopolitanism." In *Conceiving Cosmopolitanism: Theory, Context and Practice*, edited by Steven Vertovec and Robin Cohen, 1–22. Oxford: Oxford University Press.

Vidmar, Neil, and Milton Rokeach. 1974. "Archie Bunker's Bigotry: A Study in Selective Perception and Exposure." *Journal of Communication* 24, no. 1: 36–47.

Vidmar Horvat, Ksenija. 2010. "Multiculturalism in the Time of Terrorism." *Cultural Studies* 24, no. 5: 747–66.

Vujnovic, Marina. 2008. "The Political Economy of Croatian Television: Exploring the Impact of Latin American Telenovelas." *Communications: The European Journal of Communication Research* 33, no. 4: 431–54.

Ward, Susan, Tom O'Regan, and Ben Goldsmith. 2010. "From *Neighbours* to *Packed to the Rafters*: Accounting for Longevity in the Evolution of Aussie Soaps." *Media International Australia*, no. 136: 162–76.

Wayne, Michael L. 2015. "Guilty Pleasures and Cultural Legitimation: Exploring High-Status TV in the Post-network Era." *Journal of Popular Culture* 48, no. 5: 990–1009.

———. 2016. "Cultural Class Analysis and Audience Reception in American Television's 'Third Golden Age.'" *Interactions: Studies in Communication & Culture* 7, no. 1: 41–57.

"We Shape Our Tools and Thereafter Our Tools Shape Us." 2013. *McLuhan Galaxy*, April 1. http://mcluhangalaxy.wordpress.com.

"When Women Are on the Creative Team, More Women Appear in TV, Film." 2014. *Media Report to Women* 42, no. 2: 4–5.

"Wi-Fi and Cellphone Service at New York Subway Stations: Share Your Experience." 2017. *New York Times*, January 9. www.nytimes.com.

Wike, Richard. 2013. "American Star Power Still Rules the Globe." Pew Research Global Attitudes Project, February 22.

Wike, Richard, and Bridget Parker. 2015. "Corruption, Pollution, Inequality Are Top Concerns in China: Many Worry about Threats to Traditions and Culture." *Pew Research Center Global Attitudes & Trends*, September 24.

Williams, Linda. 1997. "Type and Stereotype: Chicano Images in Film." In Rodríguez, *Latin Looks*, 214–20.

Wilson, Clint C., and Felix Gutierrez. 1985. *Minorities and Media: Diversity and the End of Mass Communication*. Beverly Hills, CA: Sage.

———. 1995. *Race, Multiculturalism, and the Media: From Mass to Class Communication*. Thousand Oaks, CA: Sage.

"Winner Takes All." 2017. *Economist*, February 11.

"With Korean Dramas Booming in the U.S., Brands Should Take Note." 2014. *Hollywood Branded*, May 19. www.hollywoodbranded.com.

Wolff, Michael. 2015. *Television Is the New Television: The Unexpected Triumph of Old Media in the Digital Age*. New York: Portfolio/Penguin.

Woods, Gerald. 2016. "How People From Different Countries Watch Television?" *Solace Connect*, December 4. www.solaceconnect.com.

Wu, Tim. 2010. *The Master Switch: The Rise and Fall of Information Empires*. New York: Knopf.

Yang, Hyeseung, Srividya Ramasubramanian, and Mary Beth Oliver. 2008. "Cultivation Effects on Quality of Life Indicators: Exploring the Effects of American Television Consumption on Feelings of Relative Deprivation in South Korea and India." *Journal of Broadcasting & Electronic Media* 52, no. 2: 247–67.

Zandberg, Izabella. 2006. "A Cross-Cultural Analysis of Television Advertising in the US and Poland." Paper presented at the meeting of the International Studies Association, San Diego.

Zeng, Guojun, Frank Go, and Christian Kolmer. 2011. "The Impact of International TV Media Coverage of the Beijing Olympics 2008 on China's Media Image Formation: A Media Content Analysis Perspective." *International Journal of Sports Marketing and Sponsorship* 12, no. 4: 319–36.

Zia, Helen. 2000. *Asian American Dreams: The Emergence of an American People*. New York: Farrar, Straus and Giroux.

Zorita-Sierra, Gretchen, and Feliz Sanchez. 2012. "Decision 2012: Latinos Missing in Action on Sunday Morning Network News Shows." Washington, DC: National Hispanic Federation of the Arts.

INDEX

Academy Awards ceremony, 165

access, 62–63

adaptation: over adoption, 36; of American TV, 36; assimilation and, 45

ads: millennials on, 149–150; recollection of, 150

alcohol: consumption of, 145–150; as social lubricant, 151

Alevi Turks, 45

Alias, 76–77

All in the Family, 20

Amazon, 85

American culture, 1; as contrasting, 59–60; differences from, 70–71; exportation of, 10; foreign love of, 9

American dream, 110, 200n2

American schools, 198n1

American TV: adaptation of, 36; availability of, 2; of Chinese students, 1–2; concern with dominance, 8–12; consequences of, 11–12; controversial topics in, 4; coolness as distinct in, 74–75; corporations in, 11; defining of, 183–184; democracy spread from, 10–11; determination of, 72–74; enjoyment of, 56–63; gender in, 3; in globalization, 5; immigrants with, 2; as imperialism, 23–24; influence on race, class, gender, and national origin, *120*; patterns in, 2–4; positivity towards, 71; power of, 161–162; racial/ethnic patterns in, 3; of Soviets, 41–42, 69–70; steadiness of, 9; translation of, 2, 13–14; and world leaders, 11. *See also specific topics*

Amundson, Daniel R., 20

Ang, Ien, 32

anti-smoking message, 148

art of living, 28

Artz, Lee, 34

aspirations, 155–156

assimilation: adaptation and, 45; to homogeneity, 45–46; immigrant resistance to, 30

assumptions: from media, 22–23; re-examining of, 49–50. *See also* stereotyping

Audiovisual Media Services Directive (AVMS), 8

Australia, 204n2

Babuyan, 22

Barber, Benjamin, 33, 131

Before Twitter Period (BT), 6

Beijing Olympics, 2008, 42–43

believability, 77–78

Ben Hur, 22

Betty, a Feia (Ugly Betty), 49

the Bible, 22, 194n7

Bielby, Denise D., 26–27

The Big Bang Theory, 55

bipolar disorder, 83

birth control: foreign-born individuals opinions on, 144–145; influence on, 137–138; millennial opinions of, 144–145

Black Box, 83

Black Lives Matter movement, 98, 164–165

body size image, female, 140

ABOUT THE AUTHOR

Clara E. Rodríguez is Professor of Sociology at Fordham University's College at Lincoln Center. She is the author of numerous books and articles and the recipient of several prestigious awards for her research and teaching. She has presented her scholarly work in many countries and has advised the producers of a number of television shows and documentaries.